THE GEOGRAPHY OF ETHNIC VIOLENCE

THE GEOGRAPHY
OF ETHNIC VIOLENCE

IDENTITY, INTERESTS, AND
THE INDIVISIBILITY OF TERRITORY

Monica Duffy Toft

PRINCETON UNIVERSITY PRESS   PRINCETON AND OXFORD

Copyright © 2003 by Princeton University Press
Published by Princeton University Press, 41 William Street,
Princeton, New Jersey 08540
In the United Kingdom: Princeton University Press, 3 Market Place,
Woodstock, Oxfordshire OX20 1SY
All Rights Reserved

Fourth printing, and first paperback printing, 2006
Paperback ISBN-13: 978-0-691-12383-7
Paperback ISBN-10: 0-691-12383-7

The Library of Congress has cataloged the cloth edition of this book as follows

Toft, Monica Duffy, 1965–
The geography of ethnic violence : identity, interests, and the indivisibility of territory /
Monica Duffy Toft.
    p.   cm.
Includes bibliographical references and index.
ISBN 0-691-11354-8 (alk. paper)
1. Political violence.   2. Partition, Territorial.   3. Nationalism.   4. Human
geography.   5. Ethnic conflict—Former Soviet republics—Case studies.   6. Former
Soviet republics—Ethnic relations—Case studies.   I. Title.

JC328.6 .T64 2003
303.6—dc21   2002042463

British Library Cataloging-in-Publication Data is available

This book has been composed in Galliard

Printed on acid-free paper. ∞

pup.princeton.edu

Printed in the United States of America

P

To Ivan

Contents

Illustrations   ix

Preface   xi

1. The Forgotten Meaning of Territory   1

2. Indivisible Territory and Ethnic War   17

3. Territory and Violence: A Statistical Assessment   34

4. Russia and Tatarstan   45

5. Russia and Chechnya   64

6. Georgia and Abkhazia   87

7. Georgia and Ajaria   107

8. Conclusion   127

Appendix Tables   149

Notes   167

References   203

Index   219

Illustrations

Tables

2.1. Ethnic Groups and the Demand for Sovereignty   26
2.2. Bargaining Model: Indivisibility of Issues   30
3.1. Rebellion Variable   35
3.2. Composite Rebellion Variable   36
3.3. Spatial-Concentration Variable   36
3.4. Settlement-Pattern Variable   37
3.5. Overview of MAR Cases, according to Settlement-Pattern Variable   37
3.6. Regression of Rebellion on Settlement Patterns   38
3.7. Regression of Ethnic Violence   43
4.1. Population Data for Tatars (1989)   48
5.1. Population Data for Chechens (1989)   69
6.1. Population Data for the Abkhaz (1989)   93
8.1. Theoretical Expectations and Research Findings   138

Appendix Tables

1. Number of Independent States in the World   149
2. Minorities at Risk Cases and Key Variables   153
3. Ethnic Data for Autonomous Units of Russian Federation   164

Figures

3.1. Settlement Patterns and Frequency of Rebellion, 1980–95   39
4.1. Location Map of Tatarstan   47
5.1. Location Map of Chechnya   66
6.1. Location Map of Georgia   90
8.1. Armed Conflicts, Issue of Conflict, and Termination Type, 1989–96   143

Preface

This book began with a bag of dirt.

While doing research in Ukraine in 1992, just one year after it gained its independence from the Soviet Union, I happened by the Parliament building in Kiev. Parliament was in session, and various groups and individuals were lingering trying to get their concerns heard. One was a huge man in full Cossack regalia. In his hand was a basket, and in the basket were small, clear plastic bags. The bags were tied with a golden cord and affixed with a waxed seal that contained a trident—a symbol of Ukraine. It was not the seal, cord, or bag that mattered most, but the contents. Inside this bag were about two ounces of dirt—but not just any dirt. This was Cossack soil. Someone, a nationalist, had gone to great lengths to conceive of, design, and distribute this physical representation of Cossack national identity. To me it was a bag of dirt, but to the man it represented the Cossack nation, its land, its *homeland*. Had I not met the Cossack distributing measured and reverently packaged bits of his homeland to passersby, this book would not have been written.

Although a Cossack planted the idea of this book in my head, many friends and colleagues helped me bring it to fruition. I was extremely fortunate to have the guidance of John Mearsheimer and Steve Walt, and I thank them both for stressing the value of asking important and interesting questions and then teaching me how to go about best answering them.

I thank the many teachers, colleagues, and friends who read various parts of this book, including Robert Bates, Nora Bensahel, Michael Brown, John Colarusso, Walker Connor, Michael Desch, Paul Diehl, Alexander Downes, Tanisha Fazal, Jim Fearon, Elise Giuliano, Hein Goemans, Arman Grigorian, Ted Gurr, Yoshiko Herrera, Chaim Kaufmann, Beth Kier, Andy Kydd, David Laitin, Rose McDermott, Jonathan Mercer, Sharon Morris, Roger Petersen, William Rose, Robert Rotberg, Steve Saideman, Jack Snyder, and Ronald Suny. For help with the statistical portions of the argument, I would like to thank Bear Braumoeller, Jonathan Cowden, and Dylan Balch-Lindsay. I would also like to thank Ghia Nodia, an expert on Georgia's transition to independence, and Kakha Kenkadze and David Soumbadze, both currently officials with Georgia's government and advisers to Georgian president Eduard Shevardnadze, for generously sharing their time and thoughts on Georgian politics. Excellent research assistance was provided by Ali Ahmed, Moshe Arens, Vlada Bukavansky, Deborah Lee, Kate Regnier, Michelle Von Euw, and especially Katie Gallagher.

I am grateful for the generous support provided at various stages of this project by the United States Institute of Peace, the MacArthur Foundation, the Smith Richardson Foundation, and the John M. Olin Institute for Strategic Studies at Harvard University, where I was a post-doctoral fellow from 1998 to 1999. My time as a postdoctoral fellow and then the assistant director of the Olin Institute provided the ideal environment to work on my manuscript. I am indebted to Sam Huntington and Steve Rosen for being such wonderful and supportive colleagues.

Portions of this book appeared or will appear in "Multinationality, Regions, and State-Building," "Indivisible Territory, Geographic Concentration, and Ethnic War," and "The Case of Two-Way Mirror Nationalism in Ajaria." I thank the publishers for permission to use the material here. I would also like to thank my editors at Princeton University Press, Dalia Geffen, Charles T. Myers, and Deborah Tegarden, and my indexer, Victoria Agee, for making the process of this book seem so seamless.

Finally, my family has been an important source of strength and inspiration. The impending birth of Samuel, my first child, helped me focus on revising the manuscript and delivering it to the publisher before delivering Sam to the world. I also thank my parents, Joan and Bill, my brothers, Bill and Peter, and my sisters, Anne, Jane, and Kate, for their personal support: I am proud to put my family name—Duffy—front and center. My last name, however, I share with the person to whom I owe the deepest gratitude: my husband and colleague, Ivan.

THE GEOGRAPHY OF ETHNIC VIOLENCE

1

The Forgotten Meaning of Territory

So that my generation would comprehend the
                                    Homeland's worth,
Men were always transformed to dust, it seems.
The Homeland is the remains of our forefathers
Who turned into dust for this precious soil.
  —*Cholpan Ergash, Uzbek poet*

No matter how barren, no territory is worthless if it is a homeland. History is replete with conflicts in which people fight to the death over what appears to be territory of questionable value. This is because territory is simultaneously a divisible, quantifiable object and an indivisible and romantic subject.

As a physical object, territory can be divided and later redivided. It can be explored, inhabited, mined, polluted, exchanged, sold, bought, and farmed. Borders and boundaries can be redrawn, place-names changed, and people moved from here to there.

Yet in many places of the world, borders and boundaries seem fixed in time and in the imagination. The name of the land has remained the same for generations, and the people inhabiting that land would rather die than lose the hope or right of return. In this context territory takes on a meaning that far exceeds its material and objective description. It becomes not an object to be exchanged but an indivisible component of a group's identity.

Territories are objects that are physically divisible; at the same time they become intractably and eternally indivisible. How else can we explain why, in places like Jerusalem and Kosovo, men and women not only are willing to die but also allow their sons and daughters to die just to remain in their homeland?

The central theme of this book is that different actors—states and ethnic groups—view the same territory in different ways. This is not because states are generally rational and ethnic groups are generally irrational. Rather, it is because territory means different things to states and ethnic groups. Chapter 2 introduces and explores a theory of ethnic violence that places the dual meaning of territory at the center of a general explanation of why some ethnic conflicts become violent and others do not. I call it the theory of indivisible territory. Territory is a sine qua non of the state and can be an irreducible component of ethnic group identity. For both, control over territory may become a matter of survival and, consequently, an indivisible issue. When both sides in a conflict regard control over a disputed territory as indivisible, violence is likely.

In fact, if we ask ourselves why presumably rational actors—in this case, political elites representing states and ethnic groups at a hypothetical bargaining table—ever resort to violence, we are left with a puzzle. The puzzle stems from the often observed fact that there are almost always solutions short of violence which benefit both or all sides of a conflict more than could violence. Violence is costly, and it is risky, so whyever try it? The answer lies in the "almost always" qualification. Social scientists have in fact isolated three key obstacles to a rational settlement of disputes short of violence: (1) private information; (2) a commitment problem; and (3) an indivisible issue.[1] The private-information obstacle focuses our attention on the fact that parties to a dispute often have a large incentive to conceal their true aims and goals, as well as the costs and risks they are willing to sustain to reach those goals. In such cases, over- or underestimations can lead to suboptimal outcomes (namely, war). The commitment problem addresses the issue of trust over the long term: if I agree now, and I am the weaker party, how can you, as the stronger party, credibly commit to honoring whatever agreement we reach short of war? Finally, the indivisible-issue obstacle comes up in conflicts over values that either literally cannot be divided (one thinks here of the apocryphal tale of Solomon's decision to divide a baby in half to satisfy two women who claim to be the mother) or that for one reason or another, the two parties consider indivisible.[2] Territory, or more specifically, *homeland* territory, often has this characteristic.

Understanding ethnic war therefore requires an understanding of how two actors come to view control over the same piece of ground as an indivisible issue.[3] For ethnic groups, the key factor is settlement patterns—that is, where groups live and whether they are concentrated in a homeland and a majority or a minority. Settlement patterns bind the capability and legitimacy of an ethnic group's mobilization for sovereignty. Where both capability and legitimacy are high, as they are for groups concentrated in a region of a state, ethnic groups are likely to consider control over disputed territory an indivisible issue and demand sovereignty. However, states are likely to view control over a territory—even a worthless or costly territory—as an indivisible issue whenever precedent-setting effects come into play. Precedent setting operates when a state faces more than one potential secessionist. The state fears establishing the reputation that it allows the division of its territory. Only when both an ethnic group and a state, usually for different reasons, view the issue of territorial control as indivisible will violence erupt. If, however, the ethnic group does not demand sovereignty (that is, make an indivisible claim to the territory) or the state sees its territory as divisible, ethnic war is less likely.

A key contribution of this book is to detail the important differences between political actors in ethnic conflicts and how these differences play themselves out in disputes over territory. Ethnic groups (and nations) are not states. Although reducing ethnic groups to the ontological equivalent of states may make for elegant and parsimonious theories, my research makes it clear that such theories can be of only limited use.[4]

Finally, the central subject of this research is *violent* ethnic conflict. At its root, ethnic conflict is about groups of people arguing with other groups, where the "other" is usually characterized by differences in race, language, or religion. The vast majority of ethnic conflicts do not involve violence.[5] Here, however, my focus is on the subject of violent ethnic conflict—both its presence and its absence. The book's central question is, Why do some ethnic conflicts turn violent, but not others? I do not attempt to explain why ethnic conflicts arise in the first place, only the conditions under which they are more or less likely to escalate to violence.

The Importance of the Issue

Today nearly two-thirds of all armed conflicts include an ethnic component. Ethnic conflicts are almost twice as likely to break out as fights over governmental control and four times more likely than interstate wars.[6] Ethnic conflicts are the most prevalent form of armed conflict and are unlikely to abate in the short or long term. The number and intensity of ethnic conflicts across the globe directly and indirectly threaten the lives of millions. Since World War II alone, millions of people—both those capable of bearing arms and those incapable of doing so—have died as a result of their membership in a specific ethnic group. Understanding the conditions under which ethnic conflicts escalate to violence—especially extreme forms such as genocide—may help political elites and policy makers prevent such fatal outcomes more effectively, or at least reduce their destructiveness when they do happen. The structural explanation I offer holds out the possibility of facilitating this worthy goal.

Beyond highlighting policy options that can work, this book sheds a cautionary light on a number of policy proposals that either are unlikely to work or may prove counterproductive. Marc Trachtenberg proposes one potential policy measure, which my research suggests is problematic.

If the problem in what used to be Yugoslavia is that different ethnic groups there can no longer live together peacefully, and if for reasons having to do with precedent, proximity, and spillover effects in general, the Western world decides that the continuation of such violence is intolerable, then there is no compelling reason that intervention should be limited to preventing starvation or controlling atrocities . . . there is no reason why the outside powers should rule out as illegitimate the very idea of trying to get at the root of the problem—for example, by arranging for an orderly, equitable, and humane exchange of populations.[7]

Trachtenberg's recommendation of population exchanges seems an intuitively sound policy, yet the current empirical research does not make it clear that the exchange and separation of ethnic groups will "get at the root of the problem" and quell ethnic violence.[8] My research shows why.

Ethnically based violence may also expand from conflicts within state boundaries to those involving other states.[9] In the most famous example, World War I, an essentially ethnic conflict between Serbia and Austria-Hungary eventually engulfed all the great powers, resulting in a shattering destruction and loss of life. Similar fears appear today in the cautious approach that European governments are taking to the caustic Balkan environment. Ethnic wars have created refugee flows, disrupted trade, and closed transportation routes, all of which have the potential to destabilize the international system.[10]

The theory of indivisible territory presented in chapter 2 directly addresses these issues by detailing how ethnic conflicts escalate into violence. It demonstrates that without an understanding of what territory means to each actor in a potential negotiation, averting potential conflicts is all but impossible. The theory, which addresses the origins of ethnic violence, also bears on the resolution of such violence. Concerns over control of territory does not wither as a result of armed combat.[11] Instead, the fact of combat usually only reinforces the argument that because more brethren have died defending the land, it is even more incumbent on a new generation of fighters to regain or maintain control over that land.

The Literature

A review of the recent literature on ethnic violence illuminates the ways in which my theory is different from past approaches. Territory as a factor—its meaning and implications—is largely missing from previous considerations. A number of approaches have been proposed to explain ethnic violence, but each provides only a partial explanation for why ethnic violence erupts.[12] These approaches can be divided into three rough categories: material, nonmaterial, and elite.

Thesis: Material-Based Approaches

A number of scholars have approached the subject of ethnic violence by focusing on the material conditions of ethnic groups within a state. This approach has three major strands: development and modernization, relative deprivation, and intrinsic worth.

Political-development and economic-modernization arguments focus on the relative development of regionally concentrated ethnic groups within a state's borders.[13] As the economy and state structures modernize, individuals should transfer their loyalties from their ethnic group to the state, leading to a demise in ethnic identity.[14] This in turn should cause ethnic conflict and violence to diminish. In this theory, any ethnic conflict and violence that remain are the product of uneven development and modernization.[15] Equalize economic development, and ethnic conflict disappears.[16]

The development and modernization approach has not fared well empirically. First, development and modernization have not led to a decline in the salience of ethnic identities or regionally based ethnic conflict and violence. Violence continues to plague Spain and Northern Ireland, for example. Second, violence plagues rich and poor regions alike. In the former Yugoslavia, secessionist demands and violence broke out in the richest regions first, not in the poorest. Only after the federation was fully compromised did violence break out in the backward region of Kosovo. Economic development alone cannot explain the emergence of ethnic conflict and violence.[17]

The group of scholars arguing for relative deprivation focus on resource competition among individuals who identify with a group. They claim that violence stems principally from perceptions of a decline in economic or political conditions after a period of improvement.[18] The resulting competition for resources sparks collective action among individuals, who invariably form groups. As one group mobilizes, other groups are spurred into action. As these groups compete, conflict and violence erupt.[19]

Although the idea of relative deprivation seems intuitively correct, it is impossible to test this theory adequately. Within any given society, individuals and groups have different notions of what constitutes a relative decline or improvement in their standard of living.[20] The theory provides no guidelines on how to measure the perceptions of individuals in a society and how to aggregate those perceptions across groups.

A third major type of material-based argument comes from the international relations literature and focuses on a territory's intrinsic worth, a value that does not vary among actors.[21] In this theory, actors are more willing to use force to secure valuable territory.[22] This argument has two variations: strategic worth and intrinsic value. Often the two are inextricable.[23] Strategic worth describes the security value of a given piece of territory. Is the territory astride major routes of communication? Does it share an interstate border? Does it contain natural barriers to invasion from other states or from states considered historical enemies? Intrinsic-value arguments focus on the wealth or resources that inhere in a territory. Does the territory contain a concentration of mineral or natural resources? Does it possess an infrastructure or industry of value? Does it have space for population expansion or arable land that could support an expanded population? If the loss of the contested territory threatens to undermine the security or economic survival of an actor, then that actor is likely to resort to force. This argument contains a powerful logic, and, as we will see, this logic does explain some variation in outcomes.[24]

Although material conditions do affect relations between states and ethnic groups, explanations based only on material conditions underplay the ethnic dimensions and consequent tensions that might also contribute to conflict. State policies, for example, are not only economic or strategic, nor do they have only economic or material ramifications. Consider the Aral Sea basin. The Soviet state controlled the development and distribution of economic resources throughout the Soviet Union. It adopted policies and industries that undermined both the economic well-being of ethnic groups living in the Aral Sea basin and the cultural heritage of some groups. The huge hydroelectric dams and energy projects that benefited the rest of the Soviet Union caused the Aral Sea to dry up. Areas once teeming with fish are gone, and salt from the sea has caused severe damage to herding areas. The professions of fishing and herding are not only vital to the economic well-being of the indigenous populations of the region but also constitute part of their cultural heritage and national identity. In this case, economic development, or mis-development, by the state has caused these groups to suffer in both economic (material) and cultural (nonmaterial) terms.

Material-based explanations tend to overlook the frequent conjunction between material and nonmaterial factors. They thus oversimplify the motives of the actors. They cannot provide an explanation for why some groups are willing to risk death, internment, or mass deportation for seemingly worthless territory, or why those groups sometimes seek independence even when economic conditions are certain to be more desperate than those they are fighting to leave behind.

Rather than exclusively seek to ensure their material well-being, ethnic groups may rationally choose violence as a means of securing a cultural and historical livelihood that may link them to a particular place.[25] Control over economic development can provide for material needs as well as secure a part of the group's identity. In other words, even if we could redistribute wealth from richer to poorer regions or alleviate economic disparities between groups, such material redistribution would not necessarily eliminate the underlying fears and resentments between them. Finally, these approaches provide no necessary or logical reason why, among all the potential values over which two actors might struggle, material values matter most. The priority of material values is simply assumed. This assumption, as we will see, leads to significant weaknesses in the ability of material-based approaches to offer a general explanation of violent ethnic conflict.

Antithesis: Nonmaterial-Based Approaches

Another group of scholars has written about particular ethnic conflicts and the personalities and events that caused them to escalate. This literature crosses several disciplines, including anthropology, political science, psychology, and sociology. These scholars typically focus on such factors as the identity, history, and cultural heritage of groups to explain ethnic violence. The two most common variants are ancient hatreds and security-dilemma explanations.

ANCIENT HATREDS

Ancient-hatreds arguments explain violent conflict as stemming from long-standing historical enmities among ethnic groups. They tend to place great weight on the linguistic, cultural, racial, and religious ties of individuals within a group. These ties are passed down from generation to generation. Individuals so socialized are considered as being inside the group—they, together with "me," constitute "we." Those outside this socialized group are "they."[26] Because individual identity is so directly tied to that of the group, when the group is threatened, individuals, as members of that group, also feel threatened.[27] Ethnic violence emerges when each group attempts to maintain its boundaries against what it perceives as the depredations of historical enemies.

The ancient-hatreds argument suffers on three counts. First, many ethnic conflicts are not ancient. They may be modern phenomena that can be traced back for only decades as opposed to centuries. The notion of a Bosniak, for example, which differentiated a Bosnian Muslim from a Bosnian Croat or Bosnian Serb, emerged only in the late 1960s. Second, this argument cannot explain why a group that fights wars also cooperates with the group it is fighting against some of the time. Ethnic groups cooperate with one another most of the time.[28] Third, this explanation cannot account for why some cases escalate to violence and others do not.

SECURITY DILEMMA

The second nonmaterialist explanation places ethnic violence in the context of a security dilemma.[29] The central driving force is fear.[30] When the authority of a multinational state declines, the central regime can no longer protect the interests of ethnic groups, creating a vacuum in which ethnic groups compete to establish and control a new regime that will protect their interests. When considering the future composition of a new regime dominated by opposing groups and the probable treatment of their own group within such a new regime, ethnic groups fear widespread discrimination and even death. Imagining a worst-case scenario, each group attributes offensive capabilities and hostile intentions to competing groups.[31] The likely result is violence.

Although the security-dilemma explanation is logically quite powerful, we can find many cases in which fear was not the motivating factor for ethnic violence. The logic of the security dilemma was originally invoked to explain how actors not interested in aggression might nevertheless end up fighting a war. It does not address other motivations such as greed or aggressiveness.[32] In his efforts to mobilize Serbs to attack Bosnia in 1992, Slobodan Milosevic, for example, was probably more motivated by greed or personal ambition than by fear. The collapse of central authority may make some actors fearful, but greed or outright aggressiveness cannot be dismissed as possible motivations for others.

The main difference between nonmaterialist approaches and material-based arguments is that nonmaterialists recognize that individuals, as part of groups, can be mobilized in order to protect elements of their identity. But in many such explanations, the mechanism of violence reduces to the claim that ethnic groups fight because they "naturally" want independence to ensure the protection of their identity and well-being.

Further, nonmaterial-based approaches tend to overemphasize the local or bottom-up aspects of conflicts of interest while downplaying or even ignoring the concerns of a state as an actor in the international system.

Protosynthesis: Elite Manipulation

A third approach emphasizes the role of political leaders in exhorting the masses to violence. Elite-manipulation approaches straddle material and nonmaterial explanations; some scholars focus on the material incentives that leaders use to rally support, and others turn to nonmaterial incentives, such as a leader's charisma and ability to evoke history and national identity.

Elite-manipulation approaches assume that passive masses can be stirred to violence by the oratorical skills of charismatic leaders.[33] Thus nationalism is a tool used to maintain power. The most common recent version of this approach is the delegitimized Communist leaders attempting to hold onto office. Many of these leaders hit upon the convenient idea that they had been ardent nationalists all along. Their privileged access to the state media enabled them to reconstruct national identities, placing themselves at the vanguard of a new national mobilization.[34] Given that many formerly Communist states were multinational, nationalist rhetoric by leaders seeking legitimacy often directed national passions against members of other groups, leading to increased violence. Milosevic, for example, invoked both the history of the Serbian nation as a victim of atrocities dating back for centuries and the threat by the secessionist republics of Croatia and Slovenia to the economic well-being of Yugoslavia. According to Milosevic, Serbs needed to rally to avoid falling victim again to the Croats and to save the Yugoslav economic system from collapse.[35] This explanatory approach has a strong *prima facie* appeal. Nationalist leaders certainly appear to have been responsible for much violence in the twentieth century.

Nevertheless, elite-manipulation theories present at least four problems. First, they misconstrue and underestimate the power of nationalism. They afford nationalism little independent effect. Elites are assumed not to believe in the nationalist cause, and the masses are assumed to be passive victims of the elites' charged rhetoric. The theories provide no evidence that the distribution of demagogues is greater in areas that turn to violence and fail to explain violence in cases in which either the elites or the masses are genuine nationalists. Second, even when elites manipulate symbols, myths, and histories for personal gain, their constructions become embedded in history, perception, and interpretation. Elites are then beholden to this constructed reality if they want to stay in power.[36] Third, elite-manipulation explanations overpredict violence. If leaders can arouse a passive nation to violence, why should they not be able to dissuade an aroused nation from taking up arms? This explanation does not address such cases either logically or empirically. Finally, some elites succeed, and others fail. A recent failure is Slovak prime minister Vladimir Meciar's attempt to inflame an ethnic conflict over borders and minorities. Meciar recommended a population transfer of ethnic Slovak and ethnic Hungarian minorities living in neighboring countries. He was excoriated domestically and internationally.[37] Such cases highlight a chief weakness of elite-manipulation approaches: they cannot be generalized.

Although the literature can be divided into material and nonmaterial-based approaches, none of the scholars mentioned earlier argues that his or her chosen explanation exhausts the useful range of approaches. Each approach explains some occurrences of violence. None by itself, however, constitutes an adequate basis for a general explanation. Material-based approaches suffer when explaining why some ethnic groups and states risk their survival in pursuit of materially worthless land.[38] Nonmaterial-based approaches feature violence as the inevitable consequence of human nature (in this case, the desire to exist in a bounded ethnic community). None explains why some conflicts are much more intense than others or why some groups appear to coexist more easily with others.

Territory As an Indivisible Subject and a Divisible Object

An emphasis on territory and how it informs the motives of actors helps us to better understand the emergence of violence in three ways. First, by examining territory in relation to settlement patterns and homelands we learn how ethnic groups go about legitimating their claims and mobilizing their populations. Second, recognizing the different meanings of territory allows us to better understand the differing behaviors of states. Finally, because violence is an interactive process, seeing how different types of actors view disputed territory helps us to understand how they end up in violence together.

As we will see more fully in the remaining chapters, territory is both a material resource—an object that can be divided and exchanged—and a nonmaterial value—a subject that can be neither divided nor exchanged. The next chapter isolates the conditions under which this logic operates more or less intensely.

Research Methods and Procedures

In this book I examine principally the type of violence that pits ethnic groups against states.[39] This type of violence is more common than other types, for example, group-to-group violence within a state.[40] I have focused on this single category in order to achieve depth and detail. Yet the explanatory scope of the theory introduced here is wide enough to explain other categories of violence. As will become clear in chapter 2, if the state is dominated by one ethnic group with concerns about the integrity of the state *and* the defense of an ethnic historic homeland, then, according to my theory, the state will behave like an ethnic group. This pattern is exemplified by the Israeli-Palestinian struggle. Similarly, two states, each dominated by an ethnic group, might engage in an interstate war for worthless land because the ethnic groups see the disputed land as part of their respective and mutually exclusive homelands. This pattern is exemplified by the conflict between Turkey and Greece over Cyprus. Such interstate wars resemble ethnic wars more than they do wars of conquest.[41]

The main hypotheses of the theory of indivisible territory and ethnic war involve the settlement patterns of ethnic groups and fears of precedent setting by states. If an ethnic group is a majority, concentrated in a region of a state, and is located in its homeland, then it is most likely to see control over a particular territory as indivisible, demand independence, and therefore end up in violence. If a state contains two or more ethnic groups capable of seceding, then it is likely to see its territory as indivisible and resort to violence to maintain its borders. To test these and other hypotheses, I employ two methods. Statistical analysis tests the relationship between key variables (for example, settlement patterns and resources) and the likelihood of violent ethnic conflict, and case study analysis investigates and scrutinizes the logic of this explanation in comparison with alternative explanations.[42] Each method compensates for some of the weaknesses of the other. Although the statistics are not well suited to capturing the element of strategic interaction, they nevertheless help to establish the validity of the more general claim that certain aspects of territory explain ethnic violence. The case studies, however, suffer from being only four of hundreds of potential cases of ethnic-state violence. They may include a bias that I failed to notice in selecting them to test the theory. Yet, where the statistical analysis does not allow us to gain a sense of the interactive element among the combatants, case studies help us enter the minds of the decision makers.

Statistical Analysis

To determine the relationship between territory and violent ethnic conflict, I employ the Minorities at Risk (MAR) data set.[43] Because ethnic conflict is assumed for the inclusion of cases and the data set includes the presence and absence of violent political activity, MAR is an excellent data set for testing my theory. In this project Gurr and his colleagues categorized 275 politically active communal groups from World War II through the 1990s. They included groups that had (1) experienced systematic economic or political discrimination vis-à-vis other groups in a state and/or (2) undertaken some sort of political action (violent or nonviolent) to secure their collective interests. Information for each group includes the level of concentration of minorities, as well as different levels of political action, ranging from no action to full-scale rebellion.

Because this theory is ultimately a model of conflict bargaining, and the decisive variable that produces violence is a lack of issue divisibility among the actors (that is, strategic interaction in bargaining), a direct statistical testing of all the mechanisms of the argument is not possible. Instead, the statistical analyses are used as plausibility probes regarding the more general question of whether the likelihood of ethnic violence varies with (1) different settlement patterns and (2) concerns about precedent setting. In other words, the statistical tests address whether settlement patterns and precedent setting matter, rather than how they matter. The statistics show, for example, that the concentration of an ethnic group in a region is practically a necessary condition for violence and that the dispersion and urbanization of ethnic groups are sufficient conditions for nonrebellion. They do not, and cannot, show that this violence emerged because of actors' specific concerns, such as majority rule or fears of establishing a reputation for allowing a division of its territory.

Case Studies

The particular mechanisms of the theory are tested more systematically by way of process tracing.[44] I examine four case studies, in which two states interact with two component ethnic groups actively seeking greater autonomy and control over their homelands, formerly part of the Soviet Union. These cases consist of Russia in relation to the Chechens and Tatars and Georgia in relation to the Abkhaz and Ajars, roughly from 1990 to 1994.

These cases serve as a good laboratory because they offer variation on both the independent and the dependent variables (for example, settlement patterns and violence due to ethnic conflict). They also control as much as we can hope for in the social sciences for such variables as history (both states had similar forms of government—one-party, communist systems), culture and religion (all four groups more or less adhered to Islam), administrative status (each had equal administrative status in the Soviet Union as an autonomous republic), and the interstate system (their emergence as independent states at approximately the same time produced similar structural constraints and opportunities).

Such case control comes with methodological costs. Perhaps the most glaring cost is the active nationalities policies of the Soviet system, which deeply influenced the geographic disposition of ethnic majorities and minorities in this region. Therefore I distinguish those aspects of ethnic group behavior that might be unique to the region from those that are not.

Yet, for all the problems, there are also benefits, notably the vast amount of readily available census data and number of maps. The Soviet Union was very good at keeping track of its populations. One of the most comprehensive resources available on the visual distribution of populations is the 1964 *Atlas Narodov Mira* (Atlas of the nations of the world).[45] A multitude of other maps are available from authoritative sources such as the United States Central Intelligence Agency (CIA). These two sorts of data provide an accurate picture of the landscape: the census data provide the raw numbers and percentages of group members and the maps graphically depict where people reside.

In conjunction with these census and cartographic data, many primary and secondary accounts describe the play of events in this period. I consulted primary sources such as newspapers, along with the speeches and interviews of politicians involved in the decisions over whether to negotiate or to fight. The nature of nationalist discourse and statesmanship requires an examination of speeches and interviews in light of the audiences to whom their message is directed. Mintimer Shamiyev, the leader of Tatarstan, for example, was more nationalistic when speaking before Tatar nationalists than in interviews that he knew would receive a broader audience. As I researched the case studies, I kept the possibility of such strategic behavior in mind when analyzing the discourse, interpreting what it meant depending on the context. Relatedly, in some cases decision makers might represent a territory as indivisible in order to create the most advantageous bargaining position. We would like evidence, such as diary entries or memorandums from private meetings, to suggest that the decision maker truly believed the territory was indivisible. When such evidence is not available, as is often the case, one needs to scrutinize the behavior of elites and populations. We would expect pragmatic, uncommitted, and self-serving elites to be less consistent in bargaining and less likely to risk violence. Elites who are true believers or committed nationalists are likely to be both more consistent and more willing to risk violence. If elites and their populations willingly put themselves in harm's way to achieve independence, this is a good indication that they truly see the territory as indivisible.

I weigh evidence testing the theory of indivisible territory in light of competing explanations. So, for example, in each case, I consider whether elite-driven or material considerations better account for the emergence of violence or peace.

Plan of the Book

Using the idea of the indivisibility of territory as a foundation for explaining ethnic violence, in the following chapter I set forth the theoretical framework. I begin with an examination of the two types of actors in theory: states and ethnic groups. I argue that ethnic violence is a function of how these actors view territory, which is intricately connected with each type of actor's conception of survival. I lay out two conditions for ethnic violence: if the state regards its territory as indivisible and an ethnic group demands independence, then violence is likely. If either of these conditions is absent, then a negotiated settlement might be achieved.

Statistical tests of the propositions of the theory are laid out in chapter 3. Although due to limitations in available data not all of the variables in the model can be tested, the basic argument about the centrality of territory in explaining ethnic violence receives strong support. The tests show that settlement patterns must be part of any general explanation of ethnic violence. Furthermore, the presence of resources is not a good indicator of violence, whereas the ethnic profile of a state (for example, uninational, binational, or multinational) is.

Further support for the argument is developed in chapters 4 through 7, which detail the case studies in depth. Chapters 4 and 5, respectively, examine Moscow's relations with the Tatars and Chechens from the late 1980s until 1994. The Moscow-Tatar interaction ended in a negotiated settlement, whereas the Moscow-Chechen one turned into a civil war. In the Moscow-Tatar interaction, we find the Tatars representing their interests in divisible terms. Although the Tatars would have liked to control their homeland, their weak demographic presence in the region precluded them from representing Tatarstan as the domain of Tatars only. Economics were at the heart of this conflict, not identity. In the Chechen-Moscow interaction, both sides represented their interests as indivisible. The Chechens, concentrated in their homeland, viewed Moscow as an illegitimate imperial power bent on destroying Chechnya and Chechen identity. In the Chechen view, the conflict that emerged after 1989 was not new but the continuation of a three-hundred-year old struggle that began with their ancestors and would continue with their own deaths, if it came to that. Because both sides viewed control over the territory in indivisible terms, there was no room for compromise. The result was war.

Chapters 6 and 7 move us to Georgia for an examination of Tbilisi's interactions with the Abkhaz and Ajars. As in the previous set of cases, civil war emerged in one (Abkhazia), a negotiated settlement in the other (Ajaria). In Abkhazia we find a minority that sees itself under siege. Most Abkhaz live in Abkhazia, yet they constitute only a small minority (18 percent) of the population. Fear of a loss of identity in a Georgian-dominated state induced the Abkhaz to seek greater autonomy. At first Abkhazia's terms made the territory divisible, as the group sought a loose confederal arrangement. However, once Georgia dispatched troops and Russia came to Abkhazia's aid, Abkhazia's demands shifted. In its view, the territory became indivisible. The state of Georgia represented its interests in indivisible terms all along. This explains why violence marked this interaction. The Ajars represented a completely different situation, in which regional actors spent much of their time convincing the state that they were not a threat, that they saw themselves as part of the broader Georgian nation. The state, however, under siege from multiple secessionist movements, the machinations of power politics by Russia, and its own version of virulent nationalism, had difficulty seeing the Ajars as friends. Although Georgia represented its interests as indivisible, it ultimately recognized that the Ajars were not a threat, and violence was averted.

Taken together, these two pairs of case studies provide for a good deal of variation. In two cases we find civil war breaking out, and in two other cases negotiated settlements were achieved. And the variation in outcomes occurs within each of the two states: both Russia and Georgia either negotiated or fought in one of the two cases.[46] Along with the variation, these cases also offer a fair degree of control. As mentioned earlier, all four ethnic groups adhered to Islam more or less. All experienced the breakup of the Soviet Union at the same time, and all faced similar international constraints and opportunities.

Chapter 8 begins by summarizing the basic argument and introducing both a competing argument—that institutions such as socialist-style federalism can better explain actor capability and legitimacy endowments— and how my theory fares against this argument in explaining the nature of the disintegrations of Czechoslovakia and the Federal Republic of Yugoslavia. It then discusses the limitations of the analysis and concludes with a discussion of its key theoretical and policy implications. Three main theoretical implications and three policy implications follow from this analysis. I argue that, theoretically, it is wrong to assume that ethnic groups are irrational actors, even if they seem to be fighting for worthless territory or a dire economic situation following independence, that some interstate wars resemble ethnic wars more than is commonly recognized, and that elites alone are not responsible for the worst manifestations of nationalism. On the policy side, I argue that for a peaceful resolution to a dispute, both stability and justice must be pursued, that we need to consider how the origins of conflicts affect whether and how they are resolved, and that resettlement and partition must take into account the notion of homeland for true peace to be achieved.

Conclusion

I have a number of goals in this book. The first is to emphasize the vital role that territory continues to play in domestic and interstate affairs. Scholars in international relations sometimes suggest that with globalization and transnationalism, the value of territory is diminishing. Yet, if this were the case, ethnic groups would not be so desperate to control their homelands. Nor would states and the international community hesitate to allow them to do so. In current accounts of ethnic violence, this close connection between identity and the occupation and control of a self-imagined territory has largely been forgotten, both in social science theorizing and in policy making. Forgetting territory keeps us from understanding the dynamics of groups that are, in essence, competing for control over territory.

Second, I want to show that although elites play an important role in inciting ethnic conflicts, audience participation matters as well. This is not a new insight, but it has been largely overlooked by analysts who place the burden of ethnic conflict almost exclusively on the shoulders of elites. The masses are not blind followers.[47]

Third and finally, this focus on territory and indivisibility should provide further evidence that discourse is a vital component in interactions. Even if discourses are not "real," they have real, material consequences. Tales about historic homelands and about the generations of ethnic brethren who gave their lives to defend those homelands may seem half-baked and artificially constructed, but they often resonate with those who tell them and those who listen to them. They consequently affect the cohesion, unity, and mobilization of ethnic groups. These recounted and recast tales also provide information about where a particular group places its ethnogenesis, which in turn reveals the territory its members would like to control. Regardless of their objective validity, these historical discourses have a real impact on the relations between and among ethnic groups and states.

2

Indivisible Territory and Ethnic War

> Of course, the need for a "homeland," a
> national space of one's own, is a central tenet
> of nationalism. Indeed, nationalism is always,
> whatever other aims it may have, about the
> possession and retention of land.
> —*Anthony Smith, The Ethnic Origins
> of Nations*

This book asks a simple but important question: why do some ethnic disputes turn violent and others do not? In other words, what causes ethnic war?

The world is populated with multiethnic states: 82 percent of all independent states comprise two or more ethnic groups, which are often involved in disputes either with each other or with the state itself.[1] Although such disputes do not always lead to war, they often do, as we know from recent history in the Balkans, Rwanda, East Timor, and elsewhere.

As noted in chapter 1, an extensive body of excellent research in bargaining theory tells us that rational actors in a dispute will generally prefer a solution short of violence. And nonviolent conflict resolution is what happens most of the time. However, bargaining theory highlights three categories of obstacles that can explain how two rational actors who prefer a solution short of violence nevertheless end up at war: problems of commitment, of imperfect or private information, and of the indivisibility of issues.[2] In recent years, several scholars have taken up the subject of internal conflict in this framework.[3] But no one has yet explored the problem of issue indivisibility as an obstacle to the nonviolent resolution of ethnic and secessionist conflicts. This book focuses on the issue of the indivisibility of territory as a contribution to our understanding of violent ethnic conflict and war.[4]

This chapter presents a theory of ethnic violence that explains the conditions under which we can expect ethnic groups and states to escalate disputes over territory to violence. It demonstrates that the likelihood of violence depends on how the actors in a dispute view the territory at stake and how they represent their interests over that territory. If both actors maintain that their interests over the territory are indivisible, then they are unlikely to reach an agreement over who should control that territory. The tragic, preeminent case is Jerusalem. Both Jews and Palestinians see parts of Jerusalem as indivisible.[5] According to Yisrael Meir Lau, one of Israel's chief rabbis, "Jerusalem is one and cannot be divided"; similarly, Sheik Sabri, the mufti of Jerusalem, has stated, "We cannot permit any non-Muslim sovereignty over the entire area of Al Aksa [Jerusalem], either above or below ground."[6] So far, both sides have flatly rejected resolutions that grant sovereignty to one or the other group, or schemes for sharing sovereignty. Both groups see the territory as indivisible and represent its control in zero-sum terms. The perception of indivisibility in large measure accounts for why no solution to the status of Jerusalem has emerged and why violence continues to plague this area.

Jerusalem, however, may be an exceptional case. Settlement patterns powerfully influence whether ethnic groups will represent a territory as divisible or indivisible. The settlement pattern of a group in a territory, especially if that territory is its homeland, influences how that group will bargain with competing groups or with the state over control of that territory. Groups concentrated in a region of a state are more likely to represent control over territory as an indivisible issue. Dispersed and urban groups are far less likely to see territory as indivisible. States that include more than one ethnic group capable of seceding are more likely than other states to represent the entire state territory as indivisible. Such states are preoccupied not with homelands but with precedents. They fear that if they allow one group to secede, they will face other secessionists. When both sides see the issues as indivisible, although perhaps for different reasons, nonviolent solutions to the dispute become all but impossible.

A Theory of Indivisible Territory and Ethnic War

Ethnic disputes sometimes turn violent; other times, they are resolved without bloodshed. This section presents a theory that explains when ethnic wars are likely to occur and elaborates the logic underpinning that theory.[7]

Let us assume that the likelihood of ethnic war is largely a function of how the principal antagonists—a state and its disgruntled ethnic minority—think about the territory in dispute.[8] Violence is likely if two conditions are met: (1) the ethnic minority demands sovereignty over the territory it occupies, and (2) the state sees this territory as indivisible from the rest of the state's territory.[9] If either of these conditions is absent, the two sides can cut a deal that averts armed conflict.

When will an ethnic group seek direct control over the territory it occupies (that is, demand sovereignty), and when will a state consider its territory indivisible? The key to understanding ethnic group demands is their settlement patterns. Ethnic groups will seek to rule territory if they are geographically concentrated in a particular region of a country, especially if that region is a historic homeland. They will show little interest in controlling territory when they are either widely dispersed across the state or concentrated only in cities. For states, the key issue is precedent setting: states will refuse to surrender territory to one ethnic group when they fear it might lead other groups to demand independence, setting in motion a process that may unravel the state. Understanding the importance of territorial control to both ethnic groups and states requires understanding the different ways in which each actor links territorial control to its long-term survival.

Territory and Survival

Controlling territory is of great importance to ethnic groups and to states because both actors believe their survival depends on it. Nevertheless, each sees the relationship between territorial control and survival differently. For ethnic groups, territory is often a defining attribute of their identity, inseparable from their past and vital to their continued existence as a distinct group. States are defined by borders and therefore tend to view challenges to those borders as threats to their very existence. The different ways in which ethnic groups and states link their survival to the control of territory largely influences whether territorial disputes end in negotiations or in war.

Ethnic groups are composed of individuals who share (1) a common trait such as language, race, or religion, (2) a belief in a common heritage and destiny, and (3) an association with a given territory.[10] These shared ties are often intricately connected, as the Welsh national anthem illustrates:

> Wales! Wales! I am devoted to my country.
> So long as the sea is a wall to this fair beautiful land,
> may the ancient language remain.

All Welsh share a common lineage and language, and these have deep roots in a particular and distinctive land. Without a Wales, the Welsh could not exist. The territory of Wales is *the* Welsh homeland.

The key to understanding what motivates ethnic groups and their concern for survival is the notion of territory as homeland. Homelands contain "the fundamentals of culture and identity. And, as such, [they are] about sustaining cultural boundaries and boundedness. . . . The other is always and continuously a threat to the security and integrity of those who share a common home."[11] A homeland is therefore a special category of territory: it is not an object to be exchanged but an indivisible attribute of group identity. Regardless of a territory's objective value in terms of natural or man-made resources, ethnic groups rationally view the right to control their homeland as a survival issue. Thus, in places like Jerusalem and Kosovo, men and women continue to risk their lives to establish or maintain control of their homelands. Homeland control means that a group's language can be spoken, its culture expressed, and its faith practiced. This intimate connection between homeland territory and the preservation of identity distinguishes ethnic groups from states when the state is not an expression of the ethnic group.

States view the link between territory and survival differently. A state is the center of political relations for a specific population over which it has the recognized authority to establish and enforce laws—if necessary, by violence.[12] Whereas states provide for the survival of their citizens, including members of ethnic groups, no higher authority provides for the survival of states.[13] As a result, they constantly worry about the physical capacity of other states to compromise their survival.

A key consequence of this deep-seated concern for survival is that states tend to view power in material terms, and they fixate on obtaining, maintaining, developing, measuring, and mobilizing material resources for defense or conquest.[14] Thus, the state's focus on physical survival often overrides subjective or sentimental attachments to land. This perspective contrasts with that of ethnic groups, who view territory as intricately bound with their identity and, ultimately, their survival as a group. Two examples illustrate this difference in perspective. The state of Israel, for example, is perfectly willing to negotiate control over Jerusalem if doing so would improve its security. But Orthodox Jews would never do so, preferring to put their physical survival at risk in order to save Jews from a fate worse than death: the loss of control over a territory that in their view defines what it means to be a Jew. Similarly, in 1999 the Federal Republic of Yugoslavia grudgingly accepted loss of control over Kosovo under threat of destruction from NATO, but Serbs refuse to consider Kosovo lost.

In sum, both ethnic groups and states care about survival, but they define survival and its relationship to territory differently. It remains, therefore, to consider the conditions under which ethnic groups will demand sovereignty and states will regard the disputed territory as indivisible.

Ethnic Groups and the Demand for Sovereignty

Ethnic groups will demand sovereignty when two conditions hold.[15] First, their capabilities must give them a reasonable chance of gaining control of the territory they desire. Second, they must believe that their cause is legitimate. In this section I explain how group settlement patterns affect capability and legitimacy, and how these in turn affect the likelihood of a group's sovereignty demand.

Settlement patterns describe the physical distribution of ethnic groups within states.[16] There are essentially four patterns: concentrated majority, concentrated minority, urban groups, and dispersed groups. Concentrated groups live almost exclusively in a single region. For example, before Yugoslavia broke apart in 1991, ethnic Slovenes were concentrated in one region (now the independent state of Slovenia), in which they constituted 90 percent of the population. Concentrated groups can be majorities or minorities (here the operational meaning of *majority* is equal to or greater than 50 percent). By this definition, the Slovenians were a concentrated majority. Other groups live concentrated in a single region but do not constitute a majority of the region's population. For example, in Abkhazia, a region in the former Soviet Republic of Georgia, ethnic Abkhaz were a concentrated minority because in 1989 they represented only 17 percent of the population, yet most Abkhaz live in the region. Urban groups are concentrated in one or several cities. Eighty-eight percent of ethnic Russians and Russian speakers living in the fourteen new states created from the wreckage of the Soviet Union, for example, live in urban areas.[17] Dispersed groups are those whose members are scattered across a state. The Roma and pre–1945 European Jewry exemplify this pattern.

Although the categorization of these ideal types of settlement is relatively straightforward, their application is more complicated. Actors may disagree as to which lands constitute the claimed territory and whether the named lands constitute the homeland in whole or in part. This logic might be better explained by way of an example. In Sri Lanka, the Tamils and Sinhalese represent two ethnic groups.[18] The Tamils perceive themselves to be a minority group in Sri Lanka, fighting for the self-determination of their homeland of Eelam, in the Northern and Eastern Provinces of Sri Lanka.[19] The Tamils constitute roughly 11 percent of the Sri Lankan population of about 18 million, but they are about 65 percent of the population of Eelam. The Sinhalese, although a majority constituting 74 percent of the population of Sri Lanka, imagine themselves as a minority. This is because they see the Sri Lankan Tamils as one part of a greater Tamil nation, combining the approximately 1 million Indian Tamils within Sri Lanka and an additional 60 million across the strait in the Indian state of Tamil Nadu.[20] Although the Sri Lankan Tamils are fighting exclusively for the autonomy of Eelam, the Sinhalese see the Sri Lankan Tamil drive toward independence as the first step of an invasion of their country by Tamils from abroad and the unification of the entire area in a greater Tamil homeland. In short, to understand how a group perceives its vulnerability and legitimacy, we need to look at both what it perceives to be its homeland and where that homeland stands relative to potential and actual rivals and threats. In this case, the Tamils have represented their case as a concentrated majority under siege in their homeland of Eelam.[21] The Sinhalese have presented their cause in similar terms, fearing being overrun by Tamils not only in the Northern and Eastern Provinces but throughout greater Sri Lanka. Both sides feel equally justified in mobilizing and fighting for control of the territory. Neither side is willing to acknowledge the fears of the other, yet each side has a keen sense of its own status vis-à-vis the contested territory.

Ethnic-group settlement patterns affect both the capability and legitimacy of a group's mobilization for independence. They therefore predict the likelihood that such a demand will be made. *Capability* refers to the capacity to wage a successful fight for independence. The number of group members influences the resources (including armed combatants) that can be brought to bear in the fight. These resources include control over economic, political, and social networks (and their more formal counterparts, institutions), access to communications and media that are vital to concerted action, and money or other goods that can be exchanged for weapons, food, medical supplies, or mercenaries.[22]

Each of the four group settlement patterns has different capability implications. Urban groups have the highest capabilities. Residence in an urban area implies access to media and money, as well as dense networks (especially economic ones). Urbanites tend to be more closely connected than nonurban groups and better informed about state policies that affect them. As a result, urbanites are likely to be the most efficient mobilizers.

Concentrated majorities have capabilities second only to those of urban groups. As majorities, these groups can be expected to mobilize more fighters and resources in pursuit of sovereignty than minority or dispersed groups. They are also more likely to have dense networks and to control local institutions.

For concentrated minorities, capability is indeterminate: some groups are the largest in their region, others may be the smallest.[23] When the group is relatively small, it is unlikely to control many local resources or dominate networks. This disadvantage hampers the group's efforts at mobilization.

Dispersed groups will have the weakest capabilities. Because members are scattered across a state, dispersed groups are unlikely to have the ability to gather together the fighters necessary to achieve sovereignty in any particular region or develop the dense networks that facilitate coordinated action. Effective mobilization will therefore prove difficult.

Legitimacy refers to the perceived justness of the cause; because it determines the *effectiveness* of mobilizing capability, legitimacy directly influences a group's decision to seek sovereignty.[24] Legitimacy enhances resource mobilization because group members are more willing to sacrifice wealth and risk their lives in pursuit of a just cause. Two principles of legitimacy link settlement patterns to a group's demand for sovereignty: homeland and majority rule.

The homeland principle is the idea that a people with deep roots and a historical attachment to the land have a right to control it. Control over the homeland is vital because it determines how economic and political resources are distributed, how many foreigners can immigrate, which languages are recognized, sponsored, and spoken, and which gods may be worshiped. Losing control of homeland territory may therefore result in a loss of the capacity to reproduce nationals and, by extension, of national identity. In Canada, for example, the main motivation for the Québécois' demand for sovereignty is the protection of spoken French. Without the French language, the Québécois would soon cease to exist *as* Québécois. Canada's opposition to Québécois' demands has been constrained by the widely perceived legitimacy, even among English-speaking Canadians, of a "Québec for Québécois."

The homeland principle incorporates notions of investment and tenure that are often used to justify ethnic-group mobilization for sovereignty. *Investment* refers to a group's contribution to a given territory: a group's development or sacrifice in defense of the land may be advanced in order to establish a legitimate claim to its control.[25] For example, although ethnic Serbs constituted a tiny minority of Kosovo's population, Yugoslav leader Slobodan Milosevic argued that Serbs were entitled to control Kosovo because in the fourteenth century Serb ancestors had sacrificed their lives resisting marauding Ottomans. Most historical myths include tales of heroism against marauding bands in defense of the homeland. Blood spilled by a nation's predecessors continues to legitimate claims to territory. The Boers invoked the deeds of ancestors as a way to legitimate their claims in their fight against the British; a Boer war song expresses these sentiments.

Leave us alone! Leave us alone!
You shall not rob us of our own;
We will be free! We will be free!
Our birthright shall our standard be.

Our fathers' sweat, our fathers' blood
Have soaked the ground on which they stood;
Our mothers' tears, our mothers' toil,
Have hallowed this Afric soil.

This is our land! This is our land!
Reclaimed by our fathers' hand;
Reclaimed once, we claim it now,
As made a garden by our plough.

We ask, what has to us been left?
We will no longer be bereft!
For Fatherland and freedom dear,
We die, or live, and vanquish here![26]

The principle of tenure is based on the identity of the first people to inhabit a territory.[27] Groups often claim the right to control a territory if their ethnic ancestors settled it first. Serbs consider Kosovo the cradle of the Serbian nation because it was the seat of a medieval Serbian empire. Albanians go even farther back in time, tracing their ancestors to ancient Illyrian tribes. Both groups see Kosovo as their legitimate homeland. Both have a strong attachment to the region, and both have battled with pen and sword to defend their claims. The Albanians, however, have something the Serbs do not: a majority.

The majority-rule principle is simple: if one group comprises 50 percent or more of the population in a given region, it should be entitled to govern. As a principle of legitimacy, majority rule is important for three reasons. First, in contemporary liberal states, it is widely regarded as a foundational democratic principle, if not the most important one.[28] Wherever democracy is viewed as legitimate, claims based on majority status must also be viewed as legitimate.[29] Second, a majority is quantifiable and easily recognizable. Outside observers and participants in a dispute can agree more easily on whether a group constitutes a majority than on the validity of tenure or investment. Finally, majority rule often facilitates ethnic group mobilization. As Thomas Schelling points out, "People require some signal, preferably a signal so plain and so potent everyone can be sure that everyone else will respond similarly, thus affording one another the greater immunity that goes with action in large numbers."[30] Majority status therefore explains both how some ethnic groups are able to overcome collective action problems and why states are often reluctant to conduct plebiscites, referenda, and formal censuses.[31] States face high risks in denying greater political autonomy to groups that have a majority within a given territory. For example, although Belgrade claimed the right to protect minority Serbs in Kosovo before 1999—by brutal means if necessary—the fact that more than 90 percent of the regional population of Kosovo was (and still is) ethnic Albanian seriously undermined the legitimacy of Belgrade's position.

Each of the four settlement patterns has different legitimacy implications. Concentrated majorities have the highest legitimacy. They enjoy the legitimacy of majority rule, and because they are less likely than urban or dispersed groups to be recent arrivals, they are more likely to claim homeland legitimacy as well. The combination of high capability and high legitimacy makes these groups the most likely to demand sovereignty and risk violence toward that end.

Concentrated minorities have mixed legitimacy. Although they may be fighting for control of a homeland, the lack of majority status in that homeland is sure to hinder the effectiveness of their mobilization efforts. Regarding capabilities, these groups are also less likely than concentrated majorities to have sufficient resources to risk violence in pursuit of independence.[32] In short, these groups are less likely to demand sovereignty than concentrated majorities but more likely to do so than either urbanites or dispersed groups.

Urbanites are especially weak on the legitimacy dimension. They are usually recent immigrants who, unlike concentrated majorities and minorities, lack a strong sense of attachment to the land they occupy.[33] As a result, those urbanites who are passionately devoted to a homeland are usually attached to a distant land, rather than to the city in which they reside. Two consequences follow. First, attachment to a land other than the city of residence makes group claims to majority status unlikely, even in those rare circumstances when numbers support their cause. Second, because their employment skills tend to be transportable, in a crisis urban groups are more likely than other groups to flee than to fight.[34] Ethnic Russians living beyond the Russian Federation, for example, did not take up arms to keep the union together when the Soviet Union collapsed, even though they controlled many key institutions and had the best jobs and the most money. For the most part (excepting Russians in Kazakhstan and Ukraine who settled before the twentieth century and are viewed as "native" to the areas), these new-minority Russians simply packed their bags. Large-scale migration, not violence, has been the norm. Thus, although their potential capabilities are the highest among the four group patterns, their legitimacy is the lowest; and without a willingness to act, potential capabilities are largely irrelevant. States should therefore be less worried about urbanites than about concentrated-majority or concentrated-minority groups.

Dispersed groups combine low legitimacy with low capability. Their scattered presence precludes them from claiming majority-rule legitimacy (even when they view a region as their homeland), and they will find it difficult to mobilize potent military forces. States should therefore be least concerned about dispersed groups. Table 2.1 presents a summary of these relationships.

In sum, variations in settlement patterns explain variations in group capacity and legitimacy, which in turn predict variations in the likelihood

TABLE 2.1
Ethnic Groups and the Demand for Sovereignty

Settlement Patterns	Capability	Homeland Legitimacy	Majority-rule Legitimacy	Likelihood of Sovereignty Demand
Concentrated majority	High	High	High	High
Concentrated minority	Indeterminate	High	Low	Moderate
Urbanites	High	Low	Low	Low
Dispersed	Low	Low	Low	Low

that a group will risk violence to gain sovereignty. But when does ethnic war actually break out? In the next section I explain when states are likely to resist an ethnic group's demand for sovereignty, thus causing a war.

The State and Its Territorial Integrity

States will regard territory as indivisible when they believe that allowing one ethnic group to gain territorial sovereignty will set a precedent that encourages other ethnic groups to demand self-rule. In this section, I explain (1) why multinational states are the only type of states that worry about precedent setting; (2) how precedent setting influences political leaders in multinational states; (3) why precedent setting explains state intransigence better than arguments on the economic or strategic value of territory; and (4) why it may provoke multinational states to oppose dissatisfied ethnic groups quickly and violently.

For states facing an ethnic group's sovereignty demand, the key question is whether the secession of the group will set a precedent for other groups, thus spurring subsequent secessions. A state's ethnic profile (the number of ethnic groups it contains) determines whether this precedent-setting effect applies. There are three types of ethnic profiles: uninational, binational, and multinational. Uninational states are ethnically homogeneous. Ethnic Poles, for example, comprise 98 percent of Poland's population. Ethnic secession is not possible in uninational states. Binational states contain two well-defined ethnic groups. In the former Czechoslovakia, for example, Czechs and Slovaks were concentrated in western and eastern regions of the state respectively. In binational states, precedent setting will almost never be an issue because one secession cannot provoke subsequent secessions.[35] Czechoslovakia's "velvet divorce," for example, was peaceful because after Slovak secession, no other potential secessionists remained to threaten the integrity of the new Czech and Slovak states.

Multinational states contain more than two ethnic groups. They are by far the most common type of state, comprising roughly 90 percent of the distribution of state ethnic profiles worldwide.[36] Indeed, two-thirds of all independent states contain three or more concentrated ethnic groups, making these states particularly concerned about precedent setting. Examples include India, Myanmar, and Russia, all of which govern concentrations of many distinct racial, linguistic, and religious groups.

In multinational states, precedent setting powerfully constrains the government's willingness to bargain over territorial control. Virtually all states are likely to be concerned about precedent setting. In Roger Fisher's view, "A precedent is a fact which cannot be undone by accompanying the action with a statement that it is not a precedent. The fact demonstrates to oneself as well as to others what actions one is prepared to take under particular circumstances."[37] A state may therefore press a position, not necessarily for the immediate consequences but with the hope of establishing (or avoiding) a precedent for the future. Precedent setting can thus become one way in which a seemingly worthless piece of territory is elevated to the status of a vital interest: the loss of the territory itself matters far less than the precedent its loss might set. The practical effect of precedent setting is to make a state's entire territory indivisible.

The logic of precedent setting influences leaders in multinational states in four ways.[38] First, leaders are acutely aware that actions taken toward one ethnic group may serve as an example of what is acceptable for other ethnic groups, thereby becoming a principle of legitimacy. As a principle of legitimacy, precedent setting works by assuming an equality of status among political units. If all units are considered equal, rights granted to one political unit must count as legitimate rights for all similar units. This factor of equality creates particular problems for multinational states that grant equivalent status to their component ethnic groups. During the final months of the Soviet Union, for example, Soviet premier Mikhail Gorbachev deliberately tried to deter Russian leader Boris Yeltsin's bid for Russian independence by elevating the status of autonomous republics (for example, Chechnya and Tatarstan) to the same level as union republics (for example, Latvia and Ukraine). The union republics had long been guaranteed the right to secede under the Soviet constitution, but the autonomous republics had not. Because sixteen of the twenty-one Soviet autonomous republics were located in Russia, if Gorbachev had succeeded, the newly independent Russia might have faced sixteen entitled secessionists.[39] In short, unless a clear historical factor distinguishes one group's status from all others (thus justifying special treatment), multinational states will view disputed territory as indivisible, thereby increasing the likelihood of war.

Precedent-setting logic also explains why states sometimes bargain hard for worthless territory yet in other cases give up economically or strategically valuable land. Consider a hypothetical country with two dissatisfied ethnic groups, each concentrated in a different region. One region is economically backward and a net drain on state resources, and the other contains oil, gold, and defensible mountains. Although allowing the backward region to secede may seem rational—the loss would leave the state better off—this sets a precedent that encourages the oil- and gold-rich region to secede, thus endangering the state's survival. Even assuming that the material and strategic value of the state's ethnic regions were equal, the logic of precedent setting suggests that the threat of *cumulative* losses may jeopardize the state.[40]

Third, precedent-setting logic also explains state intransigence better than the most compelling alternative explanation, which is that states will be unwilling to give up control over territory that contains valuable resources, either economic (for example, diamonds, gold, petroleum) or strategic (defensible mountains, rivers, or even plutonium). Because gold, petroleum, and defensible mountains equal power, and power equals survival, states may calculate that their security demands unequivocal control over territory containing these resources. The problem with this argument is that although states will bargain harder for strategically valuable territory—because strategic and especially economic issues are divisible—states can often negotiate arrangements that compensate them for anticipated losses. For example, once Russia's independence set a precedent for other union republics, such as Ukraine and Kazakhstan, to declare independence, Russia was surrounded by weak states containing valuable strategic and economic resources. In Ukraine, for example, Russia faced the possibility that key elements of the Soviet Union's nuclear-weapons manufacturing and defense system—including surface-to-surface ballistic missiles with nuclear warheads—might fall under the control of a new and potentially hostile state. Ukraine faced a proximate and much larger potential adversary in Russia and for this reason should have sought to keep these weapons and control of their manufacturing facilities in order to protect itself from a potential threat from Russia or any other state. Yet Russia and Ukraine cut a deal that left Ukraine with the Black Sea fleet and Russia with possession of all Soviet nuclear weapons. The divisibility of economic and strategic goods explains why states are often willing to negotiate over resource-rich territory. Precedent-setting logic explains why states sometimes risk violence over worthless territory.

Finally, precedent-setting logic explains why a state faced with an ethnic group's demand for sovereignty might respond both quickly and violently. If willingness to countenance one secession might provoke subsequent secession demands, it follows that a swift and forceful response to a first demand might set a precedent that deters subsequent demands.[41] Milosevic's decision to move troops to Slovenia, for example, sent a clear signal to other independence-minded republics that sovereignty was not negotiable. Thus the more quickly and violently a multinational state acts to prevent secession by any group, the fewer secessionists it is likely to face.[42]

Modeling the Interaction of Interests

Because bargaining is an interactive process, failures and successes in bargaining are not necessarily the result of one actor adopting a position that represents its interests as indivisible. Therefore, we need to consider the intersection of the actors' interests in bargaining situations.

Issue divisibility dramatically reduces the likelihood of violence, whereas indivisibility increases its likelihood. To reiterate, because they experience an attachment to the land which has little to do with the land's strategic worth or resources, ethnic groups, especially concentrated majorities and concentrated minorities, are more likely to represent independence as an indivisible issue. States with more than one group capable of seceding are more likely to present the same territory as part of a larger indivisible whole due to their fears of precedent setting. If both the state and the ethnic group calculate that control of the disputed territory is indivisible, violence is likely; if neither does so, violence is unlikely. This logic is shown in table 2.2. What we are looking for in these cases, then, are situations that cause both sides to represent the issue of contention as indivisible and what happens when just one side does.

This theory explains why the Israeli-Palestinian conflict is so difficult to resolve. "Land for peace" is a classic state strategy for accommodation in negotiations.[43] But so long as the state of Israel is controlled by conservative Jews, the lands of Judea and Samaria are not divisible: they appear as indivisible components of Jewish identity.[44] The Palestinian Arabs, for their part, do not yet have a state. They do, however, lay claim to much of the territory of Palestine as a homeland. At various times the Palestinians have invoked both majority rule and tenure arguments to support their case. Israelis have responded with the tenure and investment principles, and later, as the Jewish population increased due to immigration, with majority rule. The same territory is currently represented by both sides as indivisible. So long as both sides represent the issue of control over this disputed territory as indivisible, conflict will continue.

TABLE 2.2
Bargaining Model:
Indivisibility of Issues

	Actor 1	
Actor 2	Indivisible	Divisible
Indivisible	Violence likely	Violence possible
Divisible	Violence possible	Violence unlikely

The move from a representation of interests—divisible or indivisible—to the likelihood of violent conflict is a matter of probabilities. When both sides represent their interests as indivisible, the probability of violence increases; no deal can be made. If either or both represent their interests as divisible, then the probability of violence decreases; a deal can be made. We may hypothesize the following:

- If both a state and an ethnic group represent their interests as indivisible, then the chance of reaching a settlement short of war is unlikely.
- If either a state or an ethnic group represents its interests as divisible, then the chance of reaching a settlement short of war is possible.
- If both a state and an ethnic group represent their interests as divisible, then the chance of reaching a settlement short of war is likely.

These hypotheses will be tested in subsequent chapters. An important consequence of modeling ethnic violence in this way is the suggestion that a key to avoiding violence is in encouraging actors to advance divisible issues. If even one of two parties to a dispute advances a divisible issue, the chances that a solution short of violence can be reached are dramatically improved.

A Caveat: Actor Rationality and the Costs of War

Until this point I have left out any direct discussion of the costs of war. War is costly, and states and ethnic groups would prefer not to fight to obtain their desired ends. Classic deterrence logic tells us that decision makers bent on conquest will calculate the strength of their adversary and will fight if the balance favors them by a significant margin. If the balance does not favor them, they will hold off. Every state has an interest in maintaining enough military capability relative to its largest independence-minded component group so that it can always attack and suppress that group if necessary. The ethnic group will then have to face a state that in all likelihood has the capability not only to meet but to quash any movement for self-determination.[45] This seemingly inevitable defeat does not mean groups challenging the state are irrational. Ethnic groups might risk a "hopeless" war for at least five possible reasons. First, it is not certain that secessionists will lose; they may be able to inflict high enough losses on the state to achieve some of their aims.[46] Second, the decision to fight may not rest, or rest clearly, with the ethnic group. The group may be propelled into violent conflict by the state. Ethnic groups have limited aims and are located within a distinct territory. Thus for many, such conflicts are defensive in nature. The group will seek control over a limited piece of territory, not territorial aggrandizement. Third, even if a group calculates that the chances of victory are slight relative to the risks of violence, its members may initiate violent conflict because they fear that to wait might expose them to an even worse outcome, such as genocide.[47] Fourth, sometimes leaders provoke a crackdown to gain support internally or externally. Internally, the fact that the state shows its "true" colors by resorting to violence helps mobilize coethnics. Externally, ethnic groups might gain international sympathy if the state is seen as wrong or too harsh in its use of force. Groups with large diasporas might provoke a crackdown in an effort to involve foreign powers on their side. Fifth, conditions may have become so dire that there is essentially nothing to lose by fighting. Groups in the process of being rounded up for mass murder are in this category. One thinks of the example of the Warsaw Ghetto Uprising of World War II, in which thousands of Jews being warehoused before transportation to death camps organized a desperate resistance against the Nazis, who were holding them prisoner in a special district of Warsaw.

For all these reasons, resorting to violence and war usually does not mean irrationality or the failure to maximize utilities. Rather, each actor defines its utility differently. Ethnic groups want to control territory because it means securing their identity. A secure identity, in turn, guarantees the group's continued existence and survival. States desire territorial integrity even if guaranteeing that integrity means that they might have to devolve political power.[48] Regardless of a group's size, if it manages to secede, it sets a precedent. Therefore states may agree to negotiate changes in political structures but not in borders. For states, secure borders equal survival.

Summary

This chapter introduced a theory to explain why violence breaks out between some states and their disgruntled ethnic groups but not others. The key to explaining violence, I argue, is understanding the different

ways in which states and ethnic groups think about the connection between control of territory and their survival. For ethnic groups, control of
territory ensures survival by protecting group identity. For states, control
of territory is directly linked to physical survival. To resort to violence,
both states and ethnic groups must calculate that they need to control
the same piece of territory to guarantee their survival. Whether an ethnic
group is likely to risk violence in pursuit of territorial sovereignty depends
on its settlement pattern. Ethnic groups that form a concentrated majority in a particular region of a state, especially if that region is considered
their homeland, are more likely to press for independence than ethnic
groups that are dispersed or urbanized or that constitute concentrated
minorities. States will oppose an ethnic group's sovereignty demands
with violence, regardless of a territory's material worth, when letting go
of that land might set a precedent that encourages or legitimates subsequent demands by other dissatisfied groups. If an ethnic group is willing
to accept an outcome short of full independence, or if the state sees its
territory as divisible, ethnic war is unlikely to break out. When an ethnic
group demands independence and a state fears precedent setting, ethnic
war is almost certain to occur.

In this chapter I have argued that the choice between violence and
accommodation in disputes over territory is conditioned by the expected
utility of fighting for control over that territory. I have proposed that to
understand which outcome is likely, we need to assess the different meanings of territory and the survival interests of states and ethnic groups.

Although precedent setting may also be seen as a legitimacy principle
for states, the ultimate challenge is not proving that the cause is just but
maintaining order and borders. The survival of the state is perceived to be
at stake. If a multinational state determines that precedents may be set,
then it will probably do its utmost to retain control of every piece of
territory in its charge and will represent its interests in the territory as
indivisible.

I have highlighted how both capabilities and legitimacy are important
in assessing whether ethnic groups will risk violence. Having no capabilities means not fighting. However, capabilities alone cannot explain
why some fights occur, especially in cases in which the state has overwhelming force at its disposal. To mobilize support for the cause, each
side has to make the case that its cause is legitimate. This is simpler in
some cases than in others. I have highlighted two principles of legitimacy
that might be invoked: majority rule and homeland. I have argued that
the majority-rule principle is the most powerful in that it both enhances a
group's capacity to fight and gains credence from being one of the core
tenets of democratic rule. The homeland principle is also quite powerful
in legitimating claims over who is the rightful owner of a given territory.

As we will see in subsequent chapters, much ink and blood have been spilled defending these principles.

The next chapter tests the proposed relationship between territory, settlement patterns, precedent setting, and the likelihood of violent ethnic conflict. For data I rely on phase 3 of the Minorities at Risk data set.

3

Territory and Violence

A STATISTICAL ASSESSMENT

> The force of the people . . . operates only when
> concentrated; it evaporates and disappears with
> extension.
> —*Jean-Jacques Rousseau, The Social Contract*

This chapter offers two tests of my theory's main hypotheses. The first test focuses on the part of the argument that deals with the aggrieved ethnic group and examines my hypotheses about the relationship between certain settlement patterns and violence. The second test considers the interests of the state as well, examining the effect of five factors on the likelihood of violence: (1) the relative impact of settlement patterns; (2) attachment to homeland; (3) the duration of residence in a region; (4) precedent setting; and (5) the richness of resources in a region.

The findings regarding settlement patterns and the likelihood of violence are striking.[1] Two findings stand out. First, a group's concentration in a region of a state serves as practically a necessary condition for violence, whereas urbanism and dispersion are practically sufficient conditions for nonviolent political activity. This statistical finding is important because although there is a sense in the social sciences that the concentration of ethnic groups "should" matter, no researcher has yet determined empirically whether this is the case or offered a satisfactory explanation for how the concentration or dispersion of ethnic groups influences politics and war. Second, the richness of resources in a region is negatively associated with violence. This finding counters the conventional wisdom that states fight for rich regions and not poor ones. The analysis presented here supports the idea that something other than the material value of a territory accounts for ethnic violence.

Two Statistical Tests

The data I employ for the two statistical tests are from phase 3 of the Minorities at Risk (MAR) data set.[2] MAR is appropriate for testing the theory's propositions for two reasons. It is the largest data set on issues related to ethnicity and conflict. Unlike data sets of civil wars, which exclude cases in which no war results, MAR accounts for outcomes in which violence was absent, as well as civil war.[3] MAR is also well suited to testing my theory about the relationship between ethnic groups and states, because the unit of analysis in MAR is ethnic groups, and it specifies several levels of group violence against the state.[4]

The dependent variable is the same for both tests: violence between the state and the ethnic group. This is captured by MAR's REBEL variable. The range of activity moves from "none reported," which is indicated by a score of 0, to "protracted civil war," which is indicated by a score of 7. Intervening levels of rebellion (from "local rebellion" to "guerrilla activity") fall between 0 and 7. The values correspond to the levels of activity presented in table 3.1.

TABLE 3.1
Rebellion Variable

Label	Value
0	None reported
1	Political banditry
2	Campaigns of terrorism
3	Local rebellion
4	Small-scale guerrilla activity
5	Intermediate guerrilla activity
6	Large-scale guerrilla activity
7	Protracted civil war

For some of the analysis, I collapsed these values to "no rebellion," "low-intensity rebellion," and "high-intensity rebellion." Because large-scale guerrilla activity and protracted civil war involved similar levels of engagement among the participants, including the willingness to engage the state (or groups controlling the state) and the resources needed for such engagements, I collapsed them together under high-intensity rebellion. Protracted civil war involved rebel militaries fighting from base areas, and large-scale guerrilla activity engaged more than one thousand armed fighters in more than six armed attacks per year, and those attacks affected large parts of the area occupied by the group. The remaining, lower levels of rebellious activity involved fewer resources, manpower, and engagements.[5] The collapsed categories are summarized in table 3.2.

The REBEL variable is coded for five-year periods since 1945, based on the highest level of violence within each five-year period.[6] Because

TABLE 3.2
Composite Rebellion Variable

Label	Value
0	No rebellion
1	Low intensity (political banditry to intermediate guerrilla activity)
2	High intensity (large-scale guerrilla activity to civil war)

most of the background data used to code the cases (such as population figures) are from the 1980s and early 1990s, I examined three inclusive periods from the data set: 1980–84, 1985–89, and 1990–95.[7] I collapsed these three time periods to derive a "maximum level of rebellion" score for each group over the entire sixteen-year period.

In the first test, the independent variable group is settlement patterns; this assesses whether settlement patterns are associated with different levels of violence or rebellion. I derive settlement patterns from MAR's group spatial concentration measures (REG, or region) as listed in table 3.3.

These REG variables underpin the analysis here to create the composite variable "settlement pattern." Settlement pattern collapses the six values (plus six subvalues) into four, which correspond directly with those of the theory of indivisible territory. Table 3.4 presents these values.

I supplemented a good deal of majority and minority status data for

TABLE 3.3
Spatial-Concentration Variable

Label	Value
REG1	Group concentrated in one region
REG2	Majority in one region, minority in nearby areas
REG3	Dispersed minority in one region
/1	Living separately
/2	Living interspersed
/3	Degree of integration unknown
REG4	Majority in one region, others dispersed
REG5	Predominantly urban
REG6	Widely dispersed
/1	Living separately
/2	Living interspersed
/3	Degree of integration unknown

TABLE 3.4
Settlement-Pattern Variable

Label	Value
0	Dispersed (REG6 coded)
1	Urban (REG5 coded)
2	Concentrated minority (REG1–4 coded)
3	Concentrated majority (REG1–4 coded)

cases missing information in MAR (the total number of cases is 270). Nonetheless, quite a few of them (83) are still missing data, as indicated in the total in table 3.5. Table 3.5 reveals that slightly less than a majority of cases (48.3 percent) are concentrated majorities. Urban groups are the least common in the data set, followed by concentrated minorities and the dispersed, equally.

Settlement Patterns and Violence

I regressed rebellion (using ordinary least squares) on three dichotomous measures of settlement patterns: concentrated minority, which takes on a value of 1 if the group constitutes a minority of the population in a region and 0 otherwise; urban, which takes on a value of 1 if the group lives largely in cities and 0 otherwise; and dispersed, which takes on a value of 1 if the group is scattered across a state and 0 otherwise. Concentrated-majority groups are the baseline category (the constant).

This test determines whether, as my theory predicts, concentrated majorities displayed higher levels of violence than other types of groups. The constant term provides information on the mean level of violence of ethnic groups that are concentrated majorities. The mean level of violence among these groups is 2.78, substantially higher than the scores for the three other types of settlement patterns.[8] Concentrated minorities, dis-

TABLE 3.5
Overview of MAR Cases, according to Settlement-Pattern Variable

Settlement-Pattern Value	Label	N	% of cases
0	Dispersed	40	19.3
1	Urban	27	13.0
2	Concentrated minority	40	19.3
3	Concentrated majority	100	48.3
Total		207	100

TABLE 3.6
Regression of Rebellion on Settlement Patterns

Variables	Coefficient	Standard Error
Constant/Concentrated majority	2.780*	.353
Concentrated minority	−1.605*	.490
Urban	−2.447*	.472
Dispersed	−2.105*	.418
Number of cases		207
R-squared		0.170

*$p < .01$, one-tailed test.

persed groups, and urban groups have lower levels of violence (the coefficients are statistically significant and negative). Urbanites display the lowest level of violence overall. The results of this first regression analysis are summarized in table 3.6.

This test provides strong support for the hypothesis that particular settlement patterns increase the likelihood of violence. It clearly shows that concentrated majorities are the most prone to violence. Further, it shows that concentrated majorities are two and a half times more likely than concentrated minorities and approximately four to five times more likely than urban and dispersed groups to engage in rebellion. These results are shown in figure 3.1.[9] Of all ethnic groups engaged in large-scale rebellion, 78 percent were concentrated majorities.[10] The other three categories together made up the remaining 22 percent of groups engaged in large-scale rebellion. Only 37 percent of concentrated majorities that were involved in ethnic conflict did not engage in any sort of violence; of the 63 percent that did engage in some sort of political violence, 25 percent were involved in large-scale rebellion (see figure 3.1). Concentrated minorities were substantially less active: 68 percent were not engaged in any type of rebellion, and of those who did, only 10 percent engaged in large scale rebellion. Dispersed groups revealed levels similar to concentrated minorities: 80 percent were not engaged in any rebellion, whereas only 5 percent were involved in large-scale rebellion. Urban groups hardly engaged in rebellion: 93 percent of urbanites were not involved in any rebellion. Only one urban group was engaged in large-scale rebellion, a case that may reflect a coding error.[11] These data clearly show that concentrated majorities are the most rebellious and worrisome group for states, and urbanites are the least worrisome, thus supporting a principal tenet of my theory.

Consistent with the theory of indivisible territory, the lack of violence among dispersed groups can be explained by a reduced capacity for mo-

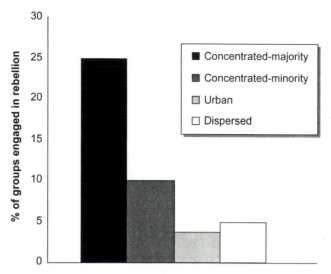

FIGURE 3.1. Settlement Patterns and Frequency of Rebellion, 1980–95

bilization: members of this group are too spread out to form networks and to organize in violent protests against the state. But what then explains the reticence of urban groups?[12] Although urbanites are concentrated in cities, their lack of attachment to the land is a good predictor that they will not mobilize to control that land. In fact, compared with those concentrated in regions, urbanites also had among the lowest mean scores for nonviolent protest during the 1980s.[13] Urbanites, it seems, do not even "voice" their grievances, but simply "exit" the political arena, to use Hirschman's terminology. The 1992–95 war in Yugoslavia supports this claim. It was the Kraijina Serbs in Croatia, and not those in Zagreb, who took action. As Misha Glenny laments, "These urban Serbs were among the greatest victims of the war, whose plight, however, is one of the least well known."[14]

The confounding case of urbanized ethnic violence between Protestants and Catholics in Northern Ireland may be attributed to the centrality of Belfast. Violence has plagued Belfast for decades. Even if Belfast is an exception to the rule, this exception bolsters my argument about the importance of ethnic groups' attachment to territory and homeland. In chapter 2 I argued that one of the primary reasons ethnic groups take up arms to secure their objective is that they view the territory in question as part of their identity; to put it another way, control of the territory means control over their identity. Both Protestants and Catholics view Northern

Ireland as rightfully theirs and vital to their identity: the primary conflict of interest hinges on whether Northern Ireland should be part of the United Kingdom or of the Republic of Ireland.[15] Because of the meaning of this territory as a homeland to both, it is not surprising that these groups have resorted to ethnic violence. The theory of indivisible territory, in other words, can readily explain this exceptional case.

At every level, dispersed minorities and urbanites do not seem prone to political activity, whether directly or indirectly. This finding is important for three reasons. Although it cannot tell us why the most concentrated groups—urbanites—are the least engaged in violence, it clearly demonstrates that demographic concentration *alone* cannot predict the likelihood of violence. This is important because to explain the outbreak of violence, both capability and legitimacy are necessary. An ethnic group must possess not only the capability for action but also a legitimate cause to justify mobilization. Second, the lack of violent activity by widely dispersed and urban ethnic groups means that, statistically speaking, dispersion or urban status is a sufficient condition for not resorting to violence, as well as to other types of political activity. Third, this analysis clearly indicates that concentrated majorities are the most worrisome for states.

A Full Test of the Theory of Indivisible Territory

Because violence depends on the interaction of ethnic groups and states, explaining it requires consideration of both actors' positions and of all the hypotheses. A more comprehensive test of the theory goes beyond the settlement patterns of ethnic groups. In this second test, the dependent variable is the same (REBEL) over the 1980–95 period.[16] This test, however, has two sets of independent variables: one focuses on ethnic groups, and the other on the state. To test the part of the theory dealing with ethnic groups, I included a settlement-pattern variable, as in the first test, and added a homeland variable and duration variable. The settlement-pattern variable used to test the entire theory is a collapsed version of the four patterns employed in the first test: 0 indicates the group is not a concentrated majority in a region, and 1 indicates that it is. Because the concentrated-majority variable is so central to my theory, I replaced the missing values with predicted values. I did this using a probit model with fifteen independent variables to predict a concentrated majority. The independent variables were chosen on the basis of a plausible correlation with a concentrated majority. This model correctly predicted 165 of the 192 cases, or 86 percent of the values originally available.[17] With the interpolated data for the missing cases included, concentrated majorities are 100 (37 percent) of the cases, leaving 170 (63 percent) nonconcentrated majority cases. My theory predicts that concentrated majorities are more likely to be engaged in violence than other groups.

The homeland variable indicates whether the ethnic group sees the territory in which it is residing as part or all of its homeland. Here, 0 indicates that the group does not view the region as its homeland, and 1 indicates that it does. The vast majority of cases, 208, or 78 percent, comprise groups in which the ethnic minority resides in homeland territory. The remaining 57 cases, or 22 percent, reside in territory that is not considered the group's homeland. An example of the latter is the Slovaks in the Czech Republic. The theory predicts that ethnic groups residing in their perceived homeland are more likely to be engaged in rebellion than those that are not.

The duration variable indicates how long a group has lived in the place. It consists of three values: 0 indicates residence since 1945, 1 indicates residence beginning between 1800 and 1945, and 2 indicates residence since before 1800. It is based on MAR's TRADITN2 variable. A review of the cases reveals that most ethnic minorities settled in their place of residence before 1800: 216, or 80 percent. Only 32 cases (12 percent) involved groups that immigrated in the nineteenth or early twentieth century, and 22 (8 percent) immigrated since 1945. My hypothesis is that the longer a group has resided in one place, the more likely it is to be involved in violence.

In terms of relationships between these variables, I found that concentrated majorities tended to live in territories they regarded as their homeland (91 of 99 cases, or 92 percent) and most (90 of 100 cases, or 90 percent) immigrated before 1800. Concentrated minorities showed patterns similar to those of concentrated majorities: 88 percent (35 of 40 cases) lived in their homeland, and 83 percent (33 of 40 cases) settled before 1800. By contrast, 65 percent (17 of 26 cases) of the urban groups were *unlikely* to live in their perceived homeland, and they were six times more likely than the other types of ethnic minorities to have immigrated to the region after 1945, although a slight majority (52 percent, or 14 of 27 cases) settled during the nineteenth and early twentieth centuries. For the dispersed groups, only 58 percent (22 of 36 cases) lived in their perceived homeland, but most settled before 1800 (31 of 40 cases, or 78 percent).

The other part of the theory focuses on state-level factors. I include two independent variables: ethnic profile and resource richness. The ethnic-profile variable aims to capture the number of potential regional secessionists confronting the state. Thus, this variable was coded for whether the group resides in a state that (1) has only dispersed groups, (2) is homogeneous or contains one concentrated group with dispersed minorities,

(3) contains two concentrated groups with or without dispersed minorities, or (4) contains three or more concentrated groups with or without dispersed minorities.[18]

There are some points about the ethnic-profile variable. Ethnic groups residing in states with three or more concentrated groups constituted 91 percent ($n = 245$) of the cases in MAR. The worldwide distribution of such states stands at 67 percent, or one-third lower. Because ethnic conflict is a prerequisite for inclusion in MAR, this descriptive statistic alone reveals that groups in states with three or more concentrated groups are at a greater risk for ethnic conflict than those in other types of states. Yet, because these states are so overrepresented in MAR, I was not confident about using the ethnic-profile variable in the regression equation. There is too little variation, leading to a lack of statistical significance. Running the equation with it or without it, however, did not change the findings in either estimation (which is what we expect statistically). The equation reported here includes the variable: 0 indicates that the ethnic group lives in a state that does not contain three or more concentrated ethnic groups, and 1 indicates it does. According to my theory, states with three or more concentrations of ethnic groups are more likely to regard territory as indivisible because of fears of precedent setting and, as a result, to resort to violence more readily than states with other ethnic profiles.

The resource-rich variable indicates whether the region in which the ethnic group lives contains valuable man-made or natural resources such as minerals, dams and river systems, pasture and farmlands, industries, and strategically important locales (for example, mountain passes or heights).[19] It is included in the equation as a dummy: 0 indicates no valuable resources, and 1 indicates the existence of a valuable resource. This variable (which I created and is not in MAR) allows precedent setting to be tested indirectly by examining the leading alternative hypothesis, that states will resort to violence to control wealthy regions more readily than poor regions. If we find no relationship (if the coefficient is not statistically significant), or if violence is employed to gain control of poor regions more often than of rich regions (that is, the coefficient is negative), then this lends credence to the claim that the fear of precedent setting might be operating (as even poor regions are seen as indivisible and worth resorting to violence to keep). Table 3.7 presents two variations of the model of the theory: one in its pure form and the other after correcting for missing values on the key independent variable, concentrated majority. To control for any possible spillover effects of one group's activities provoking another's in the same country, I used the "cluster" command in Stata on the country code variable (CCODE), which specified that the observations are independent across groups located within the same country.

TABLE 3.7
Regression of Ethnic Violence

Variables	Missing Data not Replaced		Missing Data Replaced	
	Coefficient	Standard Error	Coefficient	Standard Error
Ethnic group level				
Concentrated majority	1.864***	0.407	1.604***	0.373
Homeland	0.838***	0.375	0.966***	0.350
Duration	0.362**	0.185	0.363**	0.178
State level				
Ethnic profile	0.172	0.563	0.140	0.545
Resource rich	−0.736*	0.467	−0.468	0.443
Constant	−0.681	0.601	−0.716	0.570
Number of cases	188		235	
R-squared	0.22		0.17	

$*p < .1.$ $**p < .05.$ $***p < .01$, one-tailed test.

Overall, the statistical analysis in table 3.7 confirms the main hypotheses of the theory. Concentrated-majority status predicts violence, just as it did in the first test. Groups living in what they perceive as their homeland also seem to engage in violence more readily. The longer a group has lived in a region, the greater the chances of violence.

The state-level hypothesis, that precedent setting matters more than resources, also received support. First, even given the limitations of the ethnic profile variable described in table 3.7, the coefficient is positive (although not statistically significant), indicating that ethnic groups in states with three or more concentrated groups are more likely to experience violence (perhaps because of states' fears that they will set precedents).[20] Second, ethnic groups living in resource-rich regions were less likely to be involved in violence than groups living in resource-poor regions. The coefficient was negative and statistically significant in the variation in which the missing values were not replaced, and it was just barely insignificant ($p = .11$) in the variation that included the replaced values. This suggests that states sometimes believe that resources are divisible. Further, the fact that violence is occurring more often in resource-poor regions than in resource-rich regions confirms the idea that states, as well as ethnic groups, are willing to fight over worthless territory. This lends further support to the notion that something other than the value of resources must be motivating violence.

In sum, these tests establish that concentration in a region is almost a necessary condition for rebellion and civil war, whereas dispersion and urbanism are practically sufficient conditions for nonviolence. Yet the statistical evidence shows only an association between the proposed variables and the likelihood of violence. This is an important empirical finding in itself, but it tells us little about causation or what explains the correlation.

This is my argument in summary: settlement patterns influence capabilities and legitimacy claims. With the notable exception of urbanites, concentrated ethnic groups (especially concentrated majorities) are engaged in rebellion more often and at higher intensities because they have greater capability and legitimacy than dispersed or urban groups. Further, out of fear of setting precedents, states are most likely to directly (and one might predict, aggressively) engage those groups considered most likely to set off a series of secessions, regardless of the value of the territory. All of this makes sense logically, and the statistical analysis supports this logic. But is the logic supported historically?

To determine whether the logic of the theory is supported historically, it is necessary to examine a handful of carefully selected case studies. Case studies allow us to look for appeals to legitimacy and then to attempt to measure which appeals appeared to give states and ethnic groups the most leverage with (1) domestic coethnics, who will be asked to risk death and economic privation in pursuit of autonomy or statehood, and (2) other interested states, which may be asked to intervene either diplomatically or militarily on behalf of the appealing group.

In the next two chapters I examine the relationship between two ethnic groups and their interaction with a state. The strategic interaction between Moscow, Kazan, and Grozny reveals a state concerned about precedent setting and ethnic groups wanting greater autonomy. Whereas Moscow and Kazan negotiated a bilateral treaty regulating their relations, Moscow and Grozny engaged in a full-scale civil war over the question of Chechen secession which has yet to be resolved.

4

Russia and Tatarstan

Scratch a Tatar, you'll find a Russian.

In the late 1980s the collapse of the Soviet Union touched off a chain reaction in which many of the former union republics and autonomous republics began to seek independence. Among them was Tatarstan, which did not end up as a sovereign state. Although it had been demanding independence from Russia, it eventually moderated its position, and in 1994 a bilateral treaty that regulated political and economic relations was signed.[1] In this chapter I show how the Tatar settlement pattern affected the group's demand for independence; although Tatars viewed Tatarstan as their homeland, they simply did not have the legitimacy or capability to launch an ethnically based independence campaign.[2] Realizing this, Tatar leaders represented their interests as divisible, stressing their desire for control over the economy rather than the protection of a Tatar identity and control over Tatarstan. On the other side, the Russian position was clearly dominated by an unwavering concern for precedent setting. Russia's position on the subject of independence was indivisible, but Tatarstan's divisible position provided room for negotiation and an ultimate settlement.

This chapter has five sections. The first section sketches the historical background of the Tatars and the evolution of their settlement pattern, the second section considers Tatarstan's bargaining prior to the collapse of the USSR, and the third considers its position in post-Soviet Russia. The fourth and fifth sections demonstrate how my theory best explains the process and the outcome of the bargaining that took place between the two actors by examining questions of Tatar legitimacy and Russian fears of setting precedents.

Tatars and Tatarstan

Descendants of nomadic Tatar tribes who migrated from southern Siberia, the Tatars first appeared in the lower Volga basin in the eighth century and were converted to Islam during the tenth as a result of contact with traders and migrants from the south. From the ninth to the twelfth centuries, they formed a political-administrative entity that was centered in Bolgary Velikie. Conquered by the Golden Horde in the thirteenth century, the Tatars joined the conquerors as they continued west into areas populated by Russian city-states. Following the disintegration of the huge Mongol Empire over the course of the fourteenth century, the Tatars established the khanate of Kazan in 1445 in the Volga-Kama region, which they ruled until 1552, when their capital, Kazan, was conquered by Czar Ivan IV (the Terrible) and incorporated into the Russian Empire.

With Russian occupation came Russian settlements. Though the territory of contemporary Tatarstan is small (approximately twenty-six thousand square miles), its geographic location and natural resources have made it desirable to Russia throughout the centuries. Tatarstan is five hundred miles east of Moscow and lies on the banks of the Volga River, which connects central Russia with the Urals, northern Kazakhstan, central Asia, Siberia, and the steppes to the south. Tatarstan's strategic location is depicted in figure 4.1. The Tatar nation's early history, first as conqueror of the Russian Empire and then as the vanquished, was only the first in a series of oscillating conditions that would mark subsequent relations between Tatars and Russians. Beginning with Russian settlement of the area in the sixteenth century, competition for "cultural, territorial, and ideological (both political and religious) control of the non-Russian peoples of the Middle Volga"[3] dominated Russian-Tatar interactions. During the eighteenth and nineteenth centuries, intergroup tensions manifested themselves as sporadic Tatar revolts against a growing Russification and attempts at forced conversion to Orthodox Christianity. By that point Kazan had become the center of Slavic colonization and of Moscow's assimilation and missionary efforts, but the Tatars, determined to stem the spread of Russian influence in the area, managed to retain their language and religion.[4] Nonetheless, the familiarity that accompanies the passage of time, along with growing realizations on the part of both groups that the other was there to stay, led to some degree of rapprochement and a learning to live together, keeping the area intact in spite of the aforementioned tensions and fears. A working relationship between the two groups developed as the Russian Empire spread eastward, with the Tatars increasingly functioning as middlemen between the Christian imperial center and the newly conquered Turkic people, facilitating economic and political transactions between the two. Such a role bridged the gap between the Russians and the Turkic people, helping them, over the centuries, to learn to coexist.

Tatarstan's central location gave the Tatars prime access to numerous tradesmen and trade routes, and by the late nineteenth century the significant prosperity they enjoyed as a group led to the formation of a large

FIGURE 4.1.   Location Map of Tatarstan

middle class. They had a high literacy rate and a national consciousness that developed from an awareness of increasing Russian nationalism and its consequent threat to the Tatar way of life. Recognizing the need to educate their children so they could lead materially and spiritually productive lives, they set about developing an educational system whose creation was plagued by a national apprehension: only children who learned Russian could take full advantage of economic opportunities, but the resulting Russification and "de-Tatarization" necessarily threatened Tatar identity.[5] Debates on language and religion were thus brought to the fore, and the group was forced to address the difficult question of what exactly constituted, or should constitute, a Tatar. By the turn of the nineteenth century a clear agreement arose among the group that a distinct Tatar identity existed, with a homeland in the Volga region; nonetheless, a multitude of competing views emerged over what, precisely, were the identity's specific parameters.

Tatar identity did not coalesce further in the early part of the twentieth

TABLE 4.1
Population Data for Tatars (1989)

Distribution of Tatars	Number of Tatars	Portion of Tatar Population
Throughout FSU	6,649,000	100%
In RSFSR	5,522,000	83
In Tatar Republic	1,765,000	32
Elsewhere in Russia	3,757,000	68

century. The borders of contemporary Tatarstan, created by Soviet territorial engineers, were explicitly designed to divide Tatars across several political-administrative units to prevent the formation a large Turkic-Muslim nation in the Volga region. By the 1980s, this engineering's success manifested itself in the continual weakening of Tatar ethnic identity. In 1989, 68 percent of all Tatars in Russia lived outside the republic, as indicated in table 4.1.

Within Tatarstan, ethnic Tatars were a minority, constituting only 48.5 percent of the republic's population.[6] Ethnic Russians comprised 43.5 percent of the population. In addition, the physical distribution of Tatar settlements within Tatarstan revealed a relative lack of concern for geographic ethnic cohesion, as Tatars were highly intermingled with ethnic Russians and Russian speakers, especially in the urban areas. They also had high rates of intermarriage with ethnic Russians: 20 to 38 percent of Tatars had mixed marriages.[7] Further, only about 50 percent of all Tatars considered themselves Muslim, only about 20 percent practiced Islam, and 60 percent of Tatar children born since 1981 had been given non-Muslim names.[8] The Tatars constituted a dispersed group.

Given the lack of a clearly defined Tatar identity at the end of the nineteenth century and the progressive weakening of what existed of that identity over the course of the Soviet era, it should come as no surprise that "the newest Tatar national movement" had a "long road . . . to travel to reconstruct its national high culture."[9] In fact, when Tatarstan *did* start to push for national independence as the Soviet Union began to collapse, it proved simply unable to muster a campaign centered on ethnic issues. The course of this campaign is the subject of the next section.

The First Stage in Tatarstan's Independence Bargaining: The Death of the USSR

Tatarstan's moves toward independence in the early 1990s cannot be understood in the absence of a clear grasp of Soviet and Russian politics.

As the Soviet Union grew weaker and weaker, the future of the checks on Russia became tenuous. Autonomous republics in Russia that during the Soviet era had enjoyed some degree of protection (due to the presence of a higher form of authority in the USSR) were now faced with the imminent possibility of having to be subordinate to the Russians, with no mediating political body serving as a buffer.

In the case of Tatarstan, initial fears of impending Russian dominance centered primarily on economic issues. Greater independence would give the residents of the autonomous republic the increased control over their own trade and industry that they felt they deserved. By contrast, status as a subordinate republic within a post-USSR independent Russia might further decrease what little economic control Tatarstan had. At that point, the push for sovereignty was not a matter of ethnic identity: 60 percent of all Russians in the republic supported greater independence from Moscow, apparently for economic reasons.[10] As it was, residents of Tatarstan were already forgoing a great deal of their prosperity in favor of other sectors of the federal system. Though Tatarstan produced 25 billion rubles' worth of output annually, it had no ministry of industry. Consequently, it controlled very little of the earnings from its industry and resources: 80 percent of its enterprises were directly subordinate to the Soviet Union and 18 percent to Russia, leaving only 2 percent for Kazan.[11]

What was Tatarstan's solution? It pushed for status as a union republic, independent from Russia but bound by the laws of the USSR, which almost all residents of the republic, for reasons of protection from Russia and for easier facilitation of economic and political transactions among the republics, sought to sustain.[12] Union republic status, it was believed, would lift Tatarstan to a position where it could enjoy the economic control and benefits that it deserved; Tatar elites pointed repeatedly to the example of Lithuania, which, despite having roughly the same territory and population as Tatarstan, enjoyed a per capita income that was seven times as high.[13] Tatarstan's goal, then, became the achievement of a status *equal* to Russia's within a preserved USSR.

Tatarstan's quest for equal status with Russia was greatly enhanced and legitimized by the political maneuvering of Soviet president Mikhail Gorbachev in early 1990. At the time, Gorbachev was seeking to engineer unprecedented political and economic reforms while simultaneously attempting to preserve the complex web of political relationships that held the USSR together.[14] Many of the union republics, however, had already begun to press for independence.[15] To undermine these independence movements, Gorbachev attempted to drastically alter the political structure of the Soviet Union:[16] in April 1990, upon his insistence, the Supreme Soviet of the USSR passed the All-Union Law on the Demarcation of Powers between the USSR and Members of the Federation,[17] which declared that both the USSR's union republics and the autonomous republics were equal subjects of the federation. Intended to dilute the political power of the union republics, the law had the consequence of granting to *both* types of republics the right to secede. Thus, it was hoped, union republics seeking independence would now pause before setting an example for those territories *within* their lands that now also had the right to follow suit. With sixteen of these autonomous republics contained within its borders, Russia's territorial integrity became seriously threatened.[18]

Gorbachev's attempt to preserve the union backfired. In June 1990, in response to what were perceived as the president's threatening efforts to reel it in, Russia declared itself a sovereign state. Two months later, on August 30, 1990, Tatarstan took the opportunity to guarantee what it saw as its own political freedom by declaring, in turn, itself sovereign from an increasingly powerful Russia.[19] The Tatarstan declaration, which was passed unanimously by the Tatarstan Parliament (with one abstention), proclaimed the constitution and laws of the republic supreme throughout its territory. It also was intended to serve as the basis for Tatarstan's participation in the anticipated drafting and concluding of a unionwide treaty and treaties with Russia and other republics. According to Tatar leader Mintimer Shamiyev, who was still hoping for the preservation of the USSR, the Tatar Republic had to "establish treaty-based relations with Russia, defining the division of powers on a number of positions of mutual interest," and the declaration did "not only proclaim Tatarstan's sovereignty, but . . . also define[d], in general terms, the principles and mechanisms for its implementation within a union of sovereign states."[20] It is important to note once again, however, that Tatarstan did not define itself in *ethnic* opposition to Russia; part of the declaration of sovereignty contained a guarantee of the equal use of Tatar and Russian as the republic's official languages. Although at that point fears of Russian strength had quite clearly shifted the debate to a level higher than that of simply protecting economic control, Tatarstan's actions were nonetheless aimed only at preventing a strong power from eroding its political freedom, and *not* at restraining an enemy viewed as encroaching on Tatar identity. Had this been the case, the Tatarstan Parliament would not have been so quick to preserve Russian as one of the republic's official languages.

Still, relations between Russia and Tatarstan deteriorated rapidly. When, in a last-ditch effort to reformulize relations among the USSR's union republics, Gorbachev presented a draft of the Union Treaty in November 1990 and a referendum in March 1991 to poll the populace on its reception, Tatarstan took the opportunity to distance itself further from Russia.[21] Many republics had added questions on the local political situation alongside those on the Union Treaty, with Russia asking whether it was worthwhile to create the position of Russian president. Tatarstan refused the polling of the additional question in its territory, a slap to Russian leader Boris Yeltsin and a further signal that Tatarstan insisted on a separate status.[22] Moreover, one month later, in April 1991, the Tatarstan Parliament reiterated its sovereignty by declaring the supremacy of Tatarstan's legislation over that of Russia, and in May, Shamiyev announced that Tatarstan would sign the Union Treaty, but "only as a member of the USSR, with the subsequent conclusion of a treaty with the RSFSR [Russian Socialist Federal Soviet Republic]."[23] His republic, he explained, was seeking a "profound reshaping" of its relations with Russia, to include "principles of mutual respect for sovereignty and real equality on the basis of a bilateral treaty."[24]

When the election for president of Russia was held in June 1991, it became the first test case measuring the resolve of Tatarstan residents to pursue their quest for an independent status. Although the Tatarstan Parliament officially decided that the republic would not take part in the presidential election (but would hold elections for its own republican president), it also decided not to prevent residents of Tatarstan from participating on their own if they so wanted. It adopted a decree that directed the republic's electoral commission to organize the elections of the Russian president in the republic but declared that the results would have no juridical consequences for Tatarstan.[25]

The concession, I argue, was an attempt to accommodate the multiple sets of views within the republic and was a sign that the desire for separatism was far from complete. The largest nationalist organization, the Tatar Public Center (Tatarskii Obshchestvennyi Tsentr, TPC) was, in fact, a *moderate* group whose agenda sought the enhancement of Tatarstan's regional and economic status, and not the advancement of a distinct Tatar identity. Though its platform called for Tatar as the republic's language and for the cultural and spiritual consolidation of all Tatars within the Soviet Union, its main agenda was to achieve greater economic sovereignty.[26] Extremist nationalist organizations did exist, namely the groups known as Ittifak and Azatlyk, but they were small and never drew a large following. These groups invoked the concepts of homeland and duration of inhabitation, which ethnic struggles often cite, making the claim that "[h]alf of Russia's territory is Tatar lands" and that "the time has come to raise the question of annexing to Tatarstan the lands that belonged to the Tatars of old, lands where they now dwell."[27] Their demands for a "Tatarstan for Tatars," their support for a right of return and citizenship for any Tatar living beyond the republic, and their condemnation of Russian-Tatar marriages were, however, counterbalanced by equally extreme groups on the other side. Organizations such as the

Democratic Party of Russia (DPR) and Soglasie (Agreement) advocated even closer ties with Russia and were largely composed of ethnic Russians within the republic who feared the emergence of hostile relations should Tatarstan become independent.[28]

Perhaps most indicative of the need for an accommodation of opinion, though, was the fact that none of these groups ever managed to draw even a fraction of the population as active members. Although Tatarstan had a population of 3.6 million in the late 1980s, the TPC, the largest nationalist group, had only 2,000 activists at its height, and Azatlyk had approximately 500, Ittifak about 300, and Soglasie only 50.[29] According to polling data, by December 1992, two-thirds of the electorate supported none of the political parties.[30] Given the resounding lack of opinion expressed by most Tatar residents, it comes as no surprise that the Parliament was unwilling to forbid participation in Russian elections should any constituents express the desire to do so.

As the election for the presidential posts for both Russia and Tatarstan approached, however, Tatar nationalist organizations managed to garner increased support among the general public and to stage what would become the largest demonstrations of the independence movement. They resented that Russian presidential elections were taking place on Tatar soil, and at the end of April 1991, some 10,000 rally participants demanded the recall of Tatar deputies from the Russian Parliament. A 15,000-person demonstration on May 21 included members of Ittifak who went on a hunger strike.[31] By this time, the newspaper *Novosti* had noted the daily rallies and protest meetings, and that the issue of ethnicity was becoming increasingly prominent in the struggle for power in the republic. As one reporter put it, the moderates were demanding the quick adoption of a Tatarstan constitution that would nullify Russian laws in the republic, and radicals announced that their goal was "the creation of a Tatar state and a change in the demographic situation in favor of the indigenous [Tatar] nation."[32] Leaflets posted around Kazan put the situation in the following stark terms: "We are witnessing the end of the Great Russian yoke that many peoples in our country have suffered under for more than four centuries. No referendums or treaties can hold together the two collapsing *matryoshka* dolls: the Soviet Union and the lesser empire, the so-called Russian Federation."[33] According to those demonstrating, continued Russian control over Tatarstan was a threat to the Tatar people.

Although such demonstrations represented a significant step in the progression of the Tatar independence movement toward a more ethnically defined agenda, even at their height, they drew only 0.4 percent of the total Tatar population. Compared with demonstrations in the Baltic republics (4–27 percent of their populations), this was relatively weak support.[34] The nationalist fronts in the Baltics also enjoyed much greater participation levels: among Estonia's population of 1.5 million, for example, the Popular Front had an estimated membership of 300,000 to 900,000; in Lithuania, with a population of 3.7 million, the Lithuanian Restructuring Movement (Sajudis) had an estimated membership of 180,000; and in Latvia, whose population was 2.6 million, the People's Front of Latvia claimed 250,000 members.[35] Although, as we shall see, the Tatar demonstrations had two significant effects on the course of the independence movement, such displays were not necessarily representative of public opinion as a whole within the republic.

The first significant effect of the nationalist demonstrations was nearly immediate. On May 28 the Tatarstan Parliament, probably surprised that such a degree of mobilization could be achieved in the thus-far quiet republic, capitulated to the demands of the protesters and ruled that the only elections to be held in Tatarstan would be for the president of Tatarstan, and not for that of Russia.[36] It was only a halfhearted capitulation, however, as residents of Tatarstan who *did* want to vote for a Russian president were allowed to do so and were provided with some support, though any official organization of the vote, as planned, was absent.[37] Voter turnout was 63 percent, with 35 percent of eligible voters casting a ballot for the Russian election and proving that a good portion of Tatarstan residents disagreed with those who had staged the vocal nationalist rallies only weeks earlier.[38] Shamiyev won the presidency of Tatarstan; running uncontested (and with a turnout of 63 percent), he garnered 71 percent of the vote.[39]

The second effect was that the presence of nationalists on the Tatar political scene forced Russia to take the independence movement seriously. This presence helped to make Shamiyev's tough stances seem more legitimate and representative than they probably were. I believe that Shamiyev never intended to seek full independence but was willing to use whatever rhetoric and other devices were necessary to maneuver himself into a position that in the end would garner as much autonomy as possible. Thus the nationalist presence was one of the primary devices that Shamiyev used to gain a more favorable bargaining position, making it seem as if he really *was* accountable to a population demanding sovereignty. Russia would have been less likely to take Tatar demands seriously had it perceived the population as inactive and uncaring. When the nationalists became *too* threatening, as they did in October 1991 when a rally of two thousand demonstrators ended with an unsuccessful storming of the Parliament, Shamiyev clamped down, closing the capital and declaring an end to all militia movements.[40] For the most part, however, he was happy to grant them a larger role on the political scene than their numbers deserved, as their mere presence forced Russia's bargaining position closer to the middle to meet more moderate Tatar demands.

Thus, with a presidential victory in hand, Shamiyev set about regulating relations with Russia and the USSR. Downplaying recent attempts by the nationalists to add an ethnic dimension to the independence movement, he stressed control over economic resources.[41] He warned that Tatarstan would set up its own banking system to collect federal taxes and argued that to ensure that the funds would make it to the federal coffers and back to Tatar enterprises, Tatarstan would need to pay them directly to the USSR, bypassing Russia.

Russia's response was increased pressure on Tatarstan to sign the upcoming Union Treaty as part of the Russian delegation. Shamiyev insisted that a favorable resolution of his republic's status was the "main obstacle to the signing of the Treaty"; thus, despite Russian hesitation, negotiations on the subject did take place. During the summer of 1991, a series of official letters detailing the working committees and objectives of the talks were exchanged.[42] Delegations from each side met in Moscow for three days, from August 12 to August 15, and agreed on the following statement:

> [We] recogniz[e] and understand the aspirations of the Russian Soviet Federal Socialist Republic and the Republic of Tatarstan, as participants in the Union Treaty of sovereign states, to renew and raise their status, to orient themselves to the use of treaty forms to regulate relations of the Russian Soviet Federal Socialist Republic with the republic of Tatarstan, taking into account their priority interests without impairing the interests of other republics and the Union as a whole.[43]

Although this statement represented distinct progress on both sides in terms of meeting the other halfway, the momentum was lost in the events of subsequent days. Only one day before the Union Treaty was to be signed, the August 21 coup against Gorbachev occurred. Shamiyev was forced to choose between the conservative Communist coup leaders and the liberal reformers headed by Yeltsin. Shamiyev, a conservative former Communist who sought the preservation of the union for his republic's benefit, flew to Moscow to meet with the coup leaders and upon his return issued a statement supporting the coup in the local press. Fearful of the coup's potential of possibly increasing Russian power, he also immediately declared that Russia's laws had no jurisdiction in Tatarstan.[44]

But rather than slow down the USSR's disintegration, as was the coup leaders' intention, the coup attempt hastened it. Yeltsin emerged victorious and substantially strengthened. Gorbachev was pushed further and further into obscurity as more republics declared their independence, and Yeltsin and his team assumed greater control over functions that previously were the reserve of the Soviet government.[45] Gorbachev tried to pass the Union Treaty, but on November 25 the union republics formally declared that they would not sign. On December 8 Russia, Ukraine, and

Belarus announced the formation of the Commonwealth of Independent States (CIS), agreeing to coordinate economic and defense policies and inviting the other union republics to join.[46] Shamiyev wanted Tatarstan to be admitted as a founding member of the CIS, but, not surprisingly, he was rebuffed, as such a concession would have meant Russia's recognition of Tatarstan as an independent state. Yeltsin continued to push for the idea of a federal treaty, similar to the Union Treaty, to regulate relations between Russia and its constituent republics, including Tatarstan. Finally, on December 17, Gorbachev and Yeltsin signed an agreement stipulating that the Soviet Union would cease to exist on January 1, 1992, and Tatarstan, in its negotiations with Russia, was left without the buffer that it had been fighting to maintain for so long.

The Post-Soviet Era: Tatarstan's Referendum and Negotiated Settlement

The August 21 coup had significant ramifications on nationalist fervor both in Tatarstan and in republics throughout the former Soviet Union. Increasing Russian nationalism that grew around the rising power of Yeltsin led to a growth of similar sentiments in the autonomous republics, as Tatarstan and other regions feared the consequences of a more dominant and belligerent Russia. At this point Tatar nationalists could make their strongest case, and highly vocalized, if not widely shared, demands for a public debate on the question of secession spread rapidly.

Once again, the Tatarstan Parliament found itself giving in to increasing nationalist pressure, and a referendum on the status of the republic was scheduled for March 1992. Moscow was anxious, recognizing that a "yes" vote could endanger the legitimacy of the Russian Federation, formed on January 1, 1992.[47] Shamiyev tried to allay Russian fears:

> I never talked of independence or even of separation. The question was not put that way. Russia succeeded in retaining its sovereignty—why should we not do the same? We see real processes of self-assertion taking place in the autonomous republics, which are impossible to stop now. The people of Tatarstan should speak about its sovereignty; the Parliament has given it this right. We have not raised any question about the borders, customs, military doctrine or our own currency. We, by all means, intend to strengthen our union with Russia and work out a treaty in the near future, which should stipulate the powers we can exercise together.[48]

On March 5 the Russian Parliament issued an appeal to the Tatarstan electorate not to vote in favor of separation, arguing that the referendum was likely to increase interethnic strife,[49] and on March 8 the Tatarstan

Parliament issued an appeal, again reiterating the idea that it was not attempting to secede.

> The question presented in a referendum does not envisage secession or non-secession of the republic of Tatarstan from Russia or its isolation from Russia as a separate state entity. . . . Tatarstan is united with the Russian Federation in a common economic and geopolitical space and builds its relations with Russia on the basis of equitable treaties and the delegation of a number of powers.[50]

Despite Russian protests, Tatarstan proceeded with the referendum. On March 21, 82 percent of the electorate participated: 61.4 percent voted in favor, and 37.2 percent against. The yes vote was higher in the predominantly Tatar rural areas (75.3 percent) than in the urban areas (55.7 percent). In Kazan the majority of voters—51.2 percent—voted *against* the referendum.[51] All in all, the referendum did not represent an overwhelming victory for those in Tatarstan who sought Tatarstan's independence, and at this point the extreme Tatar nationalists were effectively silenced.

In fact, just two days after the referendum, Shamiyev stressed that what he sought was a direct treaty with Russia in which the configuration of power would resemble a confederation. Proving that the referendum had, in effect, put an end to calls for complete independence, Shamiyev reported that defense, security, and border protection would be delegated by treaty to Russia.[52] The time had come to get down to the business of hashing out a treaty to govern relations between Russia and what would inevitably be a subordinate Tatarstan.

Yeltsin had hoped that a bilateral treaty between Tatarstan and Russia could be signed before the opening of the Russian Congress of People's Deputies on April 6, so that both the bilateral treaty and the Russian Federal Treaty could be ratified simultaneously. Instead, delegates from Tatarstan and Russia met and signed only a protocol on the results of their consultations.[53] They decided to continue talks,[54] Shamiyev declaring a year later his continuing intention to work for a solution.

> [M]any questions are not solved yet, politically or economically. . . . We will go about this without confrontation and in a constitutional way. . . . Tatarstan has begun . . . a civilized path toward a new form of relations with Russia. We're ready to take part in the federation, to make available our military-industrial capacity to Russia, and turn over our national security to Russia.[55]

Negotiations continued through 1993.[56] At the end of August 1993, Mihammat Sabirov, the prime minister of Tatarstan, announced that Kazan and Moscow had reached an agreement on finances and oil and that Russia had agreed to lift its budget blockade of Tatarstan. The agreement stipulated that Tatarstan would contribute 2.1 million tons of oil toward paying off the foreign debt of the Former Soviet Union (FSU), and that Tatarstan would be allowed to dispose of 5 million tons on its own.[57] And in February 1994, Russia and Tatarstan signed a bilateral treaty that normalized their relations. The treaty, the result of two years' negotiations, included recognition of Tatarstan as a sovereign state freely associated with the Russian Federation and a clause that recognized the republic's right to legal secession from the Russian Federation, though all involved knew that Tatarstan would never again attempt to secede and that even if it did, Russia would never allow it.

Tatarstan's Bargaining Position and Questions of Legitimacy

The outcome of the Tatarstan-Russia conflict can best be explained by Tatarstan's inability to push for complete independence—once the debate had shifted away from solely economic issues—because of a lack of popular support for such a status. Prime evidence of this is found in the republic's almost-immediate softened rhetoric and willingness to sit down for hard negotiations following the less-than-successful referendum of March 1992. Nonetheless, evidence of the republic's inability to mount a serious effort for an ethnically based separation because of legitimacy questions was interspersed throughout the four years of the independence movement.

Two characteristics of Tatar settlement patterns were pointed to repeatedly as markers that detracted from the legitimacy of attempts to secede. The first is that the Tatars were a *dispersed* group, since most ethnic Tatars lived outside the republic. This fact was highlighted by Vladimir Morokin, an ethnic Russian serving as a people's deputy from Tatarstan, in a March 1992 article in *Rossiiskaya Gazeta*. Morokin pointed out that 75 percent of Tatars lived beyond Tatarstan and that more than 700,000 of them lived in Moscow and its environs.[58] In September 1992 Valery Tishkov put the issue perhaps most succinctly in the following query: "If this is taken seriously as territorial self-determination, explain to me, what will Tatarstan's independence do for the four-fifths of Tatars who live outside Tatarstan and the 300,000 who live in Moscow?"[59]

It was thus impossible for those arguing for a "Tatarstan for Tatars" to put forth their cause as legitimate, one that truly had the intention of promoting a universal Tatar interest. Tatarstan could not be presented as a home for Tatars, given that most Tatars would *not* have been able to enjoy the fruits of the independent republic had it been allowed to secede. An ethnically based movement, then, was delegitimized from the start by such considerations. It is also worth noting that even if he *had*

intended to present the independence struggle as an ethnic one, Shamiyev would have been unable to claim the position of leader of all Tatars;
paradoxically, Yeltsin represented *more* Tatars than the elected leader of
the Tatar Republic did.

Evidence, albeit limited, of an urban-rural divide in Tatarstan, with the
rural areas tending to support a more nationalist Tatar agenda than the
urban areas, surfaced in this case.[60] Not only did the rural areas have
higher turnouts for the various elections, but they voted overwhelmingly
for Shamiyev and in support of the referendum on independence. Conversely, urban areas, in which ethnic Russians tended live, displayed much
apathy toward the electoral process, as evidenced by low voter turnout.

Perhaps more important, however, was the second characteristic of
Tatars' settlement pattern: their lack of majority status within Tatarstan.
Given that ethnic Tatars comprised only 48.5 percent of the republic's
population, an independent Tatarstan *for* Tatars would have been delegitimized by that fact that the majority of the new state's populace would
have been *non*-Tatar. Yeltsin understood this and used the concept against
those fighting for an independent state when he warned, "The actions of
ultra-nationalist forces [are] fraught with an infringement upon the rights
of the majority of the population and [will] result in a split among the
peoples of Tatarstan."[61] And although the simple fact that Tatars were a
minority within their own republic was enough on its own to severely
undermine the credibility of the independence movement, further damage was done to secession efforts by the *specific ways* in which that population was distributed. That is, in addition to being in the minority, Tatar
settlements were greatly interspersed with those of Russians, and Tatars
and Russians shared extremely high rates of intermarriage. Vladimir Belyaev, a leader of the pro-Russian Soglasie movement, noted, "There is a
better chance for peace here because almost half of the families are
mixed—Tatar and Russian. . . . It will be much harder to split people
among ethnic lines."[62]

More than four hundred years of mixing and assimilation between the
two groups had created a society in which it had become impossible to
separate the two populations. They had lived together for centuries and
had been socialized in a way that they were unable to define themselves
in opposition to each other. Most Tatars simply had no desire to separate
completely from Russians, a fact proven by the relatively small member-
ships of nationalist organizations and the low participation levels at independence rallies throughout the course of the movement. One analyst
even described the apathetic Tatar population as inert (*inertno*) and attributed the condition, in part, precisely to the high rates of intermar-
riages and births.[63]

The minority status of Tatars in the republic and the dispersion of the

Tatar people as a whole thus served to severely undermine the legitimacy of ethnically based independence attempts that arose sporadically. In addition, assimilation had resulted in high levels of familiarity. Thus, it should come as no surprise that the majority of the republic's population was simply not willing to endorse an identity-based movement.

Russia's Bargaining Position and Fears of Setting Precedents

Russia understood the legitimacy problems that a push for full Tatar independence entailed, and as such, it was never fully worried that Tatar leaders or nationalists would follow through on any of their more extreme threats and demands. This condition explains Russia's willingness to negotiate with the Tatars: they knew that if given moderate concessions, Tatarstan would eventually back down from calls for independence and would be satisfied with partial economic and political autonomy. By contrast, as we shall see shortly, Russia knew that Chechens as a group were serious about secession and that there was no hope for a Chechen retreat. They were compelled to resort to force immediately in order to rein in the Chechen Republic. The Tatars, however, could be reined in with token concessions, and thus, as reported by ITAR-TASS, Yelstin declared that force in the Tatar case was *not* an option and that Moscow and Kazan needed to deal with each other in a "calm manner."[64]

Regardless of Russia's moderation in dealing with Tatarstan's demands as a whole, however, it was *not* willing to stand idly by while the republic sent signals that secession was a possible goal. Lest any other independence-minded republics get ideas about making threats of their own, Russia was prepared to meet extreme Tatar gestures with tough rhetoric. And despite periodic Tatar insistence that secession was not the republic's intention, there were plenty of opportunities for Moscow to respond heatedly to mixed Tatar signals. In January 1992, for example, as an agreement regulating economic relations was signed by Moscow and Kazan,[65] the Tatarstan Parliament was drafting citizenship legislation, an act that Russia quite reasonably perceived as a possible step toward independence.[66]

Likewise, in September 1992, Tatarstan was criticized in the Russian press and by the Kremlin for its ambiguous stance toward independence. Tatarstan remained insistent that it was not seceding, with Tatarstan vice president Vasily Likhachov declaring, "There is no doubt that Tatarstan's policy is aimed at changing the republic's status with respect to the Russian Federation. But those who say that Tatarstan wants to secede from Russia and, moreover, is wrecking the Federation, are wrong."[67]

But Shamiyev, in an effort to reinforce Likhachov's sentiments, only added to the ambiguity: "I can plainly state that I have never in any speech declared that we would secede from Russia. We continue to declare that Tatarstan will strive for its independence."[68] And, at about the same time that the vice president uttered his declaration, a delegation sent to Moscow to carry on negotiations presented a draft treaty to the Russians stipulating that the "Republic of Tatarstan enters into relations with foreign states, concludes international treaties, and exchanges diplomatic and consular representatives,"[69] an unambiguous signal of the intention to be independent.

However, one of the greatest sources of Russian confusion, and thus insecurity, was Shamiyev's tolerance of an alternative government established in Tatarstan in February 1992 by Ittifak. The attempt at an alternative government initially took the form of a congress (*kurultay*) populated by 877 members representing Tatar peoples from all over the former Soviet Union.[70] The congress was intended to reflect the dispersion of Tatars but gave priority to the Tatar homeland: even though three-fourths of all Tatars lived outside Tatarstan's borders, they held only a third of the congress's leadership positions.

At their first meeting, the congress adopted more than twenty resolutions, including one that gave the Tatars the right to use any means "to conduct a liberation movement against Russian invaders."[71] In addition, it adopted a flag for the Tatar nation, appealed to CIS members to recognize the independence of Tatarstan, and requested recognition and full membership in the UN Security Council.[72]

At the same time, the congress voted to recall their representatives from the Russian Parliament and elected a seventy-five-member ruling national assembly (Milli Medzhlis) that was designed to be an alternative parliament to the Tatarstan Parliament. It was charged with the coordination of cultural and national autonomy for Tatars, including the preservation of language, development of education and media, and the organization of interactions with states where large concentrations of ethnic Tatars existed. In addition to adopting a resolution that gave the Milli Medzhlis the authority to initiate referenda, the congress gave the assembly the right to overturn Supreme Soviet rulings that it believed fell within its jurisdiction.

Moderate Tatar organizations and leaders, including Shamiyev, rejected the congress and its resolutions. Although Talgat Abdullin, the elected chairman of the Milli Medzhlis, told Interfax that "the congress lays no claim to power in Tatarstan," Shamiyev believed otherwise.[73] He was highly critical of the congress and threatened to take strong measures against those who advocated a war of liberation against Russia. Shamiyev urged Parliament to express its opinion on the congress's attempt "to replace or influence the legally elected Parliament"[74] and condemned the threatening and divisive tactics of the nationalists at the conference, announcing that Tatarstan would pursue independence "exclusively in a civilized and constitutional way."[75] Still, probably realizing that he would benefit from giving Russia somewhat of a scare, he refused to shut the alternative congress down.

Moscow was quick to respond, stressing that such Tatar moves toward independence could potentially undermine Russia's integrity. The Russian Parliament Commission for the National-State System and Interethnic Relations, for example, warned that interethnic relations would be harmed, economic reform would be severely hampered, and the Congress's resolutions could "endanger the Russian Federation's unity and integrity."[76] Tatarstan, as we shall see shortly, was viewed as just one domino in a series of potential secessions.

Perhaps the greatest source of Russian apprehension, though, was the adoption by the legitimate Tatar Parliament of a new constitution in November 1992, months after serious bargaining had already been under way. Many of the articles of the constitution presented Tatarstan as an independent state, with a body of citizens acting in accordance with not only its own constitutional laws but with international laws as well. Article 59, for example, declared that the republic's laws would have precedence throughout the territory. Article 61 declared, "The Republic of Tatarstan is a sovereign state and a subject of international law associated with the Russian Federation–Russia on the basis of a treaty on the mutual delegation of powers and authority."

Under article 111, which delineated the powers of the president, section 9 declares that the president "represents the republic in international relations . . . and concludes treaties with foreign states."[77] The constitution also proclaimed some moderating features: the equality and protection of the rights of all citizens (at home and abroad) of all nationalities (articles 3, 13, and 21), Russian and Tatar as the two state languages (article 4), and dual citizenship—Tatar and Russian (article 19). But because the constitution did not clearly state that Tatarstan was part of the Russian Federation, the authorities in Moscow insisted that it meant that Tatarstan was seeking a separation from Russia. The Parliament most likely passed such a constitution because at the time it was still unclear what the final outcome of the negotiations would be.

Although Russia suspected that Tatarstan would never follow through on such hints of complete independence, it was nonetheless imperative for them to respond to such leanings in an unwavering manner. The primary goal of Russian politicians at the time was to keep the Russian Federation intact, and thus such threats had to be dealt with firmly in order to avoid setting the precedent of being soft on secession. In a new Russian Federation composed of twenty-one autonomous republics and a multitude of ethnic groups that might someday mobilize for autonomy, the structure of Russia precluded Moscow from considering, much less allowing, the independence of one of these. Thus, because Moscow faced numerous potential secessionists, its bargaining position with regard to any moves by Tatarstan for independence (but, remember, not autonomy, which it was willing to negotiate) was viewed as indivisible. As described by an *Izvestiya* correspondent,

> [Russia's] concern is prompted not only by the possible complication of relations with Tatarstan and of the internal political situation there, but also by the *rather dangerous precedent*, one that could become an example for certain other autonomous republics. *A precedent that could be an appreciable spur to disintegrative and divisive processes in Russia* and could make the establishment and strengthening of Russia as a unified, integral state more difficult. The anxiety [is] justified.[78]

This anxiety was voiced repeatedly in Russian reactions to perceived extreme Tatar moves. Russian vice president Aleksandr Rutskoi issued what was perhaps the strongest statement regarding the Tatar situation when he declared that "the division of Russia is tantamount to death, not only for us, but for humanity. It will mean death to the whole world."[79] In March 1992 Yeltsin, somewhat less dramatically, stated that he feared that "the . . . actions of the leaders of Tatarstan clearly show that their political course is aimed at splitting from Russia,"[80] and he worried that such actions "might jeopardize the dialogue between the state bodies of Russia and Tatarstan to form a new type of relations within the federation. [Surely the] republic," he added, "is capable of playing a constructive role in building a free, democratic Russian federation."[81] Yeltsin himself argued that a unified Russia—and its territorial integrity—was an unconditional right that had to be maintained.[82]

From the course of events, it is evident, then, that Russia was willing to negotiate some measures of autonomy for the Tatars because it understood that Tatar nationalists were not backed by a sense of legitimacy sufficient enough to create a clear secession threat. Nonetheless, the Russians were quite unwilling to tolerate Tatar words and actions that seemed to push for complete independence from the federation, responding to them with strong rhetoric of their own in order to dissuade fellow republics backed by a greater sense of legitimacy and capability from attempting *real* secessions. The Russian bargaining position on independence, then, was made indivisible by the constant need to avoid setting precedents that might one day lead to the disintegration of the federation as a whole.

The agreement that was eventually signed by Tatarstan and Russia created an overall impression that an independence-minded republic had, through tough bargaining, gained an increased measure of sovereignty.

In reality, however, it was Moscow's position that remained unwavering: its leadership simply could not countenance an independent Tatarstan for fear that it would lead to the disintegration of Russia. The Russians knew, however, that given some concessions on autonomy, the Tatar resistance would quickly melt away. Thus, Tatarstan's leadership proved most conciliatory as they backed down from vocalized plans to secede and accepted smaller measures of economic and political control. Their reluctance to use ethnicity in the political arena was due wholly to the constraints of their settlement patterns: Tatars were dispersed and did not constitute a majority in Tatarstan. They therefore lacked the legitimacy to push for complete independence, and this lack of legitimacy ultimately explains why Tatarstan accepted a final subordination to the Russian Federation.

5

Russia and Chechnya

This is our land. Get out! We're defending our
homeland and we have nowhere to retreat.
  —*A Chechen in the face of Russian troops,*
    December 1994

Two contrasting events marked 1994 in the former Soviet Union: the
signing of a bilateral treaty and the outbreak of civil war. Although both
Chechnya and Tatarstan had initially demanded greater independence
from the Russian Federation, Tatarstan eventually moderated its demands and signed a bilateral treaty with Moscow in February of that year.
Chechnya, however, remained recalcitrant, precipitating the deployment
of Russian Federation troops in December 1994 and a subsequent civil
war. Given the apparent similarities between the two independence
movements, and given their close proximity in time, why did a negotiated settlement obtain in one interaction but not in the other?

This chapter focuses on the interaction of Russia with Chechnya.[1] As in
the other case studies included in this book, I isolate the question of how
the state—Russia—and the ethnic group—the Chechens—viewed the
disputed territory, how such views conditioned their negotiations, and
how, as a result, violent conflict became more or less likely. In this interaction, violent conflict erupted because leaders on both sides presented
their cases as indivisible: Russia for reasons of reputation and precedent
setting and the Chechens because they had the legitimacy and capability
to do so.

This chapter is divided into four main sections. The first one presents
the historical and demographic background of the Chechens and Chechnya. The second section examines Chechnya's bargaining with Moscow
over its independence bid from 1990 to 1994. The third section analyzes
the Chechen case with regard to settlement patterns and precedent setting. The final section includes a comparative analysis of the merits of
material, nonmaterial, and elite-manipulation explanations in contrast to
my theory, to explain the outbreak of war in Chechnya versus the securing of peace in Tatarstan. Although the alternative explanations account
for part of the story, they explain less than the theory of indivisible territory can. The physical distribution of Tatars and Chechens influenced

each group's bargaining with the state, and precedent setting proved to be a powerful determinant of Russia's approach in both interactions. Taken together, these positions determined whether the outcome of the disputes would be a negotiated settlement or a civil war.

Chechens and Chechnya

Contemporary Chechnya comprises approximately 6,200 square miles (16,000 square kilometers)[2] and is located along the northern slopes of the Caucasus Mountains, reaching into the flood plain of the Terek River. It borders the Ingush republic to the west, the Dagestan Republic along the east and north, and the Stavropol' Kray and North Ossetian Republic to the northwest. Across the mountains to the south lies Georgia (see figure 5.1).

Because of the republic's central and strategic location, Chechen history has been riddled with wars of conquest, and these wars have imprinted on Chechen identity a virulent determination to resist any form of colonization by outsiders. Though this determination is certainly most recognizable with regard to its most recent application vis-à-vis Russia, it has been in the making for centuries and has been directed at a multitude of would-be rulers, in addition to the group's neighbors to the north. The region's first conquerors, the Iranian Alars, ancestors of the Christian Ossetians, came in the ninth through twelfth centuries and were responsible for the Chechens' conversion to Christianity. In 1241 the area was taken over by the Golden Horde, which proved unable to secure lasting control and was overthrown by the indigenous populations in 1300. Turkish and Persian domination soon followed, and though regions subservient to the Turks were allowed to govern themselves for the most part, all taxes and issues of revenue were orchestrated by the Ottoman Empire's central government. At this time the Chechens, to secure the better treatment and benefits that came with being more akin to their rulers, began to adopt Islam as their faith.[3] Subsequent efforts by outsiders (namely, the Russians and Soviets) to dislodge this faith failed, and it has survived for centuries to become a central characteristic of contemporary Chechen identity.

As the eighteenth century came to a close and Turkish and Persian power waned, the Russian Empire moved south in its quest for imperial expansion. Having defeated the Persians and the Ottomans by the beginning of the nineteenth century, Russian efforts focused on subduing the newly obtained areas' local populations. From 1817 until 1864, the region was host to a series of struggles known as the Caucasian Wars, attempts by the peoples of the Northern Caucasus to dislodge the Russian

FIGURE 5.1.   Location Map of Chechnya

imperial yoke and the religious and cultural suppression that came with it. Most of the ethnic groups in the region were organized as tribal federations, and though these broad federations did not survive to the twentieth century, they resulted from a societal structure that centered around clans and remained a defining characteristic of Chechen sociopolitical identity through modern times: "Here, where age-old concepts of honor and mutual aid to one's kin prevail, where the custom of blood vengeance persisted, protests against the repression took the familiar patriarchal form—blood for blood."[4]

The broadest union of Caucasian peoples resisting Russian domination occurred during a twenty-year period that followed an 1839 Russian attempt to disarm the locals through searches and seizures of private residences. This Russian policy provoked the peoples of the area to join efforts under the military and spiritual leadership of Imam Shamil, the most powerful of the region's warlords; Shamil led the people of the North Caucasus quite successfully, until his defeat in 1859. Although armed conflicts continued sporadically, by the mid-1860s the Caucasus region, including present-day Chechnya, had been successfully subdued and incorporated into the Russian Empire. For the most part, the Chechens adapted their way of life to the new circumstances; though some locals sought refuge in the Ottoman Empire and some remained in the mountains to try to eke out a living in the harsh and desolate environment there, most returned from battle to their land along the flood plain and were forced to share it with Terek Cossack settlers.

The adoption of a way of life within the Russian Empire, however, was a forced necessity, and it neither erased the Chechen desire to be free nor precluded Chechen attempts, when the opportunities presented themselves, to try yet again to secure independence.[5] The twentieth century saw three distinct Chechen attempts to break from Russia, each coming, quite strategically, at a time when the larger state was weak and preoccupied with revolutions or external wars.

The first of these attempts took place during the uncertainty of the Russian Revolution. When the Bolsheviks took power in 1917, most Chechens supported them with the expectation that they would receive land and autonomy in exchange for their help after the war. Although there were calls for an independent Chechnya, in 1918 the Chechens united with other Northern Caucasus people to form the Mountain Republic (Gorskaia respublika). The first independence attempt of the twentieth century thus found the Chechens retaining their outlook of the nineteenth century: identifying with the Northern Caucasian people as a whole rather than desiring a separate nation. As the Russian civil war raged in the area, the forces of the newly established Mountain Republic took part in the effort to eliminate the enemies of the Bolsheviks.[6] And although its support was welcomed during the war, it was repaid with severe repression afterward; following the defeat of the opposition armies, the Bolsheviks, seeking to consolidate power, occupied the region, put into place a military regime, imposed direct rule, and suppressed the practice of Islam.[7]

It was only in the late 1930s, in large measure as a direct result of Soviet policies, that the Chechens began to adopt an independent Chechen identity, distinct from the other Mountain peoples of the region.[8] In an effort to cope with the multitude of minorities within its borders, the Soviet Union began to confer on certain groups official recognition. By giving them something to gain or lose, namely recognition—thus making them more cooperative—and by creating tension among the groups through competition for recognition, the Soviet Union hoped to reduce the instability that the existence of such groups presented. Thus in 1934, just before the adoption of the 1936 Soviet constitution, the Chechen-Ingush Autonomous Soviet Socialist Republic (ASSR) was created. Republican status meant that Chechens were now an officially recognized national minority, leading to the creation of a Chechen literary language, the promotion of Chechen culture,[9] and, indirectly, the consolidation of a Chechen identity.

Despite this elevation in status, the 1930s brought more struggles for the Chechens, as they fell victim to the Soviet collectivization campaigns and purges of local populations that were taking place throughout the state.[10] World War II and the 1940s brought the most brutal treatment, as a failed Chechen independence movement, the second of its kind during the century, led to the government's specific targeting of the group. While Moscow was preoccupied with the war and the Germans were gaining more control in the Caucasus region, the Chechens appealed to the German invaders for recognition of an independent Chechen state. Incensed, Soviet leader Joseph Stalin branded all Chechens traitors, accused them of aiding the invaders, dissolved the republic, and ordered large numbers of them to be deported to Kazakhstan and Siberia.[11] A total of 498,452 people were deported from the republic to "special localities," and of these, 316,317, or more than 60 percent, were Chechens.[12] Close to one-fourth of them died.

After the deportation, tens of thousands of Russians, Avars, Dargins, Ossetians, and Ukrainians were settled in the Grozny area to avert an impending economic crisis in the region. Chechens also charged that such settlements were part of a deliberate Soviet policy to make a future restoration of the Chechen-Ingush ethnic ASSR impossible.[13] Nonetheless, the ethnic balance shifted back to favor the Chechens several years later when they returned en masse following Khrushchev's 1956 secret speech that rehabilitated deported nationalities.[14] It was a remarkable return, considering the fact that the Chechens had received no support or assistance for the move from the Soviet state; Chechens wishing to return to Chechnya had to bear all of the costs and risks of return themselves, but they did so precisely because they considered the territory of Chechnya their homeland.

The strength of Chechen identity that was evident in this mass migration was still present at the close of the Soviet era and the beginning of the Chechens' third struggle for independence during the twentieth century. In what are perhaps two of the greatest indicators of cultural status, the Chechens displayed remarkable resilience and unification. First, as of 1989, 98.8 percent of Chechens retained their mother tongue[15] despite the fact that in most cases urbanization leads to a shift to Russian and discourages the use of native languages. Among all non-Russian urbanites living in the former Soviet Union, only 62 percent retained their mother tongue, compared with 84 percent of rural dwellers. Not only did both urban and rural Chechen groups retain their language at a higher proportion than was the state norm but the difference between the two groups was a mere 2 percent: 97 percent of urban Chechens and 99 percent of rural Chechens claimed the retention of their mother tongue.[16]

Second, in terms of religion, the people of Chechnya have insisted on retaining their faith despite nearly continuous religious suppression over the last two centuries. Islam remains strong in the region: nine out of ten Chechens and Dagestanis consider themselves Muslims; seven in ten Chechens, including most young people, say they not only believe in but also practice Islam, and nearly 85 percent of Chechen and Dagestani

TABLE 5.1
Population Data for Chechens (1989)

Distribution of Chechens	Number of Chechens	Portion of Chechen Population
Throughout FSU	957,000	100%
In RSFSR	899,000	94
In Chechen-Ingush Republic	753,000	82
Elsewhere in Russia	164,000	18

children born since 1981 were given Muslim names.[17] The strength of the Chechen Islamic faith has been attributed to the prevalence of Sufism among the group; because Sufism is clan based and less reliant on mosques and other Muslim institutions, it has been better able to withstand the attempts of the Russians and Soviets to force the Chechens to convert.[18]

The strength of Chechen identity at the end of the Soviet era was also reflected by the fact that, at the time, almost all Chechens lived in the Chechen Republic. According to the 1989 census, Chechens comprised 0.6 percent (899,000) of the total population of Russia. Of this number, 82 percent (735,000) lived in the Chechen-Ingush Republic, and only 18 percent (164,000) resided elsewhere in Russia, as indicated in table 5.1.[19]

In addition, within Chechnya, Chechens clearly constituted a majority: according to the 1989 census, the districts considered part of the Chechen homeland (separate from what constitutes the Ingush Republic) contained just over one million people, of whom 715,000 were Chechen, 269,000 Russian, and 25,000 Ingush. Mixing between the groups was minimal: rates of intermarriage were low, and most Russians were geographically concentrated in the urban areas. The Chechens constituted a concentrated majority.

At the end of the Soviet era, then, conditions in Chechnya had ripened to the point where a prime opportunity existed for challenging Soviets' and Russians' sovereignty over the republic. The central government, as during the Chechens' two previous twentieth-century attempts at independence, was weak, and Chechen identity had been consolidated and reinforced by the presence of most Chechens within the borders of their homeland. oFears of external domination had been kindled not only by stories of empires' past domination but also by the very real and threatening deportation experiences of many Chechens, most of whom were still alive, during the Soviet years. The Russians and Soviets had proven repeatedly their willingness to destroy the Chechen Republic, and the events of the 1990s were perceived as being no different. What follows is

a description of the Chechen attempt to secure independence as the Soviet Union disintegrated and an explanation of how Chechen settlement
patterns and Russian fears of precedent setting combined to produce
conditions that would inevitably lead to the brutal outcome of war.

Chechnya's Bargaining with Russia

Chechnya's most recent quest for sovereignty did not start out in the
violent fashion in which it ended. In fact, initial Chechen discontent centered on perceived Soviet indifference to local environmental concerns.
Chechen patterns followed those emerging throughout the rest of the
USSR: as perestroika led to an openness in Soviet politics in the late
1980s and people were allowed to voice their concerns over an increasing
range of issues, discontent with environmental conditions became one of
the primary impetuses for public mobilization. This newfound mobilization among local groups proceeded to then usher in a period of national
evaluation and reflection among many of the USSR's ethnic minorities.
In the case of Chechnya, the first mass public demonstration occurred in
the summer of 1988, in the city of Gudermes, over a Soviet proposal to
construct a biochemical plant. The main issue? Not Chechen independence from the state, but impending environmental degradation, the
need to protect the local population, and the perception that Moscow
and the Communist Party were indifferent to such concerns. These initial
concerns and demonstrations, however, gave rise to broader ones, and in
a short period they encouraged the emergence of questions about
Chechen history, its role in the union, and issues of self-determination.

Two months after the Gudermes demonstration and the subsequent
perceived inaction of the state, the People's Front of the Chechen-Ingushetia Republic, the first organization to form in opposition to the
dominant Communist Party, was formed. The front had a broad agenda
and was not necessarily nationalist. It sought to establish a democratic
system of government, to protect the environment, and to revive the
history, culture, and language of the Chechen and Ingush nations.[20]
Throughout 1989 and 1990, numerous nationalist political and social
groups began to form, and the Communists were forced to adjust their
platform to meet the demands of the people.[21] The original People's
Front became more and more marginalized as most of its agenda was
adopted by the Communist Party.

The front's replacement as Chechnya's most influential political group
came in May 1990, when the Vaynakh Democratic Party (VDP), at first
formed simply to advance the rights of Chechens without a specific political agenda, was established. Although it was initially loyal to Chechen

Communist Party secretary Doku Zavgayev, it broke away from him by autumn with an increasingly extreme platform that called for a sovereign and independent Chechen republic with equal rights in the USSR.[22] It also pushed for the reestablishment of a council of elders, a greater role for Islamic law, proportional representation in the local cadres, and an end to migrations to and from the Chechen-Ingush ASSR.[23] The VDP became the leading party within the broader-based Chechen National Congress (CNC), which was formed by intellectuals in November 1990 and quickly became the largest national political organization, serving as the republic's version of a popular front for the Chechen population.[24]

The battle to set an agenda and capture the population's support gave rise to tensions between Chechnya's Communist government and the CNC. During its first meeting, in November 1990, the CNC called for a sovereign Chechen-Ingush republic and elected Zhokhar Dudayev as chairman of its Executive Committee. Dudayev, born in a Chechen village in 1944, had been deported a few weeks later with his family to Kazakhstan. After returning to Chechnya in 1957, he had entered the military, joined the Communist Party in 1966, and become a major general of the air force. From 1987 to 1991 he commanded the strategic bomber group based in Tartu, Estonia. He was sympathetic to the objectives of the Estonian national movement and was able to observe the movement and learn how nationalist popular fronts operated. After his election as chairman of the National Congress Executive Committee, he retired from the air force and returned to Chechnya.[25] His return, and the CNC's actions, were met by equally sweeping moves on the part of the Communist-dominated Chechen-Ingush Supreme Soviet, which, in November 1990, in an effort to garner the support of the people, adopted its own nationalist decree, the Declaration on State Sovereignty of the Chechen-Ingush Republic.

The CNC nevertheless maintained that the Communist government had lost the trust of the people and that it needed to be dissolved. Continuing to stress that Chechnya should be independent and that the rights of Chechens should be protected, it called for the "unconditional recognition of the Chechen nation's right to independence, compensation for crimes committed against the Chechen nation, trials of the guilty, and establishment of a government based on democratic principles."[26]

Throughout the early part of the movement, however, it was unclear precisely what portion of the public supported the moves of the CNC and its leadership. Membership and polling data are to this day unavailable and probably do not exist at all. The first clear demonstration of public support for Dudayev did not come until the events of August 1991, which found Communist leader Doku Zavgayev in Moscow for the signing of the Union Treaty during the ill-fated coup against Gorbachev. Out of pragmatism, and hoping that they would be supported once their fellow ideologues took control of the central government, Zavgayev and his deputies backed the coup. Dudayev, much more concerned with issues of justice and nationalist considerations, took what he saw as the high ground, issuing a decree denouncing the coup plotters as criminals and appealing to the Chechen population to defend democracy and begin a campaign of civil disobedience. Large rallies were held in his support and in support of the CNC. When Zavgayev returned to Chechnya on August 21, Dudayev and his followers had taken control of Grozny, and Zavgayev was unable to regain power over the institutional structures of the republic. On September 6 troops from the CNC stormed the Chechen Parliament building and forced Zavgayev to officially resign and the Parliament to disband. Power had effectively been shifted completely to the CNC.

Simultaneously, Gorbachev survived the coup, but power devolved to Russian leader Boris Yeltsin. The coup in Chechnya, which sought to overthrow Communist-era cronies and supplant them with Chechen nationalists, fitted with Yeltsin's moves in Moscow, and at this stage, the Russians regarded Chechnya and Dudayev as potential allies in the power struggle to displace the old ruling elite. Moscow nevertheless remained concerned about how events were playing out in Chechnya and in November attempted to establish order. Viewing the CNC government as illegitimate—having taken power only by a coup—it set up the Provisional Supreme Council (PSC) and scheduled elections for November 17 for a permanent government. The newly elected government, Moscow hoped, would legitimately represent the will of the people.

Dudayev, however, was uninterested in Moscow's help and went about consolidating his position. After his troops stormed the local KGB offices, he demanded that Moscow recognize that legitimate power was in the hands of his CNC Executive Committee.[27] Russian vice president Aleksandr Rutskoi met with Dudayev and the Executive Committee on October 6, during which he warned Dudayev about the illegality of storming buildings and "told him to stop 'politicizing' the people."[28] The PSC stepped up its activities and rhetoric in response to Rutskoi's visit, declaring itself the only legitimate political authority in the republic and warning Chechens about the activities of the CNC.

Armed formations are on the rampage; buildings of state agencies have been seized; unconstitutional resolutions have been published, including some that are provoking interethnic conflicts; and television and radio are being used to discredit people disagreeable to the Executive Committee. In view of the fact that the Provisional Supreme Council is the only body of power of the Chechen-Ingush Republic Supreme Soviet, its members appeal to the peoples of Checheno-Ingushetia not to permit a further escalation of antidemocratic processes.[29]

Dudayev, meanwhile, was planning elections of his own, to take place a month earlier than the Russian- and PSC-backed ones. The PSC implored the Chechen people to boycott Dudayev's early elections and, in an attempt to establish a sense of stability earlier rather than later, requested that the Russian Supreme Soviet recognize its legal status as the permanent government of the republic. Following a report from Rutskoi about his trip to Chechnya and his observations of the worsening political conditions, the Russian Supreme Soviet Presidium officially responded by declaring that the PSC was the only legal political formation in the republic and that it had the authority to take all necessary measures to stabilize the situation. Armed formations (that is, the CNC's troops, called the National Guard) were to turn in their weapons, and elections were to be held in accordance with Russian Federation legislation.[30]

Dudayev described the resolution as a "virtual declaration of war on our republic."[31] The Executive Committee of the CNC announced a general mobilization and the expansion of the National Guard, and fifty thousand people demonstrated in Grozny in Dudayev's support.[32] The units of the National Guard were put on alert,[33] and the CNC called for the suspension of all activities by the Russian-dominated prosecutor's office, Ministry of Internal Affairs, and judicial agencies.[34]

Moscow, still underestimating the resolve of Dudayev and his support among the Chechen people, attempted to handle the crisis by negotiating with the CNC. From October 11 to October 16, talks between a Russian parliamentary delegation and the Executive Committee of the CNC centered on four demands:

1. Cancellation of the Chechen presidential election set up by the CNC.
2. Preservation of the integrity of the republic within Russia.
3. Suspension of the blockade of news media and government buildings.
4. Disarmament of armed formations[35].

Though Dudayev was willing to consider the third demand, the other three were seen as vitally linked to Chechen independence and sovereignty and thus, in his mind, were nonnegotiable.[36] So, for example, he called off the general mobilization and handed over control of the Council of Ministers building and the local television and radio studios to the Ministry of Internal Affairs (thereby meeting the third demand), but he refused to reschedule elections, guarantee the integrity of Chechnya, or disarm his troops.[37] He further rejected Russia's idea that the PSC, and not the Executive Committee of the CNC, was the only legal power structure in the republic.

Yeltsin responded with more harsh rhetoric, ordering the citizens of Chechnya to surrender their arms within three days and warning the Executive Committee that if they did not cease their illegal activities, Russia would take measures to "stabilize the situation."[38] Ignoring his demands, the Executive Committee pressed ahead with preparations for the October elections.

On October 27, 1991, the CNC-organized presidential and parliamentary elections took place. The population of Chechnya, minus ethnic Russians and Ingushetians, voted overwhelmingly in favor of Dudayev and his supporters.[39] In the eyes of the people, Dudayev was the legitimately elected president of the republic, his faction gaining control of Chechnya's newly elected Parliament.[40] Acting as the legitimate representative of the Chechen people, Dudayev issued a decree on November 1, 1991, proclaiming the sovereignty of the Chechen Republic.[41]

Russia, however, discounted the authority of the elections and maintained that they were simply one more illegitimate action undertaken by a group that had come to power in an illegitimate fashion. Pushed by Rutskoi, who was the more extreme nationalist of the two, Yeltsin declared a state of emergency in the Chechen Republic on November 7 and sent troops to Grozny. The newly elected Chechen Parliament responded by granting Dudayev emergency powers, who then ordered martial law and mobilized his troops. Hundreds of Russian Interior Ministry troops were met as they landed, disarmed without a struggle by Chechen troops, and later bused to North Ossetia. The Russian Parliament, uneasy about the unfolding situation, pressured Yeltsin to recall the troops and end the state of emergency, which he subsequently did.[42]

The episode made Moscow look like the aggressive and incompetent party in the affair. Dudayev emerged as the victor and was able to parlay his successful resistance to the Russian military offensive into even more popular support.[43] On November 9, "tens of thousands" gathered on Freedom Square to support Chechnya's independence and the new government. When Dudayev was sworn in as president by the Chechen Parliament, he turned Moscow's profession of support for democracy and legitimacy against it, arguing, "If Russia [were to] recognize the sovereignty and rights of the Chechen people, . . . the majority of the population [would] vote in favor of the status of a Union Republic,"[44] and warning at the same time that "if a new war begins in the Caucasus, people in Moscow won't sleep peacefully."[45] Even some of the opposition came over to Dudayev's side. Moscow's imposition of troops was translated into the triumph of the Chechen people over the invading Russians imperialists. As one of Dudayev's aides declared:

> We have no opposition now; resentments and disagreements have been forgotten. We are united in the face of the threat of intervention. Not tens but hundreds of thousands of our people are armed. The Vainakhs [Chechens] will fight to the bitter end. But we give fair warning: if blood is shed, we won't forgive Yeltsin, Rutskoi, Arsanov, or anyone else for it.[46]

From Moscow's perspective, the problem was that Union Republic status would have afforded Chechnya the right to secede from both Russia and the USSR. The Russians, viewing the CNC as illegitimate, were furthermore unable to come to terms with the condition laid down by Dudayev for negotiations: Moscow had to recognize him as president and the faction in control of Parliament as the legitimate bodies of power in the republic.[47] Because Chechnya remained unyielding about its independence and who represented the republic in this bid for independence, elites in Russia grew frustrated. It was this frustration that had led to the dispatch of troops in 1991. Although the purpose was simply to demonstrate that Russia would not countenance the independence of an errant republic, the effect was that it proved, in the eyes of the Chechens, that Moscow, once again, was threatening the survival of the Chechen people, and it served only to strengthen their resolve.

Stalemate: 1992–93

Throughout 1992, Dudayev continued to refuse to compromise on Chechnya's independence from Russia, and Moscow remained adamant in its refusal to negotiate with Dudayev and to recognize Chechen independence.[48] Deliberations over negotiations between the Chechen and Russian delegations, which began in March 1992, were difficult. On December 31 a suggestion for a draft agreement delineating Chechen-Russian relations was published in the local press but was quickly rejected by both Dudayev and Husein Akhmadov, the head of the Parliament, on the grounds that it violated both Chechnya's declaration of sovereignty and its constitution.[49] The year 1992 ended with little compromise on either side.

By the beginning of 1993, Dudayev had managed to consolidate his position, but Chechnya was beginning to feel the impact of the economic and transportation blockade that Russia had imposed earlier as a way to isolate Chechnya and undermine Dudayev's rule.[50] One side effect of this strategy was a sharp increase in illegal and black market activity in

Chechnya, thus increasing the anarchic conditions in the republic. The year was characterized by troubles between the leaders and their domestic opposition in both Chechnya and Russia, as much as by conflicts between the two entities. Dudayev faced mounting opposition at home as some constituents blamed him for the misfortunes of the Chechen economy. As one analyst put it, "Even sympathetic observers have called the Dudayev government's management of the Chechen economy a disaster; the blockade and other sanctions imposed by Russia, even though they were haphazardly enforced, accelerated the economic decline."[51] Between 1991 and 1993, the gross national product of the republic declined by some 65.3 percent, per capita income fell to one-fourth its 1991 level,[52] and industrial production fell by as much as 60 percent.[53]

The Chechen Parliament, seeking to distance itself from a leader who it suspected would be forced to take the political fall for the republic's economic woes, demanded Dudayev's resignation; in response, Dudayev imposed emergency rule and issued a decree dissolving the Parliament, though the dissolution never took place at the time. The reaction to Dudayev's moves proved that he had not lost all support: thirty thousand of his backers gathered in front of the Parliament building, and "somewhat" fewer opposition supporters gathered on another square.[54] While Dudayev and his supporters held previous communist administrations responsible for the political and economic crisis, the opposition continued to place the blame on Dudayev's failure to cope with the economic blockade and stated that the public would not back the leader due to the drastic drop in living standards.

Meanwhile, in keeping with its refusal to negotiate with Dudayev, Russia attempted to strike a deal with the Chechen Parliament and Yaragai Mamodayev, the Chechen prime minister. In response, Dudayev sacked Mamodayev and issued yet another decree, which dissolved the Parliament. Nevertheless, the Parliament called for a referendum asking Chechen citizens whether they wanted to retain the presidency and whether they trusted Dudayev or the Parliament, a move that Dudayev obviously did not support.[55] In June his military units stormed two buildings occupied by opposition legislators,[56] and he threatened that if the opposition Parliament continued to push for the referendum, he would use "any means" to prevent it.[57] The Parliament was eventually dissolved.

Although Dudayev's support in the Parliament had obviously waned, his popular support, for the most part, had not. Though the public was discontented with the state of the economy, it still viewed Dudayev as the legitimate leader and the only man capable of leading Chechnya to independence. Parliament overestimated the sway that the economic issue would hold among the populace and underestimated Dudayev's political staying power. According to one report, local authorities in 70 percent of the villages and towns in the republic refused to hold the referendum on Chechnya's presidency and their trust in Dudayev, and three thousand people gathered in front of the presidential palace to demonstrate in support of Dudayev and of his opposition to the referendum. Only about half as many came out in support of the dissolved Parliament.

With the Parliament's dissolution, a formal opposition government led by former prime minister Mamodayev was formed.[58] Although Mamodayev was in opposition to Dudayev, he too pushed to clarify Chechnya's status vis-à-vis Russia. Mamodayev sent a letter to the constitutional arbitration body of Russia requesting that they investigate the inclusion of Chechnya in the Russian constitution[59] and claimed that in terms of international law, Chechnya had never been part of Russia, that in fact it had been seized, and that the seizure was never legally regularized. Although Dudayev did not recognize Mamodayev's authority, the two men agreed that Chechnya's relationship with Russia should be negotiated, and both seemed committed to Chechen independence. The year 1993 had thus brought increased dissension within Chechen society but had nevertheless not changed the republic's bargaining position vis-à-vis Moscow.

Civil War

The year 1994 brought more direct conflict between the Russian Federation and its independence-minded regions, Chechnya in particular. Moscow was beginning to face the reality that a Chechen opposition was incapable of overthrowing Dudayev.[60] In seeming recognition of Dudayev's continued support, a high-level meeting took place between Russian prime minister Viktor Chernomyrdin and Chechen prime minister Mairbek Mugadev at the end of January. According to Mugadev, the two sides concluded that Yeltsin and Dudayev should meet to resolve economic disputes and engineer a political settlement.[61] Moscow again issued stipulations to Chechnya before the negotiations could begin:

1. Chechnya must stop slandering Moscow.
2. Chechnya must act as a republic within the Russian Federation.
3. The Chechen delegation must study the treaty signed between Tatarstan and Moscow.

Although Dudayev expressed his willingness to meet with the Russian leadership in March, he nevertheless stressed that he would not retreat "one iota from the idea of the state independence of the republic."[62] Aslanbek Akbulatov, the head of the Chechen delegation, underscored Dudayev's position: Chechnya was willing to compromise on details but would insist on independence.

Moves toward negotiations continued through the spring, but each side's preconditions precluded any serious progress. Although Moscow was now willing to negotiate with Dudayev and had dropped the condition that he be replaced, it was on the added condition that Dudayev himself sign the Russian Federal Treaty. Dudayev, however, refused to submit to negotiations if it meant that Chechnya had to accept that it was a part of Russia,[63] and signing the Russian Federal Treaty would have meant exactly that.

Out of frustration, Moscow yet again sought to negotiate with others in Chechnya. On April 15, for example, Yeltsin issued a decree calling for the Russian government to negotiate not only with the Dudayev government but also with other Chechen political and social movements. In a further display of Dudayev's support among the populace, including the backing of his enemies, opposition leader Mamodayev warned that Moscow's move was fraught with complications and would probably disrupt the already tenuous negotiations.[64] Dudayev was still very much in control of Chechnya's future.

At the end of May it seemed as if negotiations would finally take place between Yeltsin and Dudayev, as Sergei Shakrai, widely viewed as a primary obstacle to negotiations, was dismissed as the Russian minister for Nationalities Affairs and Regional Policy.[65] Dudayev supported this action, and Russian officials announced that Yeltsin would soon meet with the Chechen leader. Yet political intrigue persisted, and Dudayev remained wary: prior to May 1994, he had survived four assassination attempts and a parliamentary coup, and on May 27 a fifth attempt was made on his life. Accusations abounded that Moscow was sponsoring state terrorism and that it was behind this and the other attempts, as well as the sponsor of Dudayev's opposition.[66] Not surprisingly, the negotiations halted.

Throughout the summer of 1994, the opposition in Chechnya continued its unsuccessful attempts to destabilize Dudayev. With aid and arms from Moscow, the opposition Chechen Provisional Council (CPC) built up armed units and sought to unite others against the government.[67] By August 2, after declaring itself the only legal body in Chechnya, the CPC claimed to be in control of all Chechnya, except for a few small areas, though the situation on the ground indicated otherwise.[68] Not only did the western media report that Dudayev was still firmly in control, but at a large meeting held in Grozny on August 10, in which all seventeen administrative districts were represented by religious and clan leaders, the participants voted to launch a holy war in the event of a Russian invasion and advised Dudayev to declare martial law and a general mobilization. Popular support remained with Dudayev, and certainly with his objectives.[69] On August 21 a rally attended by ten thousand participants was held to show support for Dudayev; and on September 6 an astonishing two hundred thousand supporters attended a speech he gave to mark the third anniversary of Chechnya's independence.[70] In the speech, Dudayev maintained that the Chechen people had no one to fear so long as they remained united to defend their independence.

Clashes between Dudayev's forces and the opposition intensified, and there were indications that Russian troops and equipment were involved directly, although the Russian Defense Ministry issued repeated denials.[71] One of the largest assaults came on November 25, when CPC forces attempted to storm the Chechen capital. Backed by some forty helicopters with Russian markings, artillery, and tanks, they claimed to control the presidential palace.[72] The attack, however, was an unmitigated disaster for Dudayev's opponents, both in Russia and in Chechnya. Within twelve hours, Dudayev's forces decisively crushed the CPC assault, capturing Russian crews and supplying definitive proof of his long-standing claim that Chechen opposition was really the work of Russia and its agents.

The crisis continued to escalate. On November 29, Yeltsin stepped up his rhetoric, ordering the two sides to immediately lay down their arms or else face all the force Moscow had at its disposal. Dudayev ignored Yeltsin's demand, and on December 5, while stating that Chechnya was willing to hold talks with Moscow, reiterated his insistence that Chechnya's independence was not negotiable.[73] On December 9 Yeltsin responded by ordering the disarmament of illegal armed formations in Chechnya and stating that his goal was to seal off the republic by December 15.

By December 15 approximately six hundred Russian tanks and an estimated forty thousand troops advanced from Ingushetia, Dagestan, and North Ossetia and remained fifteen to forty kilometers outside the capital.[74] Their advance had been slowed by civilians blocking their approach along the way, as well as by attacks from Chechen units. Dudayev refused to agree to talks until all Russian troops left Chechen territory, realizing that although Moscow's capitulation was surely preferable to war, he held a strong hand either way. If Moscow backed off, then Dudayev could take credit for fending off Russian imperialism and maintaining Chechen independence. If Moscow decided to fight, he could wage a war of the kind the Russians feared most—another Afghanistan—at the same time benefiting from Western outcries at a Russian attack on such a small ethnic group. Russian troops did not leave until 1996, when, after taking and losing Grozny several times and suffering a huge number of casualties, Russia sued for peace.

Analysis: Settlement Patterns and Precedent Setting

Among Chechens, Moscow has always been viewed as an imperialist power that colonized the Caucasus by force and repeatedly threatened to annihilate them. Each time that Russian or Soviet power eroded, the Chechens fought wars to gain their independence. In a speech in August 1992, Chechen leader Zhokhar Dudayev demonstrated the group's hostility toward Russia and its attachment to the homeland, declaring that "[i]n the future, any armed intervention of Russia in Chechnya's affairs will mean a new Caucasian war, believe me. . . . For the last 300 years they [Moscow] taught us to survive. To survive not as individuals but as a nation. . . . Three hundred years of bloodshed are quite enough. . . . This will be a war without rules."[75] Moscow, Chechens believed, threatened their survival as a nation, and under Dudayev's leadership Chechens persisted in demanding an independent state, viewing it as the only guarantee of their survival as a people. Survival rhetoric abounded, with Dudayev accusing Moscow of robbing Chechnya of its cultural heritage and economic assets. He even rejected Russian proposals that advanced economic stability over political freedom,[76] explicitly proving his willingness, and the willingness of Chechens as a whole, to accept economic hardship in exchange for political independence and what was viewed as ethnic survival.

Chechnya's dire outlook was facilitated by Chechen settlement patterns, which supported both the capability and the legitimacy of its independence demand. Chechens were concentrated and comprised a majority of Chechnya's population; as such their capacity to mobilize was high. The widely accepted notion that Chechnya must be ruled by Chechens and the perception that Chechens had an obligation to defend their homeland provided legitimacy and was proven by Moscow's inability to dislodge Dudayev because of the support he had garnered from the public as a whole. Just as Chechen ancestors had fought to overthrow the Russian imperial yoke, so would today's and tomorrow's generations: the past was no different from the present. Dudayev was representing the position of a majority of Chechens at the bargaining table, and as such he understood that he possessed both the capability and the legitimacy to fight the state, if it should come to that.

Russia, as discussed in the previous chapter, was a multiethnic state with numerous concentrated ethnic minorities and therefore faced many potential independence movements. Consequently, Moscow was deeply opposed to granting independence to any of its dissatisfied ethnic groups, fearing this would lead to independence by other groups and ultimately threaten to unravel Russia. This concern about precedent setting explains why Russia viewed all of its territory, be it Tatarstan or Chechnya, as indivisible. Thus, to Russia, the use of force in Chechnya must have seemed preferable for two reasons. First, it was guaranteed to succeed, and at a relatively low cost in blood and treasure.[77] Second, Tatarstan had only just achieved greater political autonomy after a long and drawn-out

period of negotiations short of violence, so the resort to force in Chechnya—
a positive use of the logic of precedent setting—might discourage others
from attempting to achieve greater autonomy or succeeding by any other
means. Though Russia negotiated for several years before sending in
troops, such measures were extremely halfhearted and most likely a result
of the need to buy organizational time and perhaps even to garner domestic and international support; attempts to negotiate would make it
look as if Russia had at least tried to solve the crisis without using brute
force, thus legitimizing any future war.

On December 12, 1994, just days before the war began in earnest,
Yeltsin made a speech before both houses of Parliament and asked a rhe-
torical question reflecting the importance he attached to precedent setting. He questioned whether Russia should "negotiate the status of
Chechnya as part of Russia, and is the Parliament ready to introduce into
the constitution an amendment on the right of Chechnya to secede, in
view of the possible *domino effect this would have on other secession-
minded republics* within the Russian Federation."[78] Yeltsin's speech made
it clear that in his view, Chechen territory was indivisible and that using
force to suppress the Chechen independence movement was the only
option left. Six years later Yeltsin again stressed the preeminence of precedent setting. In his published memoirs, he stated that during the session
of the Russian Security Council in which the decision to use force in
Chechnya was made, "The general position was *unanimous*. We cannot
stand idly by while a piece of Russia breaks off, because this would be the
beginning of the collapse of the country."[79] Moscow thus had to intervene to prevent Chechnya and others from attempting to gain independence, since the accumulation of seceding actors would eventually
threaten Russia's very survival.

Comparative Analysis and Competing Explanations:
   Chechnya and Tatarstan

In the Russia-Chechnya interaction, the conflicting parties were a state
concerned about precedents and an ethnic group willing and capable of
seceding. This situation differed greatly from the predicament of Tatarstan. To test whether my theory best accounts for war in Chechnya
and peace in Tatarstan, let us examine the cases in relation to possible
alternative explanations. As I demonstrate, materialist, nonmaterialist,
and elite-manipulation theories, outlined in chapter 1, are capable of ac-
counting for some of these dynamics, my theory accounts for more of
these dynamics.

Materialist Explanations

Although it seems clear that precedent-setting concerns dominated Moscow's thinking in both Tatarstan and Chechnya, there is an alternative explanation. That is, Russian leaders viewed the disputed territories as indivisible due to their strategic and intrinsic worth. Chechnya, for example, was strategically important because it shared an international border with Georgia. Losing the republic would therefore mean a Russia that was smaller and more vulnerable to external forces. Tatarstan, however, which was located well inside Russia, had no international borders and would presumably be easier for Russia to control. The problem with this argument, however, is that during the negotiations between 1991 and 1994, it was not clear that Russia itself would remain intact. Tatarstan could have had an international border had other regions gained their independence.[80] The strategic-worth argument therefore cannot adequately explain why violence emerged in Chechnya and not in Tatarstan.

What about natural and man-made resources? Can their presence or absence explain why violence emerged in Chechnya and not in Tatarstan? The problem with this argument is that *both* Tatarstan and Chechnya contained important resources. Grozny, for example, was a major oil-refining center, and an important pipeline network transited northern Chechnya. This pipeline provided Russia needed leverage over the entire Caucasus region and played a role in Russia's dispute over exploration and drilling rights in the Caspian Sea. As for Tatarstan, it served as a major hub for transporting oil and natural gas throughout Russia. Thus, since both regions had roughly equal resources, it is impossible to argue that differences in resource levels alone can account for the different outcomes in these two cases.

Two further points cut against the materialist argument. If the oil pipelines were all that mattered, then the Russian army's job should have been done once it gained control over the territory containing the pipelines. The army, however, did not halt but pushed deeper into Chechnya in an effort to control the entire republic. It is also worth noting that Russia could have negotiated a solution that would have made the loss of complete control over the pipeline less harmful to its interests. If Moscow was worried in general about Chechen control of energy resources or being blocked in efforts to participate in an energy consortium, why was it not just as concerned in the Tatar case? Tatarstan was allowed to sell off 50 percent of its oil wealth, but in Chechnya Moscow refused even to negotiate about such resources, even though these resources, like those of Tatarstan, were divisible. Given that Moscow had demonstrated its willingness to divide such resources with Tatarstan, this argument cannot explain why it was unwilling to compromise with Chechnya.

Second, Russia was under extreme fiscal duress in the early 1990s.[81] The government had almost no income from taxes, precisely because many republics refused to pay them. Under such circumstances, the loss of revenue from any errant republic might provoke strong measures from Moscow. The problem with this argument is that Tatarstan was a rich republic, whereas Chechnya was not merely poor but a net drain.[82] Therefore, if budget considerations were driving Moscow's thinking, it should have cut Chechnya loose.

Clearly all of these factors played a role in Russia's decision to commit combat troops. But just as clearly, there were many indications—though ignored by many in Moscow—that the costs of military intervention would be high and the benefits of conquest low. Galina Starovoitova, Yeltsin's adviser on ethnic issues, told Russian television journalists, for example, that the security situation in the Caucasus, including Chechnya, did not pose a real danger to the national interests of Russia.[83] In short, materialist explanations alone cannot account for divergent Russian behavior in the two situations.

Nonmaterial-Based Explanations

If material-based explanations are weak, perhaps the variation in the two outcomes can best be explained by using a nonmaterial-based approach. According to the nonmaterialist approach, ethnic groups in contact with one another would necessarily experience conflict, as tension due to their distinct identities would necessarily arise. This explanation, however, suffers from an overall lack of variation and an inability to account for the differences between ethnic groups and their particular identities. If identities derive from the attachment of a people to its territory, in the case of Tatars and Chechens an examination of their documents and records of negotiations reveals very little difference between the way they viewed their connection to Tatar and Chechen territory respectively: both regarded their territories as sacred homelands, and both could trace their ancestors back for generations. Moreover, both viewed Russian domination and their own subordination as a threat to the survival of their identities. Tatar nationalists were as concerned about the assimilation of Tatars as the Chechens were of another round of Moscow brutality and repression. What mattered was not the identity ties to a particular territory, which were similar in both cases, but rather how such ties were represented in negotiations with the state, which were due not to the mere existence of such beliefs but rather to their level of popularity among the population, a fact influenced in large part by the settlement patterns of the populations.

Elite-Manipulation Explanations

Another explanation for different outcomes among structurally similar actors in the former USSR is given by elite-manipulation theories: one leader's charisma and skill at manipulating nationalist discourse leads to one outcome, and another leader's lack of skill leads to a different outcome. Thus, according to this idea, Shamiyev lacked the charisma and skill needed to manipulate nationalist discourse, whereas Dudayev was a talented, charismatic manipulator. This difference would explain why peace came to Tatarstan and war to Chechnya.

The problem with this argument is that *both* Shamiyev and Dudayev were charismatic and talented. The difference, however, is that Shamiyev could not tap nationalist discourse even if he so desired. There is no doubt that Shamiyev was an excellent politician, but his excellence was reflected in his decision *not* to play up nationalism to gain or stay in power. Tatar nationalism did not resonate with the broader population he represented. The strength of his opposition—in this case composed of conservative and independence-minded nationalists—was severely circumscribed by both low membership and low levels of political activism. As noted in the previous chapter, at the height of the nationalist movement, the largest rally yielded only fifteen thousand demonstrators in a population of 3.6 million.[84] Tatars simply did not come out in force to support a nationalist Tatar independence cause, and recognizing that he had a broader constituency that included both Tatars and non-Tatars, Shamiyev therefore opted for a largely economic platform rather than a nationalist one. In contrast to Shamiyev, Dudayev faced a Chechen population united around the idea of an independent Chechnya. From a population of just over a million (three-fourths of whom were Chechens), 200,000 demonstrators came out to support Dudayev and Chechnya's independence in September 1994, a time when his opposition was supposed to have been at its strongest.[85]

Overall, although it is clear that Shamiyev and Dudayev had similar talents, resources, and outlooks, and that this similarity mattered to some extent, it is also true that leaders maneuver within boundaries whose areas are determined by forces beyond their control. This is a crucial point, because it counters the tendency to see leaders as always forming public opinion ex nihilo, rather than representing a preexisting public opinion. In the cases analyzed here, for example, a minority of Tatars lived in Tatarstan, and within Tatarstan ethnic Tatars made up less than half of the population. Moreover, they were significantly intermarried with ethnic Russians. This made it difficult to form majorities in favor of ethnic-based policies in Tatarstan and to demand an independent Tatarstan for Tatars.[86] In other words, the popular basis for separatism, ethnicity, simply was not there. This was not true in Chechnya, where the largely Chechen population provided sustained support for independence. Thus, it is more likely that given the distribution of ethnic groups in each territory, any leader representing a majority would have put forward policy aims similar to those advocated by Shamiyev and Dudayev, respectively. Consequently, settlement patterns better explain why nationalism emerged as a tour de force in Chechnya and fizzled out in the Tatar republic.

The Theory of Territorial Indivisibility

I have argued that whenever both parties in a dispute come to see the value over which they struggle as indivisible, they are less likely to resolve their dispute peacefully. In ethnic conflicts, violence occurs when two conditions hold: (1) states fear setting precedents, and (2) an ethnic group demands sovereignty.

The crucial factor that explains why Moscow represented control over both Tatarstan and Chechnya as indivisible is precedent-setting. In a new Russian Federation composed of a multitude of ethnic groups that might someday mobilize for independence, Moscow feared for its territorial integrity and survival. The structure of the Russian Federation, with more than one group capable of seceding, precluded Moscow from considering, much less allowing, the secession of any of them. Out of concerns for its reputation, Russia therefore viewed control over both territories as *indivisible*.

With Chechnya, Moscow argued that it had to intervene to prevent others from attempting independence, since the accumulation of seceding actors would eventually constitute a significant territorial loss. This also helps to explain the timing of violence. Moscow became impatient and resorted to force sooner rather than later; although it calculated that it was as likely to win later, resorting to force sooner signaled that it was willing to keep the Russian Federation intact. This was especially important, as it had just signed a bilateral treaty with Tatarstan, a precedent it preferred not to repeat.

The notion of precedents presupposes the acceptance of a particular form of legal process or negotiation. Russia demanded that Chechnya renounce its independence as a precondition for negotiations—negotiations whose subject was to be precisely the legal and international status of Chechnya. The Chechens attempted the same thing, again relying on the acknowledged but unspoken power of precedence: a meeting between Yeltsin and Dudayev would have the effect of legitimizing Dudayev's status as a representative of a coherent national entity.

In the battle to avoid setting precedents, however, Russia could hope to win only halfway. In a very real sense, it had already crossed a threshold by signing an agreement with Kazan granting special economic rights to Tatarstan. Russia's negotiators were keenly aware of this risk. But interestingly, once again Russian negotiators did not demand the preconditions from Tatarstan that they later did from Chechnya.[87] Even so, Russia could not be happy with the negotiations with Shamiyev nor with the likely outcome: an increased autonomy for Tatarstan, possibly setting a precedent for other independence-minded regions.

In the Tatar interaction, one actor viewed the issue as indivisible, and the other actor viewed it as divisible. What explains this? The dispersed settlement pattern of ethnic Tatars in Tatarstan restricted any representative of the majority to the representation of divisible, that is, economic, issues. If more Tatars move into Tatarstan or are born there or more Russians leave, then any future bargaining may shift to resemble Chechnya's. Tatarstan represents an interesting case in which the assimilation of Tatars does seem to have undermined the nationalist discourse and movement.

In the Chechen interaction, both Moscow and Chechnya viewed the issue as indivisible. Moscow's views have been explained, and Chechnya's can be explained by the widespread notion that *Chechnya must be ruled by Chechens* and the fact that Chechens believed they had an obligation to defend their territory. The 1994 violence was interpreted as a continuation of a three-hundred-year-old struggle. Moscow and ethnic Russians would forever be viewed as outsiders, imperialists who had no right to conquer and control the Chechen people or their homeland. Dudayev, in other words, was representing the historically held position of a majority of Chechens at the bargaining table.

In sum, both Tatarstan's and Chechnya's negotiations with Moscow over their independence status provide solid support for the causal logic that underpins my theory. Settlement patterns largely determined whether each ethnic group had the necessary legitimacy and capabilities to push for independence, and, on the other side, precedent-setting concerns dominated the Russian state's position.

6

Georgia and Abkhazia

He who has lost his homeland has lost
everything.
  —*Abkhaz proverb*

Throughout its history, Georgia has been plagued by both internal strife
and external interference. Ronald Grigor Suny, writing about the sixteenth century, described Georgian politics as consisting of "[l]ocal
dynasts maneuver[ing] among the contenders for political hegemony,
sometimes choosing the king, other times the great empires that bordered Georgia."[1] Richard Pipes, discussing Georgian politics in the early
twentieth century, wrote, "In its endeavor to create a homogeneous national state, the Tiflis government showed little sympathy for the attempts of . . . minority groups to secure political and cultural autonomy."[2] Both Suny and Pipes could just as well have been referring to
contemporary Georgia. During the 1990s, Georgia faced two serious regional civil wars, suffered a coup in the capital for control of the central
regime, and balanced the interests of neighboring Russia in its internal
affairs.

The next two chapters investigate the territorial disputes between the
state of Georgia and two of its regions, Abkhazia and Ajaria.[3] Civil war
emerged in Abkhazia, and Ajaria acquired the distinction of being the
only region in Georgia not to witness violence in the post-Soviet period.
There are many similarities between these interactions and those we analyzed in chapters 4 and 5. As with Tatarstan and Chechnya, Abkhazia
and Ajaria were autonomous republics within the Soviet Union, and
Georgia constituted a union republic, like Russia. Further, Abkhazia and
Ajaria were dominated by ethnic groups that adhered to Islam, whereas
the population that dominated the Georgian state adhered to Christianity
(as in Russia).

There are three main differences between this set of interactions and
those examined in the previous two chapters. First, there is no variation
between Abkhazia and Ajaria on the independent variable, settlement
patterns—both were concentrated minorities—yet there is variation on
the dependent variable—civil war arose in Abkhazia but not in Ajaria.
Although this difference in outcomes seems to represent a problem for

the theory of indivisible territory, I argue that the theory nonetheless can account for the divergence. Abkhazia pursued only greater autonomy, not independence. Only after Tbilisi resorted to force and Russia provided military aid did Abkhazia represent its position of an independent Abkhazia as indivisible. Ajar identity and attachment to Georgian land goes far in explaining Ajaria's lack of a full bid for independence.

Second, isolating the state of Georgia's motivations is a tricky matter. This is because the state was dominated by one ethnic group—Georgians—which meant that as an actor Georgia regarded its survival vis-à-vis Abkhazia and Ajaria in both state and ethnic terms. As a multinational state, Georgia viewed their bids for greater autonomy as a serious threat to its territorial integrity, and as a concentrated-majority ethnic group, it felt compelled to fight over territory it perceived as part of the imagined Georgian homeland. This combination of state and ethnic interests complicates Georgia's motivations.

The third difference is the active intervention of a proximate great power: Russia. Russia's engagement in the political affairs of Georgia runs deep, and the period under investigation here—roughly 1990–94—is no exception.[4] Although the Abkhaz sought greater autonomy and felt that their claims to the territory were legitimate, the ratio of their passion for autonomy to their military capabilities makes it doubtful that they would have sought independence by arms when they did if not for the very active military support of an ever-meddling Russia.

This chapter consists of three main parts. The first part provides a broad overview of the history of the Georgians and Abkhaz, their settlement patterns, and their dispute over the territory of Abkhazia. The Georgians represented a concentrated-majority ethnic group that feared Russian political and cultural domination, as well as exploitation by ethnic minorities. These ethnic concerns combined with more traditional state concerns about the inviolability of borders as Georgia pursued its own independence course from Russia. The Abkhaz represented a concentrated minority that had consistently feared Georgian domination but possessed little capability to act on those fears. The second part details the bargaining between Tbilisi and Sukhumi over the disputed territory of Abkhazia. Both actors regarded Abkhazia as part of their homeland territory, but Georgia was also concerned about the rights of all citizens living in Abkhazia (including ethnic Georgians) and its territorial integrity. The third section relates how civil war erupted in Abkhazia. It is apparent that Georgia believed it could defeat Abkhazia in a violent confrontation. However, it could not defeat an Abkhazia backed by Russia— a factor that Georgian elites failed to anticipate fully.

Georgians and Abkhaz

This section introduces the main protagonists—Georgians and Abkhaz—and their bargaining over control of Abkhazia. Both sides viewed Abkhazia as integral to Abkhaz and Georgian identity, but the Georgian side also had state concerns about maintaining the territorial integrity of Georgia. As a concentrated-majority state, the Georgians represented their interests as indivisible. As a weak concentrated minority, the Abkhaz demanded greater autonomy, and their interests were divisible. Although my theory predicts that violence is less likely in these cases, civil war nevertheless occurred. I make the case that had it not been for the active intervention of neighboring Russia, large-scale violence would have been averted, mostly because the Abkhaz lacked the capability to resort to violence to achieve their objectives.

The Development of Georgian Identity

The territory of contemporary Georgia is part of an isthmus between the Black and Caspian Seas. To the north lie the Caucasus Mountains, and to the south lies the lesser Caucasus mountain range. Georgia borders the Russian Federation to the north and northeast, Azerbaijan to the east and southeast, and Armenia and Turkey to the south. Georgia's western border is the Black Sea. Although Georgia does not border the Caspian Sea to the east, it is connected by oil and gas pipelines to the Azerbaijani port of Baku. Other important transportation links include the main rail with links to the Russian Federation, along the Black Sea coast into Turkey, Azerbaijan, and Armenia. The main ports of Georgia are Sukhumi and Batumi which provide international shipping connections with Black Sea and Mediterranean ports (see figure 6.1).

Due to its geostrategic location in the heart of the Caucasus, Georgia has been the site of competition among successive empires seeking hegemony in the region. Conquered by the Persians, Byzantines, Arabs, Mongols, and Ottomans, Georgia succumbed to Russian imperial domination in 1801, which continued until the Bolshevik Revolution in 1917.[5]

In 1918 Georgians gained complete political control over their historic homeland for the first time. Georgia experienced independent statehood for three years under a Menshevik socialist government. It was recognized by twenty-two countries, including Soviet Russia in 1920, and entered into alliances with Western states. Prior to the Bolshevik Revolution, ethnic Armenian businessmen had dominated the urban environment and, along with ethnic Russians, occupied the most important posts in

FIGURE 6.1.   Location Map of Georgia

the government. Georgians had been on the political fringe, despite their ethnic dominance, so this was an opportunity for them to gain prominence.[6] But independence in Georgia was short-lived. Nine months after Moscow had signed a treaty affirming the Georgian Democratic Republic's sovereignty, Bolshevik troops invaded Georgia. The land then became a Soviet Socialist Republic, and in 1922, along with Armenia and Azerbaijan, it became the Republic of Transcaucasia.[7] The Georgians feared this consolidation, as it increased not only imperial centralization but also Russian domination.[8]

Georgian identity and nationalism thus developed as a defense against the pressures and the blandishments of the "higher culture" of the Russians. Georgians and non-Georgians suffered the imposition of a political system that favored Russians and their chauvinism and that suppressed any hints of nationalism.[9]

As the system evolved, however, the titular nationalities, including the Georgians, managed to express their own version of national chauvinism. Within Georgia this meant that non-Georgians were affected by Georgian chauvinism: Georgia became a protected area of privilege for Georgians.[10] Abkhaz, Armenians, Ossetians, Ajars, Kurds, Jews, and other minorities in Georgia were at a considerable disadvantage. Georgians received the bulk of the rewards: the leading political positions in the republic, the largest subsidies for cultural projects, and access to a vast economic network of black market and illegal operations.[11] Minorities in Georgia resented the imposition of a Georgian higher culture and the inaccessibility of the Georgian economy. Close kinship ties, combined with the dominance of a distinctly Georgian caste within the republic's political elite, "reinforced the exclusionary character of politics in the republic, the sense of superiority of the titular nationality and inferiority of the non-Georgians."[12]

Paradoxically, however, Georgians felt threatened by ethnic minorities living in the republic. Noticeable apprehension centered on the question of the demographic balance in Georgia.[13] Considerable alarm, for example, developed among Georgians after the 1979 Soviet census revealed that some of the non-Georgian nationalities had significantly higher birthrates than Georgians did, even though Georgians still accounted for 68.8 percent of the republic's population. A 1983 report discussing demographic trends warned that if Georgian birthrates continued to decline and non-Georgian birthrates increased, within thirty years Georgians would be a minority in Georgia.

As of the 1989 census, Georgians comprised 70 percent of Georgia's total population of 5.4 million.[14] Suggesting an ethnic group with a close affinity to its homeland, more than 95 percent of all Georgians worldwide lived in Georgia.[15] Within Georgia, Georgians constituted a concentrated majority.

Georgians are descendants of an ancient Christian nation located in the southern part of the Caucasus. Ethnically they are part of the Kartvelian people, and they call their land Sakartvelo. Three groups make up most of the Kartvelian group: the Georgians (85 percent), Mingrelians (10 percent), and Svans (1 percent). Each group speaks a distinct, yet related, language within the South Caucasian (Kartvelian) language group.[16] Mingrelians and Svans had their own census grouping until 1930, when they began to be classified under the broader category of Georgian.[17] The Georgian language is one of the oldest in the region: the script has been traced to the fourth century. The Georgians are united with Russians in their Christianity, so the primary "ethnic" dimension that separates Georgians from Russians is language. More than 98 percent of all Georgians consider Georgian their native language, and only a third claim Russian as a second language.[18] Again, these figures indicate an ethnic group with strong territorial and linguistic ties.

In short, throughout the Soviet period, the well-being of the Georgians remained a dominant issue. Threats to Georgian identity were perceived to emanate not only from the dominance of Russia and the Russian language and culture but also from the minorities and their respective languages, religions, and culture. One such minority were the Abkhaz.

Abkhazia and the Abkhaz

Religious and linguistic differences mark the Abkhaz-Georgian relationship. Although the Ottoman Empire and Islam competed for dominance in the region of Georgia against the Persian and Russian Empires, it was only in the seventeenth and eighteenth centuries that the Abkhaz converted to Islam.[19] After the suppression of two rebellions against imperial Russia in 1866 and 1877, large portions of the Abkhaz population—half of all the Abkhaz, and all of them Muslim—were exiled or sought refuge in the Ottoman Empire. Many of those Abkhaz who remained converted to the Christianity of the Russian Empire. Thus both Islam and Christianity are present among the Abkhaz, with neither commanding a strict adherence; instead the Abkhaz combined elements of each with their own traditional customs. Yuri Voronov, chairman of the Human Rights and Inter-Ethnic Relations Commission for Abkhazia, described religion among the Abkhaz as such: "[M]ost Abkhazian people are Christians, although there are Muslims too—but we generally take religious matters easy."[20] Anywhere from 20 to 70 of the Abkhaz are Muslim, and the remaining portion adheres to the Orthodox Christian Gregorian Church, "but both these religions form no more than a surface layer on the old paganism."[21]

The language of the Abkhaz is literary, resulting in the publication of books, journals, and newspapers, and it is written in the Cyrillic script as opposed to the Georgian script.[22] In 1989 more than 93.5 percent of the Abkhaz considered Abkhaz their primary language, and 78.8 percent claimed Russian as their second language. Only 3.4 percent of the Abkhaz declared a language other than Russian as their second tongue, indicating little use for Georgian.[23] According to a 1979 estimate, almost 25 percent of Abkhaz and 44 percent of Georgians living in Abkhazia could not communicate with one another. The imposition of a third language—Georgian—along with Abkhaz and Russian was viewed by minorities with anxiety, for the language determined access to higher education, government offices, and professions.[24]

Despite these religious and linguistic differences, neither Georgians nor the Abkhaz would deny that the Abkhaz are indeed a distinct ethnic group with a language and culture that can trace its origins to lands in and around contemporary Georgia. Disputes arise, however, over which group first inhabited the territory of contemporary Abkhazia and therefore can rightfully claim the region as its homeland. Both trace ancestors back for generations, and both see the region of Abkhazia as vital to being an Abkhaz or a Georgian. During the 1950s and then again in the 1980s, scholarly debates among Georgian historians challenged the Abkhaz's claims of being indigenous to the territory, arguing that the Abkhaz were "recent" settlers who had displaced Georgians.[25] Georgians seemed willing to accept that descendants of the Abkhaz had been in Abkhazia for at least three to five hundred years but argued that their

TABLE 6.1
Population Data for the Abkhaz (1989)

Distribution of the Abkhaz	Number of the Abkhaz	Portion of Abkhaz Population
Throughout FSU	105,308	100%
Throughout Georgia	95,853	91
In Abkhaz Republic	93,267	89
Elsewhere in FSU	9,455	9

own Georgian ancestors were the original settlers of the region. For their part, the Abkhaz thought (and continue to think) of Abkhazia as their ancient homeland. Abkhaz scholars regarded Georgians as the "newly-arrived, non-native population of Abkhazia," and Abkhaz intellectuals, academics, and politicians have gone to great lengths to prove the long and continued history of the Abkhaz in the region, claiming a presence of at least two thousand years.[26]

In 1989 the Abkhaz of the former Soviet Union numbered 105,308. They made up just 1.8 percent of the population of Georgia. Most Abkhaz—about 89 percent—resided in the former Abkhaz Republic, as indicated in table 6.1[27]

The total population of the Republic of Abkhazia was 525,061. The Abkhaz numbered 93,267, or only 17.8 percent, as opposed to the Georgians, who made up 45.7 percent.[28] Those claiming Abkhaz as their nationality constituted substantially less than 50 percent of the regional population, yet a vast majority of the Abkhaz in Georgia and the former Soviet Union (FSU) resided there.[29] The Abkhaz were a concentrated minority.

The Territorial Dispute over Abkhazia

During the era of perestroika, events and actors in Georgia followed a course similar to the FSU and Russia, with the autonomous entities seeking greater autonomy. At the time of the dissolution of the FSU, there were three autonomous entities in Georgia: the South Ossetia Autonomous Oblast, the Ajarian Autonomous Soviet Socialist Republic, and the Abkhaz Autonomous Soviet Socialist Republic. Whereas South Ossetia and Abkhazia were established on the basis of nationality, Ajaria's territorial division was grounded in religion. The period of perestroika intensified relations among these entities and the emerging state of Georgia, as Ronald Suny describes.

In the last years of Soviet power, Georgians rapidly developed a powerful opposition to the old order, but instead of a single, united nationalist movement,
deep cleavages tore at the fabric of Georgian society. In the multinational context of the Georgian republic . . . the policies and rhetoric of leaders, the
choices and use of potent symbols, would either work to ameliorate these divisions in a unified struggle for independence and democracy or reinforce and
exacerbate the interethnic divisions within the republic. Tragically, Georgians
made political choices that deepened social and ethnic divisions.[30]

In Tbilisi the cause of a "Georgia for Georgians" intensified, despite
the fact that a good portion of the inhabitants of Georgia were neither
Georgian nor Christian. Georgia's minorities felt threatened and mobilized in response. As Georgians protested Moscow's attempt to gain
more control over the republics, Georgia's ethnic minorities struggled
against what they saw as a "Tbilisi for Georgians." One of the most vocal
minority groups was the Abkhaz.

The Abkhaz had asserted themselves politically
in defense of their national language and culture. The year 1978 marked
a low point for ethnic relations in the Georgian Republic, when the
Georgian republican government attempted to revise the language policy
as outlined in the 1978 constitution.[31] The government sought to remove a clause that affirmed Georgian as the sole official state language of
the republic and to replace it with one that gave equal status to Russian
and other languages. Georgians hotly objected to this measure, forcing
an embarrassed Eduard Shevardnadze, who was first party secretary of the
Georgian Communist Party (1972–85), to back down and retain the
original clause privileging Georgian.[32] Non-Georgian minorities interpreted this capitulation as a retreat in the face of nationalism and as evidence of an increase in Georgian chauvinism.[33]

During the late 1980s ethnic tensions came to a head, culminating in
violent demonstrations. Abkhaz elites and politicians regularly wrote letters to Moscow to protest the status of Abkhazia. These letters were
widely blamed for precipitating interethnic violence. For example, Abkhaz Communist officials addressed an open letter to the Twenty-ninth
Conference of the Communist Party of the Soviet Union detailing Abkhaz grievances against Georgia and demanding the right to secede and
join Russia. This letter was seen as a provocation. First, it catalyzed the
Georgian opposition into demonstrations, which in turn brought the Abkhaz to the streets. On November 3, 1988, 100,000 Georgians came out
in protest demanding the end of discrimination against Georgians by Abkhaz, Azeris, Ajars, and Ossetians. On February 15, 1989, several thousand Georgians demonstrated in Tbilisi against Abkhazia's secession campaign and for depriving ethnic Georgians of equal access to leadership

positions in Abkhazia.[34] The slogans "No to secession" and "An end to discrimination" epitomized the demands and concerns of the Georgian demonstrators.[35] On March 18, 1989, on the initiative of the People's Forum of Abkhazia (Aydgylara, hereafter PFA), 30,000 people rallied in the Gudauta district of Abkhazia.[36] The PFA sought to restore the 1921–31 status of Abkhazia as a Soviet Socialist Republic, a status equal to Georgia's. On March 25, 1989, a counter-rally was held in Sukhumi, Abkhazia's capital city, with 12,000 Abkhazia-dwelling Georgians in attendance.

Tensions continued to mount, resulting in what has been termed Black Sunday. On April 4 an estimated 20,000 Georgians gathered around the Council of Ministers in Tbilisi. During the next few days, the numbers swelled to more than 100,000. Although the main thrust of the demonstrations centered on Georgia's right to determine its own fate, concerns over Abkhazia were also prominent. The demonstrations spread throughout Georgia. By Sunday, April 9, the republic of Georgia was embedded in a series of nested conflicts, with Georgians demanding their independence from Moscow and decrying Abkhazia's call for independence from Tbilisi, and Abkhazia demanding the right to secede from Georgia. The Georgian government was incapacitated and turned to Moscow in an effort to restore order. Moscow obliged. Troops from the Soviet army and Ministry of Internal Affairs were deployed. Nerve gas was used, and approximately twenty people died and hundreds were injured.[37]

Officials in Moscow and Tbilisi were hard-pressed to explain and justify the confrontations.[38] Within a week, the government changed leadership and signaled that it was willing to open a dialogue.[39] As a sign of further compromise, arrested nationalist leaders were released; Zviad Gamsakhurdia was among them.[40] Although there was some expectation that the Georgian independence movement might be stifled, April 9 became a rallying cry and only intensified Georgia's desire to secede from Moscow and Abkhazia's desire to secede and join Russia.

The April 9 events provided the Georgian opposition movement with substantial credibility and launched a Georgian independence campaign. Although divisions remained, a multitude of parties were united in viewing non-Georgians as "foreigners, recent arrivals living on authentically Georgian land, and as more loyal to imperial Russian power than to Georgian."[41]

As Tbilisi pursued its independence course, the Abkhaz struggled for their own independence, seeking to attach themselves directly to Moscow. On July 8, 1989, the PFA appealed to the chairman of the Supreme Soviet of the USSR to subordinate Abkhazia directly to Moscow. The Abkhaz did not want double subordination any longer, fearing an independent Georgia more than they feared Moscow.[42]

Although the Communists moved closer to the Georgian nationalist agenda in 1989 and into 1990, their hold on power steadily waned, increasing anxiety among the minorities, who viewed the Communists as their only hope for protection, since the Communists were the only party that did not target the minorities as a threat to Georgia. Although the opposition nationalist parties were not cohesive, they were united in their profound distrust of Moscow and of the minorities living in the republic, viewing the minorities as a fifth column of Moscow, readily available to prevent Georgia's independence.

The minorities feared that Georgian independence would disenfranchise them from the political process. They became especially concerned with two issues. First, the electoral law drafted for parliamentary elections required all registered parties to have country wide reach. Because the minorities in Georgia, including the Abkhaz, tended to support parties with limited regional reach, this law potentially excluded them from the political process. Second, the Communist Party, the only party that seemed to support the rights of the minorities, had written into its platform a clause affirming the party's commitment to Georgia's territorial integrity, a move that was seen to have direct appeal to Georgians. The only way the Abkhaz could express their views was by boycotting the elections. The Supreme Soviet of Abkhazia called a special session and declared itself a sovereign Soviet Socialist Republic, a declaration quickly overturned by the Georgian Supreme Soviet.[43]

On October 28, 1990, general parliamentary elections were held in Georgia. Six nationalist blocs competed in the elections against the Communists (the Abkhaz and Ossetian party candidates were prohibited from running). With 68 percent of the electorate participating, only two parties/blocs of the competing eleven gained enough votes to pass the 4 percent threshold for seats under the proportional voting system.[44] Gamsakhurdia's Round Table finished first, gaining control of 155 out of 250 seats. The Communists finished second, garnering 64 seats. Gamsakhurdia was elected chairman of the Supreme Soviet and formed Georgia's first non-Communist government, headed by Tengiz Sigua. The new government immediately indicated that Georgia was going to pursue independence and that it would deal with the minorities in its own way.

Gamsakhurdia's political dominance unnerved the ethnic minorities. His earlier dissident writings often invoked the peril of the Georgian nation and blamed both Moscow and the minorities for the destruction of its land, language, and culture. So his slogan "Georgia for the Georgians" was interpreted as a battle cry for the suppression of minorities.[45]

At the same time that Gamsakhurdia's party gained control of the Georgian Parliament, Vladislav Ardzinba was elected chairman of the Abkhaz Supreme Soviet.[46] Ardzinba had been one of the leading figures in pressing for an upgrade of the status of the autonomous formations and rights of ethnic minorities in the Soviet Union. Now he was to head one of the autonomous formations for an ethnic group that constituted a clear minority within Georgia and Abkhazia. With Ardzinba as chairman, the Abkhaz Parliament pressed ahead with its objective to subordinate Abkhazia directly to Moscow.

The close of 1990 was therefore marked by a declaration of Abkhaz independence from Georgia and the transfer of political power to a nationalist Georgian leadership whose rhetoric clearly and directly threatened the rights of national minorities residing on Georgian territory. It was not just rhetoric. After the Supreme Soviet elections in October and the ascension of Gamsakhurdia as leader of the Georgian Parliament, the autonomous status of South Ossetia—a region of another of Georgia's national minorities—was abolished. Gamsakhurdia justified the action by declaring that the Ossetians had the right to self-determination only in those lands that constituted the homeland of the Ossetian nation, namely North Ossetia.

Georgian Independence

The question of whether the Soviet Union would remain intact preoccupied Georgians and Abkhaz for the first part of 1991, as both Gamsakhurdia and Ardzinba were concerned about the future of their relations with Moscow.

At the beginning of March, Gamsakhurdia issued an appeal to the Abkhaz people stressing the long history that Georgians and Abkhaz shared and accused Abkhazia of seeking a confrontation. Ardzinba said his republic was a full member of the Soviet Union and on an equal footing with the union republics, implying that Abkhazia had the same status as Georgia and the right to secede (according to the terms of the Union Treaty draft circulating at the time).[47] In an interview, he stated, "Moscow has assured us rights as a sovereign republic within the Soviet Union. Why wouldn't Abkhazia support the union?" Ardzinba's point was underscored by Zurab Asinba, the deputy chairman of the PFA, who said, "Georgians want to govern us as if we were a colony. We have more of a chance at equal rights from Moscow than from Tbilisi."[48]

As with the other autonomous republics in the Soviet Union, the Abkhaz welcomed the March 17, 1991, referendum, which addressed the fate of the Soviet Union, since it provided them with the opportunity to voice their preference to join the proposed union as a sovereign republic equal to Georgia. Although Gamsakhurdia prohibited the population of Georgia from participating in the Soviet referendum, Abkhazia disregarded his prohibition. More than half of the electorate of Abkhazia, largely the non-Georgian population, took part in the voting. When asked, "Do you consider it necessary to preserve the Union of Soviet Socialist Republics as a renewed federation of equal, sovereign republics, in which the rights and freedoms of people of all nationalities will be fully guaranteed?" more than 98 percent answered yes.[49] Georgia insisted that the results had been falsified and threatened to prosecute Abkhaz officials.

Yet Gamsakhurdia's government was too preoccupied with its own independence referendum to pursue the matter. On March 31, 1991, with 91 percent of the Georgian electorate participating, 98 percent voted to restore Georgia's sovereignty.[50] A few days later, the Georgian Parliament unanimously elected Gamsakhurdia as president. The Parliament's decision was ratified by the population on May 26, when 87 percent chose him as the first popularly elected president of an independent Georgia.[51]

While Tbilisi was establishing its independence from Moscow, the Abkhaz Parliament inched closer toward establishing Abkhaz control over its political institutions. On July 9 it passed a law allowing the creation of new electoral districts on the basis of ethnicity. Whereas the Abkhaz viewed this as a way to retain some sort of representation in a republic in which they constituted only 18 percent of the population, Georgians and their representatives in Parliament interpreted it as a clear violation of their rights. Shevardnadze later equated the law with apartheid.

> The electoral law of July 9, 1991, totally ignores the norms and practice of modern parliamentarism. What is this if not apartheid de jure, the striving of the minority to dictate its will to the majority, deliberately provoking the threat of inter-ethnic clashes? The restriction of electoral rights on the basis of nationality put the Georgians living in Abkhazia, and making up almost half the population, as well as Russians, Armenians, Greeks, and other national minorities, in an obviously unequal position. This was pure racial discrimination and the establishment of an ethno-dictatorship.[52]

Gamsakhurdia issued a presidential decree annulling the electoral law. In a series of negotiations to resolve the issue of representation in the Abkhaz Parliament, the parties agreed to a new election law that guaranteed a number of seats to each ethnic group and stipulated that certain legislation would require a three-quarters majority to pass. Of the 65 seats, 28 were to be reserved for Abkhaz, 26 for Georgians, and 11 for remaining nationalities. In December 1991 the new Supreme Soviet of Abkhazia was elected into office, but only 38 of 65 deputies were elected. Voter turnout was high in the regions where the Abkhaz dominated, but Abkhazia's Georgians had become so frustrated they simply did not bother to vote.[53]

In the meantime, tensions were mounting in Georgia between the supporters and the detractors of Gamsakhurdia. In August 1991 the opposition made a move to oust him.[54] By September most of the counternationalist groups were in alliance with one another. Gamsakhurdia argued that the opposition was nothing more than a disgruntled coalition of intellectuals, ex-Communists, and criminals.[55] On October 4 the two groups clashed in front of the Parliament building in Tbilisi. Although it was unclear who fired the first shot, Gamsakhurdia's troops tried to encircle the opposition troops. Demonstrations followed the next day.[56] The clash resulted in at least one dead and several dozen wounded. Gamsakhurdia declared a state of emergency, clamped down on the media, and seemed for the moment to be in control.

In December the opposition staged a full-scale assault on the Parliament building and demanded Gamsakhurdia's resignation.[57] Tengiz Sigua (the former head of government, now a member of the opposition) argued that Gamsakhurdia had become a dictator and was moving Georgia away from its newly realized democracy toward totalitarianism. He stated that Moscow allowed Gamsakhurdia to get away with corrupting the economy, political system, and relations abroad. Moscow wanted Georgia to accede to the Union Treaty; chaos in the republic would help achieve that end.[58] He also accused Gamsakhurdia of increasing Georgia's vulnerability to Islamic forces in the region. Here he tapped into Georgian fears of the diminishing influence of Christianity and of a weakened Georgian nation.

By the end of the century a large Muslim region, centered in Kazan, could arise in Russia. In time it would move more actively to the southwest, toward Astrakhan, and could possibly end with the restoration of the Astrakhan Khanate. During this same period something like a Crimean Khanate could appear in the Crimea. Lying between them in a rather dense dotted line are Muslim Chechnya, Ingushetia and Northern Ossetia (granted, it is half Christian), and then Kabarda, Balkaria, and so on. But "lying" in their way are the Krasnodar and Stavropol Cossack areas—the only obstacle preventing an easy and natural link between Astrakhan and Crimea. Serious conflicts are very likely in this region in the near future. It is not by accident that the Cossacks so insistently raise the question of borders today. The powerful foreign Muslim states nearby, especially Turkey, are also aggravating the situation. In this setting Georgia and Armenia are tiny specks, two islands in an ocean. The policy of the Georgian president is also exacerbating the situation. Z. G. [Zviad Gamsakhurdia] is making increasingly active efforts to draw closer to Turkey and Iran. Perhaps this explains why no single Christian state is establishing contacts with us, with the result that Georgia has ended up in total isolation.[59]

While the opposition presented him as a dictator who was threatening the future of Georgians, popular support remained with Gamsakhurdia as the legitimately elected president. Nevertheless, the opposition again tried to unseat him from power. This time it succeeded. On December 17, 1991, the opposition adopted a declaration condemning Gamsakhurdia, and armed conflict broke out in the capital, resulting in approximately one hundred deaths. The guards loyal to Gamsakhurdia were unable to defend him against the opposition's forces. Gamsakhurdia was forced to flee the capital.

Outcome: Civil War

By January 2, the opposition controlled Tbilisi. A military council took power, with Sigua as prime minister. The new government announced that once the situation stabilized and a government was formed, the new Military Council would surrender its power. The council's first order of business was to declare a state of emergency and impose a curfew. Rallies and demonstrations were banned. Gamsakhurdia, after fleeing the capital, declared the beginning of a civil war.[60]

The unconstitutional overthrow of Gamsakhurdia left the Military Council with a legitimacy problem: it was accused of violating the people's will, basic freedoms, and human rights. In an attempt to gain legitimacy, the Military Council formally asked Eduard Shevardnadze to serve as head of state.[61] Shevardnadze agreed. The new government set up a state council, vested with both legislative and executive authority to replace the Military Council. It then dissolved the popularly elected Supreme Council. Shevardnadze, along with opposition-paramilitary leaders Tengiz Kitovani and Jaba Ioseliani and Prime Minister Tengiz Sigua, formed a presidium.

Shevardnadze faced a seemingly impossible set of tasks. First, he had to unite the various Georgian political factions and their respective militias around the idea that his government was the only legitimate one. Next he needed to deal with the supporters of Gamsakhurdia, whose resistance to him was understandable, given Shevardnadze's ties and influence in the former Soviet government and his alleged collaboration with the perpetrators of the coup in Georgia. Finally, Tbilisi was at war in South Ossetia, and the problem of Abkhazia's status had yet to be seriously dealt with, much less resolved.

Shevardnadze's return brought relative stability through the spring of 1992. Yet by June rifts within the larger Georgian political scene became readily apparent. Zviadists, supporters of Gamsakhurdia, were organized and active in Gamsakhurdia's home district of Mingrelia (in western Georgia and bordering Abkhazia).

Within Abkhazia, divisions between ethnic Georgians and the Abkhaz intensified. Georgians accused the Abkhaz Parliament of becoming a forum for advancing Abkhazia's moves toward independence from Georgia. Evidence to back such claims included the passage of legislation without regard for the required two-thirds majority and the creation of an Abkhaz national guard consisting of only ethnic Abkhaz and subordinate to the presidium of the Abkhaz Supreme Soviet.[62] By May the Georgian deputies of the Abkhaz Supreme Soviet stated they would no longer attend any sessions of the Parliament. In June Georgians in Abkhazia announced a campaign of noncompliance with the rulings of the Supreme Soviet and staged a three-day strike to demand new elections. The situation in Abkhazia was further complicated by the fact that its Georgian population was divided between those who supported the new government under Shevardnadze and those who remained loyal to Gamsakhurdia.

On June 13 the newspaper *Abkhazia* published the "treaty principles of interrelations between the Republic of Abkhazia and the republic of Georgia." The treaty declared that "the sides recognize Georgia and Abkhazia as sovereign states and equal participants of international and foreign-economic relations . . . [and that] the sides independently conclude treaties and agreements with other countries."[63] The treaty draft also contained provisions for the protection of minorities in the territories under Georgian and Abkhaz jurisdiction and for the establishment of either a confederation or a federation between the two entities. Georgia's territorial integrity would been maintained, but Abkhazia would be granted quite a bit of autonomy. The State Council of Georgia did not respond to the treaty draft.[64]

On July 23, after months of recriminations, the Abkhaz Parliament, in the absence of Georgian deputies, declared the independence of the republic. To pass, this legislation required a two-thirds majority in parliament, but it had only a simple majority. The Parliament maintained that this call for independence was a reaction to Georgia's declaration and reinstatement of Georgia's 1921 constitution.[65] Such moves, they argued, automatically reinstated the Abkhaz constitution of 1925, and consequently the republic of Abkhazia was "united with Georgia on the basis of a special treaty."[66] The deputy chairman of the PFA insisted that the Parliament's decision did not mean that Abkhazia was seceding from Georgia but that Abkhazia was to become a federal republic.

This time the Georgian State Council did not take long to respond. Two days later, it declared the Abkhaz Supreme Soviet's decisions regarding the 1925 Abkhaz and 1978 Georgian constitutions invalid.[67]

Tedo Ninidze, a member of the juridical commission of the State Council, argued that the "decree of the Abkhazian Parliament cannot be considered valid in as much as it cannot express the interests and opinion of the majority of the population of the Autonomous Republic, for it was adopted in the absence of a quorum."[68]

With tensions mounting between Sukhumi and Tbilisi over Abkhazia's political status, and with the different factions fighting to control Georgia at the same time, the collision of the two conflicts seemed inevitable given the fact that most Georgians living in Abkhazia were supporters of Gamsakhurdia.[69] This became an issue when a group of Gamsakhurdia supporters kidnapped twelve Georgian officials and reportedly held them in the town of Kokhori in the Gali district of Abkhazia. The Georgian government dispatched troops to release the hostages. On August 14 the Abkhaz Supreme Soviet declared the move an act of aggression.[70]

Reports came out that the leadership in Abkhazia and Georgia had agreed on the deployment of Georgian troops. The Georgian government was expected to destroy the Zviadist formations that were targeting civilians and destroying rail bridges that linked Georgia to Russia in the Gali and Ochamchira districts of Abkhazia. Following that, the troops, in conjunction with Abkhaz formations, were to redeploy along the routes to Sukhumi to secure the main rail lines that connect Georgia to Armenia, as well as rid Abkhazia of the remaining Gamsakhurdia supporters.

The Abkhaz Parliament nevertheless protested the deployment of troops, declaring it a violation of Abkhaz sovereignty. The Parliament argued that although it had permitted the deployment, the Georgian government changed the objectives: it both pursued the Zviadists and sought control over Abkhazia. As a result, troops from the Abkhaz Internal Affairs Ministry opened fire on the Georgian National Guard troops.

Although the Georgian government acknowledged that it had come to an agreement with Abkhaz officials, Shevardnadze stated that calling Georgia's troops an occupation force was absurd, since Abkhazia "is an integral part of Georgia, and the Georgian government has the right to bring troops into any part of Georgia, proceeding from national interests."[71] He added that Georgian troops would remain in the area so long as state interests required them there. The situation was further complicated by Moscow's dispatch of Russian paratroopers to the region to protect Russian military installations.

Georgian prime minister Sigua and State Council presidium member-Mkhedrioni commander Jaba Ioseliani flew to Sukhumi on August 15 to negotiate a cease-fire.[72] Gunfire persisted on August 16, and each side accused the other of violating the terms of the cease-fire agreement. Sigua threatened that "unconstitutional units" in Abkhazia would be neutralized if they failed to surrender their arms. By the morning of August 17, Georgian troops were in control of all the major towns, with the exception of Gudauta (forty-five miles northwest of Sukhumi). In an address that day, Shevardnadze stated that the Georgian government was in control and restored order throughout the territory of Georgia.[73]

A cease-fire was set up, and Georgian troops withdrew from Sukhumi on August 17. The cease-fire was quickly violated, however, when on August 18 the Georgian National Guard reentered the Abkhaz capital with a full contingent of armored vehicles. It targeted the Parliament building, shelling and storming it in an attempt to get Abkhaz leader Ardzinba to resign. The building was burned to the ground, and Ardzinba, along with fifteen hundred troops, fled the capital for the coastal town of Gudauta. Georgia had brought Abkhazia to the brink of defeat..

With the violation of the first cease-fire, fighting continued. On August 19 Ardzinba, in a telephone conversation with Shevardnadze, laid down his terms for engaging in talks. He insisted that Georgian troops had to leave Abkhaz soil and that negotiations had to take place in Russia. Shevardnadze and the Georgian State Council rejected Ardzinba's demands. Shevardnadze stated that he did not insist on Ardzinba's resignation—largely because Ardzinba had the support of the Abkhaz population in the republic—but did insist that the Supreme Soviet address the question of a political settlement for the republic. If it was unable to come to an agreement, then Abkhazia's status would be held to a referendum. This latter option was not acceptable to the Abkhaz side, however; they were not confident that other non-Georgian minorities would support their cause in a referendum.

Negotiations continued. During a meeting between Ardzinba and Georgian State Council member Ivlian Khaindrava, the two men signed an agreement stipulating the withdrawal of Georgian troops from Sukhumi on August 20 and 21. Yet on August 22 Shevardnadze stated that troops would remain in order to safeguard the rail links from Zviadists.[74] Ardzinba remained adamant that he would not negotiate with Tbilisi so long as Georgian troops remained on Abkhaz soil.

On the night of August 24–25, intense fighting resumed. Colonel Giorgi Karkarashvili, commander of the Georgian National Guard troops in Abkhazia, issued an ultimatum to Ardzinba to resign on August 26 or face an attack on his headquarters in Gudauta.[75] According to one account, Karkarashvili warned the Abkhaz in a televised address that they faced the possibility of extinction if they continued their military resistance against the Georgian troops.[76]

Russia interceded and appeared to side with Tbilisi. Russian president Boris Yeltsin stressed Georgia's unity and territorial integrity.[77] On September 3, Ardzinba, Yeltsin, and Shevardnadze met to arrange another cease-fire. On September 5 all armed formations were to lay down their weapons. A commission including representatives from Abkhazia, Georgia, and Russia would be set up to monitor the cease-fire. A limited number of Georgian troops would be allowed to remain in Abkhazia, but only to guard important railroads and institutions. Russian troops would be stationed in Abkhazia but would remain neutral and not participate in any conflicts. By September 15, conditions for the functioning of governmental bodies in Abkhazia were set, and negotiations began over the status of Abkhazia's constitutional-legal relationship with Georgia. The wording of the agreement guaranteed Georgia's territorial integrity. In fact, the first line of the document stated that "[t]he territorial integrity of the Republic of Georgia is ensured."

Russia stopped the escalation and perhaps the spread of violence along its southern frontier. It let it be known quite clearly that it did not countenance the secession of autonomous republics in Georgia, or in Russia. Yeltsin had other events on his mind when he pressed for the signing of the accords. He stated that without them ethnic wars would erupt, and the Caucasus would threaten to become "five Nagorno-Karabakhs."[78]

Ardzinba stated that he signed the agreement only "to stop the genocide and flouting of human rights in Abkhazia,"[79] and that he saw Yeltsin as the guarantor of a fair and peaceful settlement of the conflict. But because the Abkhaz side did not support the agreement, he signed it only under extreme pressure and, in the end, did not keep to the terms of the agreement. Abkhazia's representatives failed to appear at the first round of scheduled talks on September 8. Shortly thereafter, the Abkhaz side declared that Georgia had violated the primary condition of the cease-fire agreement, namely the complete withdrawal of Georgian troops from Abkhaz territory.

On October 1 Abkhazia launched an offensive against the city of Gagra. The offensive included heavy armored equipment, including T-72 tanks. The Georgian forces were surprised by the offensive and retreated. They quickly recovered, however, and within hours had reestablished the original front lines. The Abkhaz forces reconsolidated and launched another attack on Gagra and captured the city. Shevardnadze responded to the capture with the following statement: "For the first time in my life, I have found myself deceived and driven into a political blind alley. I understand that for all practical purposes, there are no methods left for resolving the Abkhaz conflict except military ones."[80]

The Georgian side, according to Russian army lieutenant general Sufiyan Beppayev, deputy commander of the Transcaucasus Military District, had complied with the letter and spirit of the September 3 accords. It had withdrawn its heavy equipment two days before the offensive on Gagra: twelve hundred Georgian troops and corresponding equipment had been withdrawn from that city.[81] Beppayev viewed the Georgian side as a victim of political treachery. Suspicion that Russian troops were directly involved grew, especially given the type and quantity of equipment that helped advance the Abkhaz offensive.

The situation in Abkhazia looked desperate, and a negotiated solution seemed unachievable. As an indication of the divide between the two parties, the head of the UN mission, Antoine Blanca, an assistant to the secretary general, said that there was little hope of resolution given that the Abkhaz leader had his own interpretation of the September 3 agreement.[82]

On October 11, by popular vote, Shevardnadze was elected chairman of the Georgian Parliament. He was the only candidate who ran for office, but with 95 percent of the electorate selecting his name (requiring a threshold of 30 percent), the vote was interpreted as a mandate for his continued leadership.[83] Even though Shevardnadze had the support of the Georgian population, he was at his wits' end about what to do with the Abkhaz conflict. Evidence mounted that Russia was aiding and abetting Abkhaz forces. According to a Georgian commander,

> It is not clear whom we're fighting. Given the current lineup of forces, we could defeat the armed units of the separatists and the confederates in a few days. But Russian planes are bombing us. Russian units are firing on our positions. Russian generals are threatening us. Yet we are in our own country, on our own legitimate territory.[84]

By the end of October Shevardnadze had broken off talks with Russia, declaring that because of Russia' "undisguised interference, including military interference, . . . in the internal affairs of sovereign Georgia, we have no other choice."[85] Russian troops were actively helping Abkhaz separatists, and therefore his main demand was the withdrawal of Russian troops from the conflict zone. If these troops were not withdrawn, then Georgia would take more decisive steps and demand the withdrawal of Russian troops from all of Georgia. The Parliament then adopted a resolution demanding the withdrawal of Russian troops from Abkhaz territory. Russia ignored the demand.[86]

Civil war raged in Abkhazia until the autumn of 1993, with Russia providing support to the Abkhaz side.[87] Shevardnadze never doubted Russian involvement. In March 1993 he said, "An analysis of recent events shows that what happened in Sukhumi was a military action for which serious advance preparations had been made. Certain circles in Russia knew exactly when it was supposed to take place and what was supposed to happen."[88] He went on to add that the military equipment used by the Abkhaz forces must have come from somewhere. Russian claims to neutrality just did not square with what was happening on the ground.[89] By the middle of September, the Abkhaz side retook Sukhumi, and Georgia's defeat in Abkhazia seemed imminent. A desperate Shevardnadze appealed to Yeltsin for help.

I appeal to you at this tragic hour for my homeland. No longer able to request anything of you, I inform you that tanks and heavy combat equipment of the Gudauta group are being massed outside Sukhumi. . . . Any minute now, its forces are going to burst into the helpless city, which lacks even minimal means of defense. . . . What have we done wrong in the eyes of Russia and the world? Isn't it that yet again in the Georgian people's history, we have wanted freedom and independence for ourselves?[90]

On September 21 the Russian government interceded as peacemaker.[91] By September 27, Abkhaz forces had complete control of Sukhumi and all of Abkhazia. Georgian forces were expelled, and Abkhazia was declared liberated. Although large-scale warfare was eventually halted as a result of Russian intercession, which balanced the warring factions, the resulting peace remains tenuous. Abkhazia has achieved de facto independence. Georgia, for its part, has accepted a Faustian bargain to maintain its de jure territorial integrity. It accepted more Russian troops on its soil and became a member of the Commonwealth of Independent States, an organization established and dominated by Russia.

The fundamental disagreement between Georgia and Abkhazia remains the same: Georgia insists on the preservation of its territorial integrity, and Abkhazia continues to demand independence from Georgia. In other words, control over the disputed territory remains an indivisible issue.

This concludes the discussion of the territorial dispute between Abkhazia and Georgia. Although a fuller explanation of events in relation to the theory of indivisible territory is in the next chapter following the case study of Ajaria, it should be clear that the settlement patterns of the Abkhaz weakened their capabilities and consequently their demands for independence. Although both the Abkhaz and Georgians acknowledged that the Abkhaz had rightful claims to Abkhazia as a homeland, homeland legitimacy was not enough to allow the Abkhaz to risk violence to gain independence. The Abkhaz's minority status, albeit concentrated, seriously undermined any independence bid. Needed capabilities came only with Russia's help. The Georgians too viewed Abkhazia as part of their homeland, but because they represented the state of Georgia, they had state concerns as well. As a multiethnic state facing multiple secessionist challenges in other regions, such as South Ossetia and Ajaria, its preeminent concern was maintaining the territorial integrity of Georgia. Georgia calculated that it could have defeated the Abkhaz in a violent confrontation, and in fact it did. Only after Russia intervened on Abkhazia's behalf did large-scale violence and civil war emerge. In the end Georgia was forced to accept Russian "help" in order to maintain its borders.

7

Georgia and Ajaria

> Deep quiet holds the breath of night;
>   My mother-land in silence lies,
> Yet oft is heard an anguished moan
>   As Georgia in her slumber sighs.
>   —*Ilia Chavchavadze, "Elegy"*

While the rest of Georgia broke out in violence in the early 1990s, Ajaria acquired the distinction of being the only region to avoid it. I argue that violence failed to erupt there largely because the Ajars did not view their identity as distinct from that of the dominant group and because they regarded the territory of Ajaria as an integral part of Georgia. The Ajar leaders identified and represented themselves to Tbilisi as Georgians, committed to the territorial integrity of Georgia. The question of territorial independence from a "Georgia for Georgians" was not an issue at the bargaining table. Rather, the issue of contention between Ajaria and Tbilisi centered on an attempt by Georgia to restrict Ajaria's preexisting political and economic privileges. Ajaria's position was divisible.

We have seen from the previous chapter that Georgia, driven by both state and ethnic concerns, refused to countenance the division of its borders. The integrity of Georgia had to be maintained, even if force and Russian intercession were needed to maintain the borders. The state's position was indivisible. Because Ajaria's interests were represented as divisible, however, a negotiated settlement short of violence obtained.

This chapter contains four main sections. The first section provides an introduction to the Ajars and the formation of their identity. The second section outlines the relationship of Ajaria and the Ajars with Georgia and Georgians. We find an intriguing situation of misperception and a problem of timing. Because Tbilisi was under siege and those who controlled the government had a narrow conception of what it meant to be Georgian, they needed time to be persuaded that Ajaria was not trying to separate from Georgia, largely because Ajars saw themselves as Georgians and their territory as integral to a larger Georgia. Once Tbilisi understood Ajaria's position vis-à-vis the rest of Georgia, the dispute over Ajaria's status dissipated and violence was averted. The third section then compares the Ajaria case with Abkhazia in light of competing explanations, and the fourth section argues that the theory of indivisible territory best explains this set of cases. Concerns over the territorial integrity of Georgia influenced Georgia's bargaining as did concerns about maintaining control over a homeland. Georgia had both the legitimacy and the capability to defend its interests (or so it thought) and represented its interests as indivisible. Abkhazia had only homeland legitimacy to tap and thus pursued only limited autonomy. Its position was divisible, becoming indivisible only after Moscow provided the needed capabilities. Civil war was the result. The Ajars did not demand independence, and thus, as postulated by the theory, one of the needed conditions for violence was absent.

Ajaria and Ajars

Whereas the Abkhaz are seen as distinct from the Georgians, the Ajars are considered ethnic Georgians, albeit Muslims. The ancestors of contemporary Ajars converted to Islam in the sixteenth and seventeenth centuries when the Ottoman Empire occupied the western portion of Transcaucasia. Their written language is Georgian, although they speak a Gurian dialect that contains numerous Turkic words. Ajars are deeply attached to their faith, and there are few Christian-Muslim marriages among them.[1]

In the 1926 census, the Soviets categorized the Ajars as a distinct ethnic group. Even though some Ajars continued to distinguish themselves from the Georgian population, in the 1939 census, the Ajars were folded into the same category as Georgians.[2]

Today most Ajars and Georgians consider the Ajars Georgian in terms of descent and familial lineage. Religion, however, is another matter and complicates the relationship between the two groups. Ajars see this as a nonissue: They are Georgians regardless of their faith. They do not see themselves as "other" in relation to the broader Georgian ethnic group. However, this is not the case for Christian Georgians. That Ajars are Muslims does not accord with their commonly held sentiment that to be Georgian means being a Christian. In contemporary discourse, most Georgians and most descriptions of Georgians describe members as professing their Christianity.[3] Thus, the Ajars are seen as a sort of contradiction and, perhaps even more perniciously, as an aberration that needs to be corrected. For the dominant Christian Georgians, the key question is whether a Georgian can be a Muslim.[4] Given the limited information about such matters, the question can be only partly explored. The following case might shed some light on this issue.

In the mid-1980s a series of articles targeting the Muslims of Ajaria appeared in Georgian newspapers but did not target the Azeri population, which is also Muslim. Why would Muslim Georgians be targeted but not other Muslims? Elizabeth Fuller advanced the argument that the attacks against the Ajars were due to Soviet fears of Islamic fundamentalism arriving across the border from Turkey into the Soviet Union.[5] Yet this explanation fails to explain why Azeris would not be targeted, since they too would be susceptible to the same feared Islamic influence.

A better explanation focuses on the demographic balance in Georgia. When the results of the 1979 census were released, Georgian (namely, Christian Georgian) intellectuals and authorities became wary of the fact that non-Georgians had higher birthrates. The Ajars were targeted precisely because they were viewed as Georgian, albeit aberrant Georgians.[6] Here was a group of Georgians with higher-than-average birthrates who simply needed to be secularized, if not Christianized (which was forbidden under the Soviet system). If they could be converted from Islam, then the Georgian group's numbers would increase and the threat of being overtaken by minorities and questionable Georgians would be reduced.[7]

If one considers that the main Georgian newspapers readily discussed (and continue to discuss) such issues, and that the Georgian Central Committee advocated and implemented policies that "called for the intensification of atheistic education in Ajaria"[8] and the official resettlement of Georgians into traditionally Georgian areas, then such an interpretation seems logical. One could go even further to make the case that there was a sort of double desperation, given the religion of these Georgians and their high birthrates. In May 1981, for example, *Zaria Vostoka* quoted the first secretary of the Ajar Oblast Party Committee as saying that a quarter of the republic's population was of school or college age and that this population had higher birthrates than did Georgia writ large. The insinuation was that these students needed to be converted before they advanced to adulthood and had (Muslim) children of their own. Secularizing or converting Ajars would make them Georgians (in the eyes of Christian Georgians). Ajars would no longer be "other."

This brings us to the question of exactly how many Ajars lived in the Georgian Republic. As mentioned earlier, Ajars were not counted as a discrete nationality after the 1926 census,[9] According to the 1989 census, the population of the Ajar Republic totaled 381,000, of whom 317,000 were Georgians.[10] With the countryside considered largely Muslim and Batumi, the capital, non-Muslim, the number of Ajars has been estimated at about 130,000–160,000, or 34–42 percent of the total population of Ajaria.[11] The number of Ajars living outside Ajaria is very small. One expert explained that this lack of out-migration is similar to the migratory (or rather nonmigratory) patterns of other Georgians.[12] Given that a majority of Ajars lived in Ajaria yet constituted a minority, the Ajars were a concentrated minority.

The Territorial Dispute over Ajaria

Whereas violence broke out in most regions of Georgia, Ajaria remained a bastion of stability, despite the fact that Batumi sought greater autonomy and the state resisted these demands. Further, Ajar calls for greater autonomy were at first met with much greater resistance than those of the other autonomous entities. Whereas Abkhazia's autonomy status was never questioned, but only its degree, in Tbilisi proposals were advanced to abolish Ajaria's autonomy altogether.[13]

The chief proponent of abolishing Ajaria's autonomy was Zviad Gamsakhurdia, who on November 14, 1990, became the chairman of the Supreme Soviet of the Georgian SSR. Gamsakhurdia's Round Table–Free Georgia coalition won 155 of 250 seats on a platform that was common to all the parties competing in the elections, including an independent Georgia, a free market economy, a multiparty system, a legal system that protected the rights of all citizens, the strengthening of the rights of Georgians, restricted immigration, and protection of the Georgian language.[14] Unlike other parties, however, Gamsakhurdia's coalition added a messianic message of a Georgia for Christian Georgians. In terms of foreign policy, he envisioned a Georgia that would serve as the mediator between East and West, Islam and Christianity.[15]

Ajars could not help but notice that while moving toward greater independence under perestroika, Georgia was also moving toward a more exclusive conception of Georgian citizenship. Further, the status of the Ajar Republic was directly and publicly threatened. Not surprisingly, therefore, Gamsakhurdia's Round Table polled only 24 percent of the vote in Ajaria in the October 1990 elections for the Georgian Supreme Soviet. The Communist Party, viewed as less hostile to the non-Georgian minorities, came in first with 56 percent.[16] In view of these results, Gamsakhurdia retreated, stating that the abolishment of Ajar autonomy would come only by local initiative.[17]

During the height of the confrontation between Batumi and Tbilisi, Tbilisi accused Batumi of separatism. Yet if one looks at the evidence carefully, one finds that although resentment over the dominance of Christianity in Georgia was heard and felt in Batumi, the issue of contention was not separatism per se but the much more limited question of whether Ajaria would remain an autonomous republic. In 1989, for example, Guram Chigogidsze, the then-chairman of the Ajar ASSR Council of Ministers, stated in a speech to the Georgian Supreme Soviet that a separatist organization in Ajaria consisted of six persons at most and did not represent the views of the population at large.[18] Similarly, Pridon Khalvashi, the head of the Ajar branch of the Georgian Writers' Union, wrote that "no separatist inclinations of any kind exist in Ajaria."[19] Overall, then, separatism among Ajars can be described as nonexistent or extremely limited.

Tbilisi nevertheless feared that Ajaria was pursuing secession. From the Ajar point of view, the debate at this point was not whether Tbilisi would have control over the republic but how much control it would exert. During the winter months of 1990–91, for example, the Ajar Supreme Soviet passed legislation that required candidates for the republic's Parliament to be permanent residents of Ajaria.[20] Two rationales emerged to explain the law, neither of which revealed secessionist tendencies. The first was that the law was intended to protect the positions of bureaucrats and cronies in the republic. The second hinged on representation and implied that parliamentarians needed to come from Ajaria in order for the Ajar Supreme Soviet to function properly and pass legislation that served the best interests of the republic's population. Neither rationale at the time provided evidence that the law reflected the emergence of a separatist. The Georgian Supreme Soviet declared the law invalid, since it violated the constitutional right of citizens "to elect and be elected to Councils of People's Deputies and other elected state organs."[21] The law was then sent back to the Ajar Supreme Soviet to be amended so that all citizens of Georgia would be eligible to run for the republic's Supreme Soviet. The Ajar Supreme Soviet did so in early February 1991.

In the meantime, Gamsakhurdia sent Tengiz Putkaradze, a fellow coalition member, to Batumi to act as Tbilisi's prefect in the republic. Ajar officials feared that Putkaradze's appointment marked the beginning of a purge. Indeed, shortly thereafter, Tengiz Khakhva, the chairman of the Ajar Supreme Soviet, resigned (at his own request), and Aslan Abashidze was elected in his place.[22] The elections to the Supreme Soviet were then delayed from March 31 to April 28, 1991.[23]

Just before the April 28 elections, rumors surfaced that the Georgian Supreme Soviet had abolished Ajaria's autonomous status. In response, several thousand workers staged mass demonstrations in Batumi to defend the republic's autonomy. Concern over Islam did play a role in the demonstrations, especially over the nationalist government's strong Christian bent, but this concern translated not into an "Ajaria for Ajarians" but into a "Georgia for *all* Georgians, Christian and Muslim." Abashidze met with the demonstrators in an attempt to persuade them that the rumors were false. Yet the demonstrators remained unconvinced and demanded that local officials be placed in positions currently held by those appointed from Tbilisi. As demonstrations continued, members of the Georgian National Guard fired shots, but no one was hurt and the violence did not escalate. The demonstrations did not end until April 24. Elections were postponed again, until June.

Shortly thereafter, Nodar Imnadze, the acting first deputy chairman of the Supreme Soviet and a Round Table supporter, was killed by security guards after he opened fire on a meeting in the Supreme Soviet building. (Abashidze was injured in the melee.) Contrary to what might have been expected, the killing of Imnadze did not ignite hostilities between Batumi and Tbilisi. In May 1991 officials from Tbilisi visited Ajaria to discuss the economic and political development of the republic. A month later Gamsakhurdia himself visited the republic and stated that while Ajaria remained "the cradle of Georgian Christianity," the new Georgian government would remain committed to freedom of conscience. He reiterated that any decision on the autonomous status of Ajaria would have to come solely from the local population.[24]

Elections to the Supreme Soviet were finally held on June 23, 1991. Voter turnout was low, at 60.2 percent overall and less than the required threshold of 50 percent in eleven of the forty districts. No single party/ bloc garnered a majority of the votes. The Round Table came in first with 48 percent, followed by the local, nationalist Ajara electoral bloc with 20 percent.[25] The Ajar Oblast Organization of the Georgian Communist Party came in third with 18 percent. Because candidates in only five districts received a majority in the first round, runoff elections were held on July 10. Turnout was even lower this time (in part because the polling took place on a Wednesday rather than on a Sunday). Round Table obtained the highest number of seats, followed by the Communist Party, and then the Ajara bloc. Ajar nationalist separatism was simply not evident.

Later in 1991, when the status of Georgia vis-à-vis the USSR was still unclear and Batumi feared provocation by Tbilisi, the Supreme Soviet of Ajaria called for the creation of a headquarters for the defense of the republic. The decree declared that Ajaria shared common Georgian interests and that the defense preparations were designed to maintain order. In flowery terms, the decree went on to say that Ajaria had always been, and would be, committed to the ideal and realization of Georgian unity.

> We remind everybody, both friends and enemies, that Ajaria is the region in which the population has not only heroically defended itself over centuries, but has also defended the whole of Georgia and has constituted a kind of shield for it. Ajaria has heroically resisted countless conquerors, has been the first to take upon itself the blows of the invaders, has been a support for our fatherland, and has held high the banner of Georgian unity. The unshakable spirit and the genetic code of our heroic ancestors are still alive in us. If the interests of our

motherland demand this, all of Ajaria will rise again and be the vanguard of its defenders.[26]

This passage raises three key points in terms of my theory of indivisible territory. First, note the Supreme Soviet's insistence that the unity of Georgia was in the interests of the republic, and that *the republic alone* should be responsible for ensuring that unity. Second, note the reference to the historic and heroic deeds of ancestors. It is the responsibility of the present generation not only to ensure the future of the next ones but to guarantee the continuation of the ancestors' deeds, which remain embodied within the present generation. Third, it shows that Ajaria was concerned about maintaining and defending Georgia. This concern was all the more prescient in light of events that took place in Georgia. During the coup of December 1991, with the overthrow of Gamsakhurdia, the republic's security forces and interior troops were put on alert, and they remained so throughout 1992 as the possibility of civil war loomed in Georgia.[27]

Largely because he continued to back Gamsakhurdia as the legitimate leader of Georgia, Abashidze came under increasing pressure from parliamentary deputies in Tbilisi. They accused him of usurping power and establishing a dictatorship.[28] The deputies attacked Abashidze's move toward an independent economic policy and claimed that because he lacked the support of both the Parliament and the majority of the population, he had sought to protect his rule by issuing weapons to those loyal to him. Finally, they stated that such an anti-Georgian leadership had never before ruled in Ajaria.[29]

Abashidze rejected such criticism as slander. His support for Gamsakhurdia and opposition to the coup was not personal, he insisted, but rather because he believed the coup seriously violated democratic principles: "I will repeat once again that deposing the republic's lawfully elected leaders was a mistake."[30] He continually insisted that he was committed to stability and to Georgia's territorial integrity:

> The situation in South Ossetia and Abkhazia cannot be compared with the state of affairs in Ajaria. Our republic is an administrative unit that is inhabited by members of various nationalities, but all of them are citizens of Ajaria, and hence of Georgia as well. *We have never had, and never can have, any territorial claims against Georgia. . . . Ajaria is historically a part of Georgia, and there has never been any instance in history in which Ajaria has created problems for its motherland* [that is, Georgia]. Reports that Ajaria intends to become part of Turkey are totally unfounded.[31]

In the same interview, Abashidze rejected the accusation that he was a dictator and denied charges that he was pro-Russian, pro-Islamic, or pro-

Turkish. Rather than harp on differences in religion, Abashidze stressed the importance of advancing the economic interests of the republic, not the cultural interests of the Ajars. What he sought for Ajaria, he stated, was a stable political system, which would allow for the development of the economy. This was highlighted in the slogan adopted by his party, Ajarian Revival: "Wealthy people mean a wealthy state." Later he expanded it to "A wealthy state is a strong state."[32]

Abashidze was quite vocal in his opposition to Tbilisi's use of force in Abkhazia. Throughout the conflict he tried to arrange meetings between the two sides. According to him, Abkhaz leader Ardzinba was willing to negotiate the status of the republic: it was Tbilisi that was unwilling to negotiate and closed off channels of communication.

> He [Ardzinba] did indeed blame the Georgian leadership in extremely categorical terms for their decision to bring in the troops. . . . I agreed with him. Our leaders were after all uncompromising too; they were responsible for turning an internal political problem into a bitter military conflict. My main concern was that Ardzinba was willing at that time to settle the question of the demarcation of functions between the center and the autonomous formations via talks.[33]

In his opinion, it was the center that had led to the current situation and the stalled negotiations over Abkhazia's status. Nevertheless, Abashidze remained committed to maintaining Georgia's political integrity. In an interview in October 1994 he stated that "Ajaria is zealously preserving Georgia's territorial integrity. This is borne out by its entire history. Ajaria cannot be separated from Georgia. It is not from Georgia we are splitting ourselves. Rather, we are distancing ourselves from those decisions which are harmful to Georgia."[34]

In another interview, he again stressed the importance of maintaining Georgia's territorial integrity: "I well remember the moment during the discussion when I suddenly realized that my disagreement [over the use of force] might be seen not so much as concern for Georgia's integrity and interests as a calculated political approach to the problem by the chairman of a similar autonomous republic's Supreme Council."[35]

Two points are worth noting. The first is Abashidze's sense that he was not only a leader of a republic within the borders of Georgia but also a representative of a greater Georgian state. As such, early in the struggle between Sukhumi and Tbilisi he adopted a vocal stance and attempted to persuade the parties to adopt courses of action that would not hurt the interests of Georgia proper (as these would hurt Ajaria as well). Second, and more interesting, is his recognition of the power of precedence in how his actions were being interpreted. Was he the leader of another secessionist republic, or did he have the interests of a greater Georgia in mind? The evidence clearly supports the second point: Abashidze was as committed to maintaining Georgia's territorial integrity as was Shevard-nadze.

Throughout the period of 1991–93, while Georgia was facing ethnic conflicts in South Ossetia and Abkhazia and civil war over control of the government in Tbilisi, the situation in Ajaria remained relatively stable. There were moments of tension between the Ajars and Georgia, but they were not of the scope (regional as opposed to ethnic) or magnitude (ballot rather than bullet) of those in other reaches of the chaotic country.

Unlike the previous set of cases, these cases were much more complicated. Here we have a contested state with a contested identity involved in a fight for its survival vis-à-vis a proximate great power—Russia—and two armed secessionist movements (Abkhazia and South Ossetia) simultaneously. In addition to the normal risks and problems of intervention by external powers, Georgia itself was dotted with military installations garrisoned by Russian Federation troops—a legacy of the collapse of the federal structure of the Soviet Union.

Analysis: Competing Explanations of Variation in Outcomes

So much for the evidence about bargaining over territory in Georgia. What conclusions can we draw from this nested, layered, and confusing sequence of events? However complicated the reality, in other words, is there a simple explanation for the outcome of each interaction? If so, which of the several explanations can offer us the most insight? We turn to these questions in the final section of the chapter. I begin with material-based explanations.

Material-Based Explanations

The first category of explanations of war and peace involve the specific strategic or economic resources of the areas in question. Was there some resource particular to Abkhazia which caused Georgian authorities to take a hard line? Further, would such resources explain Russia's intervention?

There is in fact some support for a material-based argument in the case of Abkhazia: a vitally important railway linking Russia and Georgia runs through Abkhazia. This railway was the only such link between Georgia and the Russian Federation and hence a major import and export artery. In the period under analysis, the Russian Federation was Georgia's chief trading partner, so the Zviadists' disruption of the links provoked a rapid and violent response from Tbilisi (a response that, as mentioned earlier, was later used by Tbilisi as a pretext for dispatching troops to Abkhazia).

Our interest, however, is not really in the absolute strategic value of the resource in question—in this case rail communications. Rather we are interested only in whether the relative distribution of strategic or material resources explains the variation in outcomes: in this case, specifically between Abkhazia and Ajaria. What strategic resources did Ajaria have?

Ajaria contained few resources that could be counted as vital or strategic, save Batumi. Batumi is clearly a vital industrial port. Its infrastructure is extensive, and it provides Georgia's main point of sea communications with Turkey and other trading partners. More important, Batumi is the Black Sea terminus of an important oil pipeline that begins in Baku on the Caspian Sea (one of the few pipelines not under Moscow's control after the collapse of the Soviet Union). It is therefore difficult to argue that rail communications to the Russian Federation were a much higher priority to a worried Tbilisi than the sea communications and oil pipeline through Ajaria.

In short, there is little evidence to suggest that disparity in the value the state ascribed to strategic or material resources in each area accounts for the disparity in outcomes. Furthermore, there is no evidence that Georgia chose to fight for control over Abkhazia because of resources as opposed to other issues.

Nonmaterial-Based Explanations

The essence of nonmaterial-based explanations is that ethnic groups fear each other. They do not want to be subordinate to those belonging to another ethnic group for fear of discrimination, which might lead to the loss of control over their lives and identities. Therefore, they seek autonomy or independence.

In this set of interactions we appear to have strong evidence to support the nonmaterial-based argument. Clearly the Abkhaz were passionately committed to independence from Georgia. Georgians too seem to have been equally committed to distinguishing themselves politically from the former Soviet Union and from a position subordinate to a newly independent Russian Federation. The Ajars, by contrast, did not view themselves as significantly distinguished from non-Muslim Georgians (although the reverse was not true: the Christian Georgians did see the Ajars as distinct). War obtained in the dispute between Moscow and Georgia and between Abkhazia and Georgia, but not between Ajaria and Georgia. Thus to the extent that ethnic fear can be ranged along a variable axis, this case would appear to support the argument that ethnic groups seek independence if they are fearful enough. The greater the fear the greater the demands and the greater the willingness to use violence to achieve those demands.

But there are at least three difficulties with this explanation in this case. First, even if we can characterize the Abkhaz as being dedicated to an independent state, as observed earlier, this hardly explains why violence emerged in Abkhazia. It was Georgia that moved in and set the stage for violence, not Abkhazia.

Second, the nonmaterial-based explanation cannot account for the motives of the three other actors: Georgia, Russia, and Ajaria. The problem is that Georgia and Russia already had states. Georgia's argument with Abkhazia was really about the preservation of a preexisting state, not about statehood as such. There is, in other words, a crucial difference between an ethnic group seeking a state it does not already have and a state seeking to preserve its territorial integrity. In cases of statehood seeking, the dynamics of nationalism are in full play. In cases of extant statehood, the dynamics of interstate conflict take over. In other words, Georgia's actions (especially following independence in 1991) can more simply be described as those of a state rationally attempting to secure its territorial integrity while facing an external threat.[36] As we will see, this is a better explanation for the timing and intensity of the conflict between Abkhazia and Georgia, but by itself it is insufficient in explaining all of Georgia's behavior.

Third, the Ajars should have been the most fearful ethnic group and therefore the most likely to resort to violence. Tbilisi had already demonstrated that it considered assimilation of the Ajars a viable option for sustaining Christian-Georgian predominance in the republic-state. To them the Ajars were aberrant Georgians who simply needed to be converted to Christianity. Without Islam, the Ajars would cease to exist. However, no such claims were made against the Abkhaz. In fact, the Georgians recognized the Abkhaz as a distinct ethnic group, with a distinct language and culture. When Georgia formally declared its independence in 1991, the declaration stated that it expressed the "wishes of the people." Interestingly, "the people" included the Abkhaz, to whom the declaration afforded special consideration "as an aboriginal people of Georgia."[37]

The bottom line is that the nonmaterial explanations fail to account for most of the dynamics in these cases. Do elite-manipulation explanations do any better?

Elite-Manipulation Explanations

The logic of elite-manipulation arguments is that there is a significant difference in intensity of nationalism between ethnic masses and charismatic leaders. Leaders can skillfully manipulate nationalism among the masses to mobilize for political autonomy, or against members of other groups in a preventive or preemptive way.

For such explanations to be of use here, then, we would need to establish a significant gap in nationalist aspirations between the Abkhaz people and their leaders, or the Georgian people and their leaders. Did such a gap exist? Or is it more accurate to say that the leaders who emerged in these regions represented their populations' interests?

Although we can identify charismatic leaders in Abkhazia, Ajaria, Georgia, and Russia, there is little evidence to suggest that the escalation of disputes was due to the machinations of charismatic leaders. The individual who came the closest to fitting this description is Zviad Gamsakhurdia, an outspoken Georgian chauvinist. Not only did his party—one of the most nationalist—gain the highest number of votes in the first set of parliamentary elections in 1990, but Gamsakhurdia himself, a committed Christian-Georgian nationalist, was elected by popular vote. Gamsakhurdia was a *representative* leader. Further, during the main period in which the disputes escalated, Gamsakhurdia was a hamstrung figure who had suffered a coup: his access to the media was extremely limited, and he and his forces were constantly on the run.

Although it could be argued that Gamsakhurdia in fact stirred nationalist passions among Georgians prior to his ouster, more than eight months passed between his ouster and the firing of the first shots in the Abkhaz civil war. Shevardnadze, the consummate diplomat and statesman, was in charge during this time. Gamsakhurdia, the passionate nationalist, was viewed as Shevardnadze's opposite: articulate and charismatic but diplomatically inept. Gamsakhurdia was incapable of seeing Moscow as anything other than a unitary colonial power, and as a result he is blamed for missing a golden opportunity to secure strong relations with Yeltsin during the breakup of the Soviet Union. This sense of his foreign policy incompetence goes a long way toward explaining why he was removed from power. During the crisis, Georgia got what it needed most: a statesman, not a demagogue. As we have seen above, Shevardnadze clearly identified the problem of Abkhazia as one that could be mediated, short of violence (because the Abkhaz would be quickly overwhelmed militarily, which they were).[38] Thus, while Georgian nationalism helped him field reasonably effective fighting forces, in no way did it alter the likelihood or necessity of their deployment.

With respect to Abkhazia's Ardzinba, there is simply no evidence that he was representing anything other than the wishes of the Abkhaz people—wishes that had remained constant for decades. Again, we have a charismatic leader, and again, no real evidence that the issues of contention were in any sense reframed or intensified by that leader.

For his part, Ajaria's Abashidze was criticized for being anti-Georgian in even his more modest proposals for increased regional autonomy. He simply was not a demagogue, and in fact he showed himself incapable of changing his people's opinions, much less their identity.

The Theory of Indivisible Territory and Ethnic War

We have three alternative explanations, yet none of them adequately explains the variation in outcomes. What can settlement patterns and precedent setting tell us about the likelihood of violent ethnic conflict in these interactions?

My argument is that states and ethnic groups fear for their survival, especially in periods of transition. For states, survival hinges on its territorial integrity. If a state is multinational and faces the possibility of multiple secessions from disgruntled ethnic groups which might unravel the state, then it is likely to view disputed territory as indivisible. For ethnic groups, survival is based on the group's identity, which in turn is based on control over territory, usually a homeland. If a group calculates that it has both the legitimacy and the capability to gain control over a territory, then it will demand independence. If an ethnic group demands independence and a state fears setting precedents, then violence is likely. If, however, an ethnic group does not demand independence or the state has no fear of establishing precedents, then violence is less likely. How well did the logic of my theory of indivisible territory hold up in this interaction?

The ethnic group portion of my theory appears to be refuted here for two reasons. First, we established the settlement patterns of both Abkhazia and Ajaria as concentrated minorities, yet the outcome was different in each interaction. Second, my argument may have been overwhelmed by interstate or balance-of-power dynamics. The argument is further complicated by the logical expectations, in terms of capability and legitimacy, of a concentrated-minority actor representing only 18 percent of the regional population. Because such actors are outnumbered in their own homeland, we would expect them not to risk violence, regardless of whether they possesed high legitimacy.

When we look more closely at the interactions in this case, however, my argument goes a long way toward explaining more of the variation in outcomes than any of the competing explanations. What follows is an analysis of the interactions beginning with Georgia and Abkhazia and then Georgia and Ajaria.

Georgia and Abkhazia

We need to remember that Georgia was a state dominated by a concentrated-majority ethnic group in a dispute with a proximate great power

and a concentrated-minority group. As a state under siege and as a concentrated majority, we would expect the Georgian leadership to represent
indivisible issues at the table. And so it did.

Two reasons of state explain Georgia's position of viewing Abkhazia as
indivisible: capabilities and precedent setting. First, Georgia's military capability was high relative to any of its component ethnic minorities, and
especially the Abkhaz. It could therefore feel confident that as long as the
Abkhaz were on their own, Georgia had little incentive to compromise.

Second, and more important, as a multiethnic state Georgia could ill
afford to establish a reputation that allowed secessions, for fear that other
component ethnic groups would quickly petition for independence, leading to a rump Georgia ever less capable of maintaining its own security.
In fact, Georgia was already in the throes of a civil war in South Ossetia,
so the idea of precedent setting was clearly on the minds of Georgians as
Abkhazia sought its own independence. In August 1992 Shevardnadze,
for example, allowed Russian peacekeeping troops to be deployed to
South Ossetia because he believed "this senseless war must be ended at
any price."[39] This "price," however, did not include "the inviolability of
our [Georgia's] borders or the integrity of our territory." To maintain
Georgia's borders, Georgia accepted Russian mediation in its internal affairs and Russian forces on its soil: high prices to pay for a state that only
recently had secured its independence.

Time and again, the notion of territorial integrity was advanced as the
reason for Georgia's fight with Sukhumi. But this notion took on two
different meanings. First, it meant securing the state of Georgia's internationally recognized borders. It is not surprising, therefore, that the first
line in the September 1992 cease-fire agreement guaranteed its territorial
integrity. Moreover, opinion polls from June 1993, at the height of the
war, indicated that the Georgian population overwhelmingly supported
maintaining the territorial integrity of Georgia: 95 percent believed that
the territorial integrity of Georgia had to be maintained at all costs, and
92 percent opposed independence for Abkhazia.[40] The population, like
their elite counterparts, were concerned that the independence of Abkhazia would lead to their country's dismemberment.

Second, maintaining Georgia's borders also meant keeping intact the
homeland of Georgians. Both Abkhaz and Georgian historians and an-
thropologists bickered about who had settled the disputed territory first
and could therefore claim it as their homeland. Not surprisingly, although
Tbilisi was forced to acknowledge the long tenure of the Abkhaz people,
it claimed that Georgians had settled the area first and that the Abkhaz
were recent settlers. Shevardnadze, for example, viewed it as his responsibility to maintain the motherland, the place that had given birth to the
Georgian nation. "Whoever is a politician," he said, "even if he is a man

of genius, his interests are a drop in the ocean compared with the integrity of the motherland." He continued, "Singling out provinces, and speaking about an administrative and state system dividing the country into provinces, may be a time bomb."[41] Shevardnadze's fears of setting off a "time bomb" extended to the even narrower question of the structure of the Georgian state. If the structure was not negotiable, then talk of independence for any one region, especially a region that was seen as homeland territory, was unthinkable.

Beyond these state and homeland attachment incentives to advance indivisible issues at the bargaining table, we expect Tbilisi to have advanced indivisible issues because 46 percent of those living in Abkhazia were Georgians—constituting a far greater portion of Abkhazia's population than did the Abkhaz—18 percent—or any other single group. In this technical sense, Tbilisi could therefore claim a kind of democratic-representative legitimacy in Abkhazia. Weeks into the fighting, Shevardnadze insisted that Georgia must "reinstate the rights of citizens of Abkhazia, including the 50 percent of Georgians who live in the autonomous republic, including 15 percent of Russians and 15 percent of Armenians."[42]

Although it is difficult to disentangle ethnic motivations from state ones in the struggle to prevent Abkhazia's secession, it is clear from the empirical record that Georgian nationalism had been mobilized around the negative aim of maintaining the state of Georgia against specifically Russian colonialism and secession by minorities. Thus, because Georgians viewed Abkhaz (and South Ossetian) separatists as agents of Russian colonialism, a secession would be simultaneously a reduction in state power and a diminishment of Georgians' pride and identity.

From the Abkhaz side, we expect fear of annihilation or greed (for territory) to be constrained by the vulnerability of the ethnic group within the contested territory. In fact, Georgian authorities themselves acknowledged the Abkhaz vulnerability. Georgian vice premier Aleksandr Kavadze, for example, stated that "[a]s for the forms of autonomy and management, particularly in Abkhazia, I believe the Abkhazes—unlike the Armenians, Greeks, Azerbaijanis, and other people living in Georgia—have no native land but Abkhazia. Consequently, we must do everything to ensure their rights. This is a matter of honor for our state."[43] Here was a Georgian official acknowledging that the Abkhaz had a right to the land and that it was the responsibility of the Georgian state to protect their rights: this ethnic group had nowhere else to go. Yet the same officials were fighting to preserve a state. And so in this situation, where elites were forced to choose between ethnic-identity interests and state interests, state interests took precedence.

Returning to the Abkhaz side, we expect leaders of a concentrated minority, because of a lack of capability, to represent divisible issues at the table, or more accurately, to attempt to represent indivisible issues as divisible ones. This is what the Abkhaz did. Settlement patterns played into Abkhazia's bargaining position in two ways: in the demands it made and in its use of principles of legitimacy. First, Abkhazia did not demand full independence; rather, it sought greater autonomy or confederation within Georgia. Following the initial Georgian offensive in August 1992, for example, Zurab Achba, deputy chairman of the Standing Committee on Legal Matters of the Abkhaz Republic, claimed:

> On August 14 we were busy writing documents on the model of the Federal Treaty, and we intended to separate the powers of Georgia and Abkhazia on the basis of some kind of federal agreement—and we did not want anything beyond that, since we know all too well that we couldn't possibly coexist in another kind of environment. . . . Now that it's clear that they continue killing and humiliating my people, I'm afraid we may be compelled to secede after all.[44]

Achba cited the treaty that detailed Abkhazia's desired relationship with Georgia. He said that this was not the basis for declaring Abkhazia independent from Georgia. Abkhazia would be voluntarily united with Georgia with powers divided between them on the basis of bilateral treaties and agreements resulting in what he termed a "normal federative system."

Second, as minorities in their own homeland, the Abkhaz could play for sympathy: they could reasonably argue that their vulnerability entitled them to autonomy. Although there is a distinction between a play for sympathy and a claim to legitimacy, the aim of both is similar: to increase the likelihood of support in the event of a crisis. Further, the Abkhaz argued that they were the first to arrive and settle in Abkhazia, and as such Abkhazia was *their* homeland. Combined with the play for sympathy, this resulted in an impassioned nationalism, but one constrained by the lack of capabilities from taking the form of armed rebellion. Achba pointed out that Abkhazia's fate was intimately tied to Georgia, largely because of settlement patterns.

> How is it possible to create a territorial autonomy in Abkhazia, where the population is diffused, where there is no compact settlement of Abkhaz, where we are all mixed up. This is impossible. The idea of territorial autonomy in Abkhazia cannot be realized. . . . This will be a sovereign republic, enjoying normal federative relations with Georgia. We shall deal with our interethnic problems ourselves. . . . We shall not return to an autonomy [republic subordinate to Georgia]. This is absolutely ruled out.[45]

But my argument is that in such an interaction—concentrated-majority state versus a concentrated-minority ethnic group—we expect these disputes to endure but not escalate into violence. What then explains the fact that civil war was the outcome?

In a word: Moscow. Recall that Georgia opened the war by moving against Sukhumi, which it quickly captured, causing the Abkhaz forces to flee in disarray. Had Russia not actively intervened at this point, it seems certain that the conflict would have ended, and ended with relatively little bloodshed. But Russia did intervene, and its support enhanced Abkhazia's capabilities. Russia sent tanks, planes, fuel, ammunition, and military advisers. Ardzinba was no longer constrained in the demands he could table, and he ceased all pretense at advancing divisible issues. The Abkhaz were able to take back Sukhumi and establish de facto independence from Georgia. As a result of ethnic cleansing, conducted during and after the military campaigns, the Abkhaz now constitute the largest ethnic group in Abkhazia, with Georgians making up only 15 percent, most of them in the Gali region, bordering Georgia. The Abkhaz are as committed to preventing the repatriation of Georgians as the Georgians are to returning and reclaiming this part of their imagined homeland.

For its part, Moscow had mixed motives for intervening in the conflict in Abkhazia. On the one hand, it remained committed to a united Georgia, and the Georgian government played on this concern by insisting that Abkhazia remain an integral part of Georgia. In the opinion of Vazha Lordkipanidze, the Georgian ambassador to Russia, the precedent of an independent Abkhazia might have triggered the disintegration of Russia.[46] It was in Russia's strategic interest to keep Georgia's borders together. Yet it was also in Russia's interests to have instability in Georgia. Instability would allow Russia to mediate disputes, sustain its military presence, and bolster its influence on the region.

Georgia and Ajaria

The Georgian-Ajarian dispute also featured a concentrated-majority state and a concentrated-minority ethnic group. As in the Abkhaz interaction, we expect the state to represent indivisible issues and the ethnic group to represent divisible ones. All other things being equal, we expect conflict, but not violence. Again this is what happened.

Ajaria began by representing divisible issues—increased autonomy—at the table. The logic here is the same as in the case of Abkhazia. The combination of the lack of capabilities and vulnerability implied a conflict that would not escalate into violence. After the collapse of the Soviet Union, the Ajars did advance moderate demands. Given its own fight with Moscow, however, Tbilisi at first not only resisted such claims but threatened to deprive Ajaria of its preexisting rights and freedoms. But this is not what happened, and the explanation for it has to do with the peculiar nature of the interaction between Ajaria and Georgia.

From the Georgian point of view, Ajars were fallen Georgians. The fact that they were ethnically and linguistically the same as true Christian Georgians, but nevertheless Muslim, made them different, perhaps in need of redemption by conversion. From the Ajar point of view, however, the religious distinction carried relatively little weight: Ajars were Georgians.

This meant three things. First, the Ajars were loyal to Tbilisi's stated aim of maintaining the integrity of the Georgian state; at no time did they support secessionist claims by other groups within Georgia. Abashidze did object to the use of force to solve the Abkhaz-Georgian dispute (at least before it became obvious that Russia was actively intervening—a response provoked by premature Georgian attempts at a fait accompli). However, he clearly distinguished between the legitimacy of the means employed to resolve the crisis and the legitimate aim of Georgia's policy: the maintenance of Georgia's territorial integrity.

Second, the Ajars were reluctant to involve Russia in their struggle with Tbilisi. In fact, although Abashidze kept the "Russian card" in his deck[47] and let Tbilisi see the card, he never played it, even when Tbilisi appeared poised to deny any separate identity to the Ajars by completely abolishing all parallel administrative and political structures.[48]

Third, the struggle between Ajaria and Tbilisi revealed something important to Tbilisi and the Christian Georgians: unlike the Abkhaz, the Ajars had not in fact advanced demands as a first step toward achieving de facto political autonomy. By the time the crisis passed, Tbilisi had come to see the Ajars as the Ajars saw themselves: true and loyal Georgians, whose petition for autonomy had been just that, nothing more.

Conclusion

This chapter examined a series of nested interactions between actors in disputes over territory. The overarching conflict took place between a newly independent Georgian nation-state and the Russian Federation: a multiethnic great power bordering Georgia. Moscow's interests in Georgia can best be described as foreign-policy inertia and the grasping of a superpower in rapid decline.

Georgia's interests vis-à-vis Moscow were matters of simple survival: survival as a state with intact boundaries. Georgia's leaders, Gamsakhurdia and Shevardnadze, each understood the Russian threat in a different way. Gamsakhurdia recognized the state threat. When asked, for example, whether the 1989 ethnic clashes were provoked by Moscow, he replied, "Of course. As soon as our struggle for independence intensifies, Moscow immediately stirs up ethnic conflicts and even openly threatens us with them."[49] But his response to that threat was to incite Georgian nationalism, even chauvinism. Shevardnadze recognized the state threat even more clearly, and his first response was to attempt to persuade Russia to back off. He then blundered badly, attempting to capture Sukhumi and crush the Abkhaz in a surprise attack—perhaps hoping to remove any pretext for Russian intervention.[50] Once the war was on, and Russia had begun actively arming and supporting the Abkhaz, he appealed to the United Nations, to no avail. Although Georgia could have defeated Abkhazia on its own terms, it could not defeat a Russian-reinforced Abkhazia and was forced to accept greater Russian military presence and influence on Georgian soil. Shevardnadze admitted as much: "We have to cooperate with Russia . . . otherwise Georgia will collapse and disintegrate."[51]

Georgia dealt harshly with Abkhazia for three reasons. First, Georgian ethnic identity had been attached to the notion of a Georgian state free of patronizing Russian domination. Ardzinba made no secret of Abkhazia's desire to ally with Russia, and this made it easy to see Abkhaz resistance as a smoke screen for Russian neocolonialism. The loss of Abkhazia would have been the equivalent of a diminished Georgian identity. Second, Georgia felt threatened by a meddling and formerly colonial Moscow, and as a state it could ill afford to lose the territory and resources represented by Abkhazia, however small those may have been. In the event, the rail communications through Abkhazia could hardly be characterized as small to Georgia, but they do not explain the variation in outcomes. Third, to have allowed Abkhazia's secession would have been to set a bad precedent in multiethnic Georgia, with several potential and actual secessionists. Georgia desperately sought to avoid the reputation of a state that allows secession.

Given its precarious state, why then did Georgia deal so leniently with Ajaria? The answer is simply that Ajaria did not advance demands that threatened the physical territory of Georgia or ethnic identity of Georgians. Given its settlement pattern, we did not expect Ajaria to advance indivisible issues, and it did not. Yet as noted earlier, the divisible character of Ajar demands may not have been so obvious to a Tbilisi in crisis, which it was at the time the demands were tabled. Yet after a clear referendum on the abolishment of a separate Ajar republic, and after months of solid support for Georgia's ethnic and state aims vis-à-vis South Ossetia and Abkhazia, Tbilisi came to view Ajaria as an administrative region only, not as a region occupied by a separate and potentially secessionist ethnic group. As such, precedent-setting logic did not enter into negotiations with Ajaria. Georgia was therefore able to deal leniently with Ajaria and devote its scarce resources to more pressing conflicts in Abkhazia and South Ossetia.

In sum, the bargaining positions and behavior of the actors in these cases provide excellent support for my theory. Ethnic settlement patterns and state precedent-setting concerns influenced whether the actors represented control over the disputed territory as divisible or indivisible.

8

Conclusion

Breathes there the man with soul so dead,
Who never to himself hath said,
This is my own, my native land!
—*Sir Walter Scott,*
"The Lay of the Last Minstrel"

This book started with a simple point. Territory is not only a material and divisible object but also a nonmaterial and indivisible subject. In the last century alone, millions died in wars and in other violence as a result of this simple and enduring problem. Although this dual nature of territory has never been forgotten in such diverse places as Israel/Palestine, Northern Ireland, Sri Lanka, and Spain, in academic treatments of ethnic conflicts and wars and in many attempts to implement policies designed to end ethnic violence, it has largely been forgotten or overlooked. The central purpose of this book is to both recall and underscore the crucial role of territory in explaining ethnic violence. To this end the central question motivating my research was, Why does violence erupt in some ethnic conflicts but not in others?

To answer this question, I introduced a theory of ethnic war called the theory of indivisible territory. I argued that the likelihood of ethnic violence rests on how a conflict's principal antagonists—a state and its dissatisfied ethnic minority—think about or value a disputed territory. Attempts to negotiate a resolution short of war will fail when (1) the ethnic minority demands sovereignty over the territory it occupies, and (2) the state views that territory as indivisible. Ethnic war is less likely to break out if one condition only is met, and very unlikely if neither condition is met.

The remainder of this concluding chapter contains four sections. The first introduces and reviews an important competing explanation of ethnic conflict in the Soviet Union, Czechoslovakia, and Yugoslavia: namely, the idea that the institutions of Soviet-style federalism are a better explanation for the capability and legitimacy endowments of different ethnic groups in the three states that had such arrangements. The second section then provides an overview of the main elements of the theory. The third section highlights the main findings of the statistical analysis and case studies. The fourth and final section presents a number of the theory's key theoretical and policy implications.

Alternative Explanations and Cases

In the first chapter I outlined three approaches to explain the outbreak of ethnic violence —material based, nonmaterial based, and elite manipulation—and detailed that although each captures some of the dynamics, none of them is sufficient on its own. In this section I focus on a competing argument, namely, that the institutions associated with Soviet federalism may allow ethnic groups to mobilize more readily by providing access to resources and information. I also compare this argument against my own in two additional minicases: the disintegrations of the Yugoslav Federation and Czechoslovakia.

At the broadest level, a number of scholars of ethnic conflict point to federalism as a major factor in increasing or decreasing the likelihood of ethnic violence. Arend Lijphart, for example, argued that federalism's diffusion of power makes it useful for managing ethnic conflicts.[1] Yet other scholars argue that by allowing groups greater control over institutions and resources that can facilitate collective action (mobilization), federalism has precisely the opposite effect.[2]

The theory of indivisible territory neatly explains why Lijphart can be right in some cases but, as his critics observe, wrong in others. If my theory is right, then federalism's impact depends on the nature of the issue of contention. If the basis of dissatisfaction with a status quo or with a state's criteria for distributing values has a material basis—say taxes or economic subsidies—or perhaps a political-control or educational basis—such as cabinet positions or access to education—then Lijphart is likely to be right, and federalism would serve as a useful institution to deflect calls—especially violent calls—for autonomy. When, however, the issue is homeland territory or national identity (including way of life), then federalism will only enhance the resources of actors determined to obtain independence, even at the risk of violence and civil war. This is another way of saying that a key implication of the theory of indivisible territory is that territory and identity concerns can overwhelm institutions in many settings: sandbags are all well and good, but when the big river rises, nothing man-made is going to stand in its way.

In *Subversive Institutions*, for example, Valerie Bunce argues that the organization of Communist institutions undermined them.[3] She notes that the only Communist states that broke apart were those characterized by ethnofederal institutions (for example, Czechoslovakia, the Soviet Union, and Yugoslavia). Ethnofederalism allowed for the strengthening of identities and control over resources by the units, thereby weakening the power of these states. Bunce makes it clear that the national-federal design created "states-in-the-making, complete with their own borders, elites, national communities, and a full array of economic, political, social, and cultural institutions."[4]

But how then would Bunce account for the variation in outcomes? All three states collapsed, but only one—Yugoslavia—collapsed violently. To explain the violent demise of Yugoslavia, Bunce argues that three factors "guaranteed" a violent ending: (1) a sense of injustice and the need for retribution embedded in Serbian nationalism; (2) the Yugoslav army as an extension of Serbian national interests; and (3) the presence of large Serbian minorities in Croatia and Bosnia.[5] She argues that the last factor was less important in and of itself than how it interacted with the institutional characteristics that distinguished Yugoslavia from Czechoslovakia.

The Socialist Federations: Czechoslovakia and Yugoslavia

Czechoslovakia and Yugoslavia disintegrated within a year of one another: the Federal Republic of Yugoslavia in 1992 and Czechoslovakia in 1993. The Czechoslovak disintegration was nonviolent, but not without costs or victims. The Yugoslav disintegration was extremely violent and continues to produce both high costs and victims.

Czechoslovakia had a federal structure, but its disintegration is best explained by pride on the Slovak side and economic interests on the Czech side. Its *peaceful* disintegration is best explained by the fact that Czechoslovakia was a rare binational state. The secession of either component republic could therefore not set a precedent for subsequent secessions, which would threaten the territorial integrity of either newly independent republic.

The history of the Czechoslovakian disintegration is as interesting as it is straightforward.[6] The Slovaks felt slighted by their wealthier and more numerous Czech neighbors.[7] After the collapse of communism in Czechoslovakia, Slovak leader Vladimir Meciar advanced a political agenda that would make Czechs and Slovaks equal partners in a confederal state.[8] The Czechs, led by Vaclav Klaus, demurred, calculating that the economic costs of confederation would be too high, and would further delay Czech entry into "European" institutions such as the European Union and NATO. Matters quickly got out of hand, as political elites on both sides escalated their rhetoric until the velvet divorce became a fait accompli.[9]

The Czechoslovak case highlights the limitations of institutional solutions to ethnic disputes when one or more parties consider the state's criteria for distribution of resources illegitimate and where national identity (or national pride) is involved. Meciar and a majority of Slovaks believed that the institutions they sought to change favored the Czechs disproportionately.[10] Their solution was a new institutional arrangement that shared the state's resources more equitably and gave them greater control over the pace of economic reform. Confederation and slowing the transition to a market economy were unacceptable to the Czech side. The state split without much fanfare on January 1, 1993.

In Czechoslovakia it was the stronger republic that wanted to split the state into two. Klaus's predecessor, Czech prime minister Petr Pithart, stated that "Czech selfishness played a significant role [in the breakup of the federation]. . . . We created the impression that the state was being smashed by the Slovaks but really, two motives clashed here, not one."[11] The two ethnic groups—Czechs and Slovaks—lived in different territories. Few Czechs lived in Slovakia, and only a small group of Slovaks resided in the Czech Republic. For the most part, each group occupied its own homeland. Neither side had a potential fifth column residing in the other territory, and territory was not contested between the two parties. The split was simply a matter of dividing economic resources.

The same cannot be said of Yugoslavia, where ethnic groups were concentrated in regions and laid claim to territories occupied by other ethnic groups. Bosnia, for example, was claimed as the homeland of Bosnian Muslims, Croats, and Serbs, whereas Kosovo was considered the homeland of both Kosovar Albanians and Serbs. In addition to competing claims, there were concerns about the issue of precedent setting. This explains why Belgrade attacked Slovenia.[12]

As predicted by my theory the Slovenes, a concentrated majority, were the first to seek independence (June 1991). Also as predicted by my theory, the multinational state of Yugoslavia objected to establishing the precedent of granting independence to one republic for fear of setting off a domino effect. This fear was warranted because just days after Slovenia declared independence, Croatia followed suit. Within a matter of weeks, federal troops had moved into Slovenia and then into Croatia. Although in Slovenia the fight was short, it dragged on in Croatia, in large measure because Serbs were concentrated in regions of Croatia that they deemed part of the Serbian homeland (for example, Kraijina).

This civil war eventually engulfed Bosnia-Herzegovina, a republic in which *no* ethnic group constituted a majority.[13] Like Croatia and Slovenia, Bosnia was embedded in federal institutions that disproportionately benefited Serbs and Serbia. If it could be arranged without bloodshed (as in the Soviet and Czech examples), then Bosnia would be better off on its own instead of being stuck with a reform-resistant and chauvinist Serbian "big brother." Even so, Bosnia would not have declared independence had Slovenia and Croatia not done so. Bosnia's leader, Alija Izetbegovic, argued that Bosnia would be forced to declare its independence should Croatia or Slovenia secede. Croatia and Slovenia did declare independence, and Bosnia was pressed to do so as well.[14] But why was the disintegration of Yugoslavia so violent, and why was the fighting in Bosnia in particular so brutal?

The answer lies in a factor particular to Yugoslavia and to conservative nationalist intellectuals within the Serb Republic. Like other national-isms, Serb nationalism had a strong territorial component, and this, in combination with two other factors (a Serb-controlled military and a powerful precedent-setting problem), is sufficient to explain why—in a postfederal reality in which other states asserted sovereignty over lands claimed by ethnic Serbs—violence was overdetermined. But in addition to the territorial component, there was an ideal Serb identity that con-temporary Serbs had reconstructed around an active mission to liberate Serb lands from "Turks." In other words, the new Serb nationalism had a vengeful component built into an already territorial self-conception. The language used is strikingly similar to the language of conservative Mus-lims regarding jihad in defense of the Holy Land. The reasoning—such as it was—behind Serb atrocities in former Yugoslavia was twofold. First, "if we don't do it to them, they will do it to us," and second, "anyway they deserve it because of what they did to us in [fill in the blank]."

In sum, federal institutions in these cases tended to magnify the exist-ing capability and legitimacy endowments of disparate ethnic groups. In each case, the state's distribution of values (offices, educational access, and economic aid) were bitterly resented by the other groups in the state. Violence did not erupt in Czechoslovakia because the stronger actor—the Czech Republic—had nothing to lose (in terms of identity) and much to gain (economically) from Slovak secession. Violence did erupt in Yugoslavia because Serbia, the stronger actor, had nothing to gain and everything to lose, both economically and concerning its identity, by al-lowing the secessions of Slovenia, Croatia, and Bosnia.

Summary

In sum, the proper question regarding institutions as competitors for the theory of indivisible territory is not, Do institutions explain some features of ethnic violence as well as or better than the theory of indivisible terri-tory? but rather, Under what conditions do institutions constrain de-mands for national self-determination? My theory brackets the answer. Institutions can constrain demands for political autonomy when the is-sues over which the various actors contend are not territory or national identity. Otherwise, institutions—and federalism in particular—tend to increase rather than decrease the likelihood of a self-determination claim.

This is what Bunce concludes. Bunce is a careful researcher. She sets out to explore the ways in which institutions—in this case a de jure socialist federalism that became more de facto over time—affect simmering ethnic disputes. But her explanation of Yugoslavia's descent into brutal violence, although convincing, is too specific to be generalized beyond this case. More important, she concludes that in the final analysis nationalism overwhelmed the effects of institutions. She asks: "[C]ould we dispense with the federal side of the argument and account for the end of these three states by emphasizing, simply, the national side?"[15] Her answer is yes: "The three socialist states that ended were the most nationally diverse of any in the region—as indicated, for example, by the size of their second largest national group; many of the nations in each of these cases were geographically concentrated and, thus, optimally positioned to form solidaristic groups promoting a nationalist agenda; and *it was precisely those compact nations that did mobilize and tear the state asunder.*"[16]

After providing an elegant theory of institutions and their impact on the dissolution of multiethnic states, in other words, Bunce concedes that nationalism and the distribution of groups within the state have to be considered in the analysis: "Thus, while the nation in some sense seems to be a necessary condition for secession, federalism does not."[17]

In sum, institutions such as federalism may act as a bulwark against the disintegration of multiethnic states in some circumstances but not in others. Although Bunce and other researchers have a different focus—disintegration rather than *violent* disintegration—the theory of an indivisible territory helps to bracket those circumstances.

The Theory of Indivisible Territory

My theory begins by positing territory as a survival issue for both states and ethnic groups. Assuming—for the sake of theory building—that both types of actors seek, at a minimum, to survive, I argue that there are systematic differences in the way states and ethnic groups will view the connection between territory and survival.[18]

I assume that for states, territory (maintaining borders) is a matter of physical survival. I argued that for states, a key issue is structure or ethnic profile. States with more than one ethnic group capable of seceding are likely to fear setting precedents. This fear will cause them to regard the territory as indivisible regardless of the territory's material worth.

For ethnic groups, territory should be a matter of survival for the group's identity: control over territory means control over the group's identity. I argued that the settlement patterns of ethnic groups were the key—but not the only—determinants of a group's legitimacy and capability. Majorities and groups concentrated in a region of a state, especially if that region is a homeland, are more likely to regard control over territory as indivisible than are groups that are minorities, dispersed, or urbanized. This is because concentrated and majority groups have relatively greater capability and legitimacy. Dispersed groups are likely to lack capability, whereas urbanites are likely to be recent immigrants who lack attachment to the territory in which they reside.

I then posited that the intersection of a state's and an ethnic group's bargaining positions over control of a disputed territory determined whether their dispute would escalate into violence. If both actors represent their interests over the disputed territory as indivisible, then violence is likely. If one or both do not, then violence can be averted.

The theory was subjected to two main tests: a statistical test to establish a significant positive correlation between settlement patterns and the likelihood of violence and a test of the theory's causal logic in four comparative historical case studies. In both cases, though with minor qualifications, the theory received strong support.

Data Analysis

The statistical analysis in chapter 3 showed that the type of settlement patterns by ethnic groups and the ethnic profile of states explain the likelihood of ethnic violence. Using the Minorities at Risk (MAR) data set, I organized this analysis into two separate tests of the relationship between settlement patterns and violence over a fourteen-year period. The first test examined only the ethnic group portion, and the second included the state-level factors as well. Both tests confirmed the theory's main hypotheses.

In the first test I regressed settlement patterns against rebellion. I hypothesized that concentrated-majority groups were more likely to engage in violent ethnic conflict, and at higher intensities, than their concentrated-minority, dispersed, and urban counterparts. This test showed that concentrated majorities are the most prone to violence: they were two and a half times more likely than concentrated minorities to be engaged in rebellion, and approximately four to five times more likely than urban and dispersed groups.

The second test was more comprehensive. Five factors were included to test the likelihood of violence: (1) the relative impact of settlement patterns; (2) attachment to homeland; (3) duration of residence in a region; (4) precedent setting; and (5) the resource richness of the region.

Overall, the second test confirmed the main hypotheses of the theory. Concentrated-majority status predicted violence, just as it did in the first test. Groups living in what they perceived as their homeland also seemed to more readily engage in violence. The longer a group had lived in a region the greater its chances of violence.

The state-level hypothesis, that precedent setting mattered more than resources, was also confirmed. Further, ethnic groups living in resource-rich regions were less likely to be involved in violence than groups living in resource-poor regions. I argued that this finding suggests that states sometimes believe that resources are divisible. In addition, the fact that violence occurred more often in resource-poor regions confirms the idea that states, as well as ethnic groups, are willing to fight over worthless territory. I contended that something other than the value of resources must be motivating violence.

In sum, the two tests clearly establish that concentration in a region is almost a necessary condition for rebellion and civil war, and dispersion and urbanism are practically sufficient conditions for a settlement short of violence. This is a crucial finding because it confirms that power—in the sense that concentrated groups have more capability and therefore are most likely to escalate autonomy claims to violence—does not explain why concentrated groups risk violence to attain their goals. Concentration matters, but the *most* concentrated groups—urbanites—are the *least* likely to press autonomy claims, violent or otherwise. The empirical finding, in other words, suggests that only by overlaying legitimacy and identity concerns with power can a sound explanation of the likelihood of ethnic violence emerge. Moreover, the notion that precedent setting was a key concern for multiethnic states also received strong support.

The statistical analysis, however, confirms only an association between settlement patterns and the likelihood of violence. This is an important empirical finding in itself, but it tells us little about the causal links between variables. The case studies examined in chapters 4 through 7 provide additional support for the proposed mechanisms of the theory of indivisible territory.

Evidence from the Cases

The case studies in this analysis were structured to give us a greater understanding of the dynamics of ethnic conflicts and to test the logic of competing explanations. On balance, the results of this careful research supported my argument. The first set of cases (chapters 4 and 5) examined the interaction between Russia, the state, and two component regions, Tatarstan and Chechnya. The second set of cases (chapters 6 and

7) explored a more complex relationship between Georgia as a state and two component regions, Abkhazia and Ajaria. As we have seen, the second case study raised some unanticipated but important findings.

Russia, Tatarstan, and Chechnya

At the outset, Russia's relations with its ethnic minorities were complicated by the problem of precedent setting: the very arguments Russian president Yeltsin and the Russians leveled at Soviet leader Gorbachev and the USSR were subsequently invoked by union republics and later by ethnic groups within those republics. In this first set of interactions, Russia stands as the state. It possessed an overwhelming advantage in numbers, military infrastructure, and, on paper at least, a large and sophisticated army, air force, and police force. In the bargaining between the two actors, precedent-setting logic made Russia adamant about the possibility of Tatar and Chechen independence.

The dispersed settlement pattern of Tatars in Tatarstan left the various independence movements rather poorly supplied in terms of both legitimacy and capability. This weak bargaining position best explains the nature of the demands Shamiyev, Tatarstan's leader, introduced at the bargaining table. Essentially, Shamiyev represented Tatarstan's short-term interests in economic terms—both to the Russians and, crucially, to his own people. Putting things this way made the issue of contention divisible. For its part, Russia had come to view Tatarstan as a potential precedent-setting issue, but due to the shared understanding regarding the distribution of legitimacy and capability between the two actors, Moscow treated Tatarstan rather patiently and professionally. The outcome was therefore a negotiated settlement that resulted in significant economic concessions to Tatarstan, in exchange for an agreement to delay talk of political autonomy to a distant date.

Chechnya, by contrast, was a concentrated majority with an equally charismatic leader. Dudayev, understandably concerned about (though hardly awed by) Russian military capability, nevertheless advanced Chechen independence from Moscow as an indivisible issue. Although it appears that Dudayev was not especially determined to resort to arms, Moscow's bungling, and its refusal to negotiate with Dudayev in good faith, undermined Dudayev's moderate rivals in Chechnya and hardened Dudayev's position to the point where armed rebellion became the preferred course of action. As in Tatarstan, precedent-setting logic made Russia's position on Chechen autonomy indivisible. Both sides advanced indivisible issues, and civil war erupted.

There is no question that other factors—such as the years of bad blood between Moscow and Chechnya and the Russian army's abandonment of large stocks of munitions and heavy weapons—affected Chechnya's legitimacy claims and capabilities. However, what is striking about this case is the way the concentrated-majority settlement pattern strongly influenced which of several political elites rose to the top and represented Chechen interests at the bargaining table with Moscow. For its part, Moscow instantly regarded Chechen autonomy probes as a vital threat to its security, leading to a series of diplomatic and military blunders that only escalated the conflict and squeezed out political moderates in Chechnya. This state of affairs dramatically reduced the likelihood that divisible issues would be presented at the bargaining table. On the contrary, Chechnya's Dudayev came to represent a "live free or die" position. The end result was a civil war that was never resolved and that tragically reignited in 1999.

In both Tatarstan and Chechnya, Moscow clearly attached material and strategic values to both territories, but the variation in these value assessments was not sufficient to explain the variation in outcomes. Consistent with the logic of nonmaterial-based explanations, both groups wished for greater autonomy, but the scope of that autonomy and the intensity with which each was willing to pursue its aims differed markedly. Leaders emerged who were representative of respective group aspirations. Neither Shamiyev nor Dudayev was a demagogue, however, and the elite-manipulation explanation cannot account for the variation in outcomes between Tatarstan and Chechnya. Finally, precedent-setting concerns clearly made Moscow intransigent on the issue of political autonomy for both Tatarstan and Chechnya. Variation in outcomes is therefore best explained by differences in the issues each ethnic group represented. In sum, this first set of interactions supports the importance of settlement patterns and precedent setting in explaining violent ethnic conflicts.

Georgia, Abkhazia, Ajaria, and Moscow

The second set of interactions presented a more complex situation than the first. Although Georgia stands as the state here, during the period under analysis it was simultaneously embroiled in (1) a conflict of interests with Moscow (a proximate and meddling great power), (2) a civil war in South Ossetia, (3) a civil war for control of the government and two calls for increased autonomy, (4) calls for greater autonomy in Abkazia, which became calls for outright independence once Russia came to its aid, and (5) limited calls for a demand for increased regional autonomy in Ajaria.

Tbilisi represented itself as both a multiethnic state trying to hold together what has been termed a miniempire and an ethnic group under siege by minority groups that were outbirthing the dominant Christian Georgians. As a concentrated-majority *nation*-state, Georgia demanded full autonomy from any Russian-dominated post-Soviet federal structure. Georgia's unwillingness to roll over and join Russia in a confederation angered Moscow, which soon set about undermining Georgian independence by encouraging minorities on Georgian territory to mobilize for independence.

Ultimately state concerns trumped ethnic concerns, with Tbilisi striking a Faustian bargain with Moscow. As a state, Georgia was faced with the threat of Russian military intervention on its territory. Precedent-setting logic made it intransigent regarding autonomy calls, all the more so as evidence developed that the scope and intensity of such calls were increasing due to Moscow's interference. Still, as a state, Georgia could field an armed force backed by a population of 5.4 million against component groups who could field armed forces backed by populations of 235,000 at most (assuming that other non-Georgians in Abkhazia fought along with the 90,000 Abkhaz). Its capabilities were high, precedent setting was a significant factor, and a sizable proportion of minorities in Abkhazia (46 percent) and Ajaria (39 percent) were Georgians. Georgia was therefore not about to treat autonomy calls from component minorities as divisible issues.

As a concentrated minority, the Abkhaz sought greater autonomy but would not by themselves have resorted to violence, due to their lack of any reasonable chance of obtaining independence without risking annihilation. The Abkhaz argued that a primary reason they were a minority in their own homeland was Georgia's genocidal policy of forced resettlement of ethnic Georgians on Abkhaz land. But if Georgia was adamant and Abkhazia fearful, why did indivisible demands get tabled by both sides? The answer is Moscow. Moscow's active intervention gave Abkhazia the capability it could never have achieved on its own. This effectively converted the interaction, resulting in indivisible issues being tabled by both sides and in a civil war.

The Ajars were a surprise altogether. Although I did expect them to represent their interests as divisible, which they did, they did so not because of a lack of capability or legitimacy but because they viewed themselves as Georgians. The Ajars share the descent of Georgians, but they are Muslim. So, whereas the Christian Georgians saw Ajars as tainted and therefore not true Georgians, the Ajars saw themselves as Georgian. They did not see the need to separate their territory from Georgia proper, since Georgia proper was viewed as their homeland as well. Thus they represented their interests as divisible.

TABLE 8.1
Theoretical Expectations and Research Findings

Interaction	Outcome	Does Theory of Indivisible Territory Explain Case?	Outcome Expected?
Case 1 Russia (state) Tatarstan (dispersed)	Negotiated settlement	Yes	Yes
Case 2 Russia (state) Chechnya (concentrated majority)	Civil war	Yes	Yes
Case 3 Georgia (state) Abkhazia (concentrated minority)	Civil war	Yes	No
Case 4 Georgia (state) Ajaria (concentrated minority)	Negotiated settlement	Yes	Yes
Case 5 Russia (state) Georgia (concentrated majority)	(Violence)	(Yes)	(Yes)

As table 8.1 indicates, the theory of indivisible territory fared well in this set of interactions. Fears of precedent setting and settlement patterns influenced the relative strengths and weaknesses of the actors' bargaining positions.

On the face of it, however, two aspects of the Georgian case challenge the validity of my argument. First, Georgia and Abkhazia came to blows, but Georgia and Ajaria did not; yet both ethnic groups shared the same settlement pattern. If settlement patterns explain variation in outcomes, why were the outcomes different? Second, my argument faces the challenge that the complex dynamics of ethnic conflict reduce to simple calculations of relative power whenever other states actively interfere in the interaction.

In the event, it was clear that Moscow's diplomatic and military intervention dramatically affected the outcomes. Where Moscow intervened (in Abkhazia), the outcome was a civil war. Where Moscow did not intervene (in Ajaria), the outcome was as predicted: a negotiated settlement.

This explains the variation in outcomes and answers the first challenge these interactions presented to my explanation. But what of the second challenge? My answer must be that in this case the intervention of a great power overwhelmed the dynamics. Yet this raises an interesting subsidiary question: what is the distribution of interactions that are likely to be affected by a proximate and activist great power as compared with those removed from such interference? The answer to this question lies beyond the scope of this analysis, but I would argue that the number of cases is small compared with the number of cases that play themselves out without such intervention. Further, although the theory of indivisible territory failed to capture all of the dynamics of bargaining, it did capture important aspects of many of them. The case of Ajaria is illuminating here. Had I not examined this case in light of territories and homelands, we may have missed the important fact that Ajars see themselves as Georgians and their homeland as Georgia and thus were not and are not likely to press secessionist claims.

The statistics and cases complemented each other well. Whereas the statistics could not prove that attachment to the territory motivated the ethnic groups and that precedent setting motivated the states, the case studies did show that these factors were among the deepest and most pressing concerns among the actors.

Implications and Conclusion

The theory of indivisible territory has a number of important theoretical and policy implications. In this section I highlight three from each.

Theoretical Implications

The first theoretical implication has to do with the rationality of ethnic groups and states. In the literature on ethnic conflict and violence, states are often assumed to be rational, whereas ethnic groups tend to be treated as irrational actors. This is because ethnic group members are often observed to be willing to die for a cause that hardly seems to justify such a steep price. My research makes it clear, however, that both types of actors act rationally. Ethnic groups calculate and maximize their utility just as states do, but they define *utility*—or more narrowly, *survival*—differently. Whereas Moscow, for example, seemed to think it was fighting its first Chechen war, the Chechens viewed it as the latest phase in a three-hundred-year struggle to save themselves from foreign domination.

Ethnic groups may indeed rationally calculate that it is better to risk death than to lose their identity.[19]

Second, although the theory deals exclusively with intrastate conflicts, its has implications for interstate conflicts. Specifically, some wars between states have an ethnic dimension that is linked to territory. In those cases, the dynamics of conflict should reflect, in part, the basic logic of my theory. Consider the recent Eritrean-Ethiopian war, which began in February 1999 over the Badme region.[20] This rocky and sparsely populated hinterland lies between Eritrea and Ethiopia and is of little material consequence to either. However, the ethnic group that dominates each state views Badme as an integral part of its homeland. An Ethiopian merchant put it this way: "That area, I think, is desert. It is valueless . . . [but] it's territory, you know. We'll die for our country."[21] Interstate wars of this kind resemble ethnic wars more than they resemble traditional wars over resources or geopolitical advantage; as such, my theory explains them better than it does more traditional theories of interstate war.

A third theoretical implication centers on the role of elites in shaping ethnic identities, which also has policy implications. Among the most common elements of ethnic identity is shared territory: an attachment to the land which is indivisible from a conception of self. This leaves open the important question of which of the elements of a given identity will become or be made salient and explains why the question of identity is irreducible to a particular formula or definition that remains fixed over time. This highlights the fact that ethnic and national identity cannot be meaningfully evaluated without a discussion of the role of elites. It is vital to note, however, both the importance of leaders in guiding public opinion (and mobilizing the popular will) and of the ways in which the distribution of coethnics within a given territory can constrain leaders attempting to make a particular element of national identity more or less salient.

We can envision four scenarios. In the first, leaders and masses might share the same nationalist vision. In the second, leaders might be even more committed nationalists than the masses. In the third, leaders might use nationalist discourse for personal gain. And in the fourth, leaders might be committed to both nationalism and staying in office. In all four scenarios elites are free to attempt to shape identity and interpret dramatic events as they wish, but these identity constructs and interpretations are unlikely to be equally successful in mobilizing and sustaining support for the nationalist cause. Moreover, elites may become victims of their own rhetoric, making themselves captive to policies and discourses that helped them gain power.

Elites represent groups and often respond to popular will. In all of the cases examined in this book, elites were representative. Gamsakhurdia was a committed nationalist, but so was the broader Georgian population who elected him to office. Dudayev too represented the popular wishes of his people, as did Shamiyev. Their positions regarding autonomy or independence were limited by the popular wishes of those they represented. When political leaders represent interests rather than construct them, their ability to make concessions or even negotiate is severely circumscribed. The literature on ethnic violence and policy formulation in dealing with ethnic violence do not fully reflect the fact that in some cases the masses may be as nationalistic as—or even more than—the elites who represent them.

Policy Implications

My argument has implications for policy as well. Here I discuss three: stability versus justice, conflict termination, and partition.

The first policy implication is that states face a trade-off between the short-term benefits of supporting stability for its own sake and sacrificing blood and treasure in order to forge lasting settlements to ethnic disputes in the pursuit of justice. This calculus looks entirely different from the top down and from the bottom up.

From the bottom up, the ethnic-group perspective, the trade-off looks like a sacrifice of justice to stability and is often intolerable.[22] Turning to the former Soviet Union as an example, it is clear that stability came with a high price tag: millions murdered, imprisoned, resettled, sent to the front, and so on, all for the sake of a peaceful and stable union. The implication is that for states who wish to deny nationalist claims, such measures may be required to maintain peace.

From the top down, the state perspective, the sacrifice of justice to stability seems at least fair and in many cases necessary, even if unfair to some groups (keeping in mind that for states, physical survival is the ultimate value). Nationalism played a large role in both the causes of and brutal conduct in two world wars in the last century. Thus unchecked nationalism would proliferate states, some so small that they would fall below the threshold of viability. If this process continued, the likelihood of war would increase, thus, paradoxically, making everyone worse off.[23]

My argument implies that between these two extremes is a considerable and largely unexplored middle ground and that this ground is demarcated by settlement patterns. Policymakers can use settlement patterns to identify the fault lines of ethnic disputes long before a crisis causes actors to begin the process of reevaluation, which may lead to violence. This is analogous to being able to identify a weak building prior to an earthquake and then taking steps to improve it structurally so that when an earthquake does happen, the building will remain intact (or will collapse in a way that spares lives). Dispersed and concentrated-minority nations can be made to feel less vulnerable by the establishment of social, economic, and educational policies and forums—especially sharing power by having greater representation in the state—that reduce their insecurity without threatening the state's political control of the territory. The political quiescence of urbanites means that states have little to fear from these groups. A key implication is that if states feel the need to move ethnic minorities, they should move them to urban centers, not to rural areas. Although class interests and divisions are likely to arise in urban centers, there are two reasons these divisions are unlikely to lead to large-scale ethnic violence or war.[24] First, class interests cut across ethnic identities, making it more difficult for individuals to organize into groups. Second, when class grievances do emerge, states can meet these needs through educational and employment opportunities. Such opportunities are more easily provided than land, which is not only a finite, material resource but may be a sacred and an indivisible part of another group's identity. Concentrated majorities' desire for complete independence may be modified by carefully designed federal structures and power sharing that allow them a good deal of independence, if not outright statehood. States should be wary, however, of establishing quotas for the distribution of power and services. Although concrete formulas for dividing power seem desirable for achieving equity and a balance of interests, future demographic changes may lead to instability and perhaps violence.[25]

Moreover, because legitimacy is so important, all actors could benefit from an increased openness and more dialogue about the facts and contexts of national history. In some cases such dialogues might make national independence fair and necessary, but my guess is that in most cases, they would make national independence seem unnecessary or even wrong.

The second policy implication concerns the termination of ethnic conflicts. This theory suggests that intrastate conflicts over territory are likely to be more difficult to resolve than fights over the makeup of the government (such as who should run it or the nature of its political system). The historical evidence of intrastate conflict reveals that fights over territory are three times more likely to end in a cease-fire or stalemate than in an outright military victory or a lasting peace settlement.[26] In contrast, fights over the makeup of the government are just half as likely to end in stalemate as to be resolved.[27] Figure 8.1 illustrates this.[28]

Intrastate conflicts over territory—which are invariably ethnic—are not likely to be resolved through either force or persuasion, and efforts to resolve them must take this into account. Because in such cases territory is not seen as a divisible asset, attempts to make deals to share control of the territory are usually unworkable, both in the period leading up to the conflict and at the end of the conflict. States' precedent-setting concerns

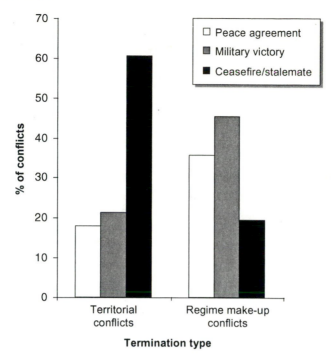

FIGURE 8.1. Armed Conflicts, Issue of Conflict, and
Termination Type, 1989–96

do not diminish with the outbreak of violence, and the death of ethnic
brethren while defending their homeland may only intensify a group's
attachment to its territory. This dynamic of extended and intensified indivisibility is not found in fights over other issues, such as the makeup of
the government, which may explain why on balance the latter are more
amenable to negotiated settlements. Resources can be divided, and positions in the government can be shared by the contending groups. In
ethnic wars, the disputed territory may have little material value to either
side, compared with the costs of continued fighting, but both sides are
willing to spill blood because of precedent-setting or identity concerns.

The theory of territorial indivisibility explains why these wars are unlikely to be resolved easily. Neither of the two cases of war I examined in
depth has been resolved. The violence in Abkhazia ended with a cease-
fire, and negotiations have taken place over Abkhazia's status. However,
a durable solution remains a distant hope. Two issues in the negotiations
have hampered progress. First, the Abkhaz remain committed to independence from Georgia. Georgia does not accept this. Second, Georgia
remains persistent about the right of return for ethnic Georgian displaced

persons. The Abkhaz will not allow large-scale repatriation for fear that this will tilt the demographic balance against them. Until either side budges from its indivisible bargaining positions, peace will remain elusive.

Abkhaz-Georgian affairs seem mild compared with events that transpired between Chechnya and Russia. The Abkhaz war ended in neither peace nor war, and so did the Chechen war. Whereas the Georgians refused to even countenance the notion of negotiating Abkhazia's status, Moscow agreed during the 1996 peace talks to allow the discussion and decision of Chechnya's status to be postponed. Yet no progress was made in these status talks, and relations deteriorated, as did Chechnya's economic and political well-being. In September 1999, only three years after Russia's defeat, war again ravaged the region, and victory is nowhere in sight.[29] Although the Chechen side has not fared as well as it did in the previous war, Moscow has failed to gain a decisive victory. For the time being Chechnya is back to a position of stasis, neither at peace nor at war. Nevertheless, a negotiated settlement is unlikely.

The difficulty of settling territorial ethnic wars suggests the limits of relying on a third-party intervention to end them.[30] Intervention in such conflicts may lead to the signing of peace accords, but if the warring parties fail to settle the underlying territorial disputes, these peace efforts will disintegrate. The Dayton Peace Accords (1995) are a prime example. The basic territorial issues were not resolved and to this day remain unsolved. Richard Holbrooke's 1995 warning that "[t]he territorial issues—the 'map'—would be far more difficult to resolve than the constitutional issues" continues to ring true.[31] Peace has been secured by NATO forces, which cannot be removed without violence breaking out again. In nonethnic wars, by contrast, both sides are more likely to change their minds about the worth of fighting once the war is under way; in such cases third-party intervention may be an effective way to stop the violence and allow the two sides to engineer a peaceful solution.

The third policy implication concerns the controversial issue of partition. In a recent article Chaim Kaufmann argues that in order to stop ethnic violence, it is essential to separate and resettle the rival ethnic groups (even if that means population transfers) and to give each group increased political autonomy. He does not advocate granting statehood.[32] However, there are two problems with this kind of partition. First, it does not account for the notion of homeland and the attachment of different ethnic groups to particular places. In fact, partition is unlikely to work unless serious attention is paid to settling ethnic groups in their respective homelands. The existence of different meanings of territory implies that ethnic groups will maintain a strong attachment to the land. Such an attachment has often been characterized as irrational, and irrationality has thus become a common historical justification for state coercion. But understanding how ethnic groups relate to territory implies that redistributing people will be costly in terms of treasure, and possibly blood. Partition as a policy is also risky in moral terms: at the extreme end, *resettlement* becomes merely a euphemism for ethnic cleansing.[33] Even a process as brutal as ethnic cleansing will fail because the people who are moved maintain the memory of their attachment to their land. In the case of both Chechens and Crimean Tatars, for example, even a particularly brutal Soviet Union could not erase the memory of the land from national consciousness. The Crimean Tatars are currently migrating—at great cost and risk—from the Russian hinterlands (where Stalin moved them en masse in the 1930s) to their ancestral homelands in present-day Ukraine. In Ukraine they have begun demanding greater representation and even political autonomy, and they have invoked both tenure and investment arguments to support their demands.

Second, Kaufmann's policy of separating and concentrating rival ethnic groups in enclaves, without granting them independence, is a prescription for more violence.[34] In effect, it would create multiethnic states with concentrated majorities, which is the most violence-prone settlement pattern. A better way to make partition work is to settle rival ethnic groups in their homelands, or at least some part of their sacred territory, and then grant them statehood.

The long history of Chechen resistance to Russian rule suggests the benefits of granting independence. Russia has engaged in wars with Chechens for centuries, wars that have resulted in the loss of tens of thousands of Russian and Chechen lives. Russia's current military strategy of rooting out every last insurgent has been tried before and has yet to work. Although attractive in theory, to be successful, this strategy requires far more troops than Russia can afford to commit, and increased deployment tends to offer only more targets for guerrilla attacks.

Russia has also been unsuccessful in its political strategy of establishing a sympathetic government through aid from Moscow. This strategy failed both in Afghanistan in the 1980s and in the 1994–96 and 1999 confrontations with Chechnya. At one time Russia may have pursued this option successfully, but that time has long since passed in Chechnya, as 1999 events revealed. On October 24, 2002, a group of Chechens seized control of a crowded theater in a working-class district of Moscow. Their demands were far from clear,[35] but they appear to have centered on an end to Russia's war in Chechnya. Most ominously, the group's spokesman and leader, a nephew of the famed (and now deceased) Chechen general Barayev, declared that the forty or so fighters he led were *smertniki*, or suicide martyrs.

After three days, during which the 600 or so hostages—some of whom were elderly or in poor health—suffered deprivation of food or the ability to use a bathroom,[36] Russian special forces pumped an opiate gas into the theater, turning the hostage takers into *smertniki*, and killing as many as 120 of the hostages.

These facts, sketchy as they are, are not in dispute; but details of the operation and its depressing outcome are less important than two questions. First, what led to the hostage taking in the first place, and second, what are the likely political consequences?

As should be clear by now, Chechens and Russians live in a different reality concerning historical facts and what past acts either side can be said to justify or necessitate. Like Palestinians and Israelis, they share a rich and intimate history, but each side chooses from that history selectively in order to justify its often brutal and counterproductive acts.

That said, even a Russian sampling of Russian-Chechen history makes it relatively simple to explain, though not justify, why a group of young Chechens, including eighteen women (many of them widows of Chechen men and guerrillas), might imagine that seizing hostages and world attention would gain them leverage in their war to force the Russian army to leave Chechnya. Chechens, for reasons ranging from geography to culture and social customs, resent central authority, and historically Russia has presented itself as the quintessential conqueror, colonial power, and central authority in the Caucasus.

But more important, strong evidence suggests that in the last three years since Russia reignited a military campaign in Chechnya, the desire for independence has been successfully sublimated into a more primal desire to survive. Such resistance as continues to exist, and to inflict a steady toll of painful Russian casualties, increasingly appears to be the result of a simple desire for retribution for continuing Russian abuses and atrocities.[37]

As to the political consequences, these follow logically. Due to deliberate and systematic distortion in the press and mass media, few Russians are aware of the true nature of the actions of the Russian army in Chechnya. Although they are daily reminded of Chechen atrocities against Russian forces—which are real—they are rarely told of the Russian atrocities that most often precede and give rise to such acts.[38] In the longer historical perspective, Chechens are viewed as a conquered and inferior people who should consider themselves lucky to be part of the Russian Federation and who no more deserve independence than would Native American tribes in the United States. Combined with outrage over the Moscow hostage-taking attack, this grants Russian president Vladimir Putin new and considerable political license to act freely against Chechnya.

But few outside Russia understand that militarily there is very little Putin can do to escalate the fighting against Chechen guerrillas in the

Caucasus. Russian forces can, and have, expanded their sweeps for arms and young men in Chechen villages and escalated their harassment of Chechen males. But beyond this, there is simply not much in the way of coercive leverage to be gained in Chechnya itself.

The great danger—and what has in fact solidified into the main political consequence of the Chechen attack in Moscow—has been Putin's escalation of the fight beyond Chechnya. This has taken two forms. First, Putin has declared the Chechen fight a fight against *global* and *Islamic* terrorism, a move supported by the United States and NATO.[39] Second, and as a consequence, Putin has declared that international boundaries—the very principle of state sovereignty—will become conditional and porous.[40] For example, he has put Georgia on notice that its border with Russia will not preclude the deployment of Russian troops on Georgian soil in the event that a counterterrorist operation becomes necessary.

The prospects for a lasting peace in Chechnya—as in the region as a whole—are therefore dim. There are three reasons for this. First, Chechens will never give up the idea that Russians have no business governing them in their own homeland. Second, Russia and Russians continue to believe that, short of genocide, Chechens have a "willingness to suffer" that frustrates any attempt to convince them to scale back their demands for independence.[41] Finally, a lasting peace in Chechnya will demand billions of dollars in reconstruction and economic assistance. Russia simply does not have it, and it is unlikely that Russia would allow foreign donors to help rebuild Chechnya.

Russia faces three options. The first, and arguably best, option is to declare victory and grant Chechnya independence. It could also opt to prosecute an unpopular, Stalin-style war. Finally, Russia could try to live with a counterinsurgency struggle for decades. Each course of action carries its own risks.

Granting Chechnya greater independence might induce other regions to seek similar political rights. In addition, it might not have a quick impact on terrorism and organized crime—issues that motivated Russians' public support for the war in the first place. Perhaps the greatest obstacle to the adoption of this policy is Russia's sense of betrayal, which followed the 1996 peace accords, particularly among members of the military (who were forced to accept a treaty negotiated by one of their own generals, Aleksandr Lebed). On a psychological level, Russia may simply be unable to accept Chechen independence.

Pursuing all-out war against Chechnya and Chechens is a difficult strategy, even assuming the existence of well-trained forces and complete control over information from the battlefield. Escalating the war effort when Russia's troops are demoralized and the public no longer believes in victory is likely to increase popular dissatisfaction and bolster support for the insurgents. Moreover, success in the longer term would require the wholesale killing of Chechens, amounting to genocide or mass deportation. If the historical precedent has any bearing, one might ask the current Russian president, Vladimir Putin, what makes him think he can solve the Chechen problem in this manner if Stalin was incapable of solving it.

A protracted counterinsurgency campaign looks as untenable as full-scale war. Russia is losing too many soldiers to maintain a viable counterinsurgency force in Chechnya. The media are becoming more critical, and popular support continues to erode. Further, with the war taking up an estimated one-third of the defense budget, Russia simply cannot afford to prosecute, either politically or financially, a long and costly counterinsurgency campaign.

In sum, Russia's best option is to grant Chechnya independence. The risks of independence seem relatively minor compared with the alternatives Russia currently faces. Although precedent setting may still be on the minds of some Russian elites, Russia currently faces no other viable independence movements. In part, this is because Moscow's resolve and brutality in prosecuting the most recent Chechen wars in 1996 and 1999 sent a clear signal that independence from Russia will not be tolerated easily. The independence option may be a bitter pill to swallow, but if Russia is to find a long-term solution to its Chechnya problem, it must begin by granting independence and then offer significant economic aid to help rebuild Chechnya and repatriate the Chechen people to their homeland. Only then can a stable and lasting peace be established.

We now know a great deal more about the dynamics of ethnic violence than we did before. As a first step in better understanding these complex and important dynamics, I have established that how people live together determines the likelihood of violence between and among them. I have done so by means of a general theory. I hope that this research serves both to further our understanding of violent ethnic conflict and as a solid foundation for policies that will make such violence less likely.

The theory of indivisible territory is not intended to completely explain every violent ethnic conflict. What it can do is explain why some ethnic conflicts turn violent and others do not. My research clearly suggests that a more careful and diligent study of the motivations of different actors and how these may lead to war can lead to general theoretical insights and improved policies. In the cases explored here, territory, both as an imagined homeland and as a real material resource, had profound implications regarding whether people lived or died. Recognizing this double meaning of territory is the first step toward a better understanding of the origins, character, and duration of ethnic violence.

Appendix Tables _____

APPENDIX 1
Number of Independent States in the World = 191

0: (11/6%)	1: (35/18%)	2: (18/9%)	3+: (127/67%)
Andorra	Antig./Barbuda	Australia	Afghanistan
Burundi	Bahamas, The	Cyprus	Albania
Holy See	Bahrain	Czech Republic	Algeria
Mauritius	Barbados	Djibouti	Angola
Monaco	Cape Verde	Dominica	Argentina
Nauru	Cuba	Estonia	Armenia
Qatar	Dom Republic	Germany	Austria
Rwanda	Grenada	Israel	Azerbaijan
San Marino	Haiti	Kiribati	Bangladesh
Singapore	Iceland	Lithuania	Belarus
Trin./Tobago	Ireland	Netherlands	Belgium
	Jamaica	New Zealand	Belize
	Japan	Norway	Benin
	Korea, North	Oman	Bhutan
	Korea, South	St. Kitts/Nevis	Bolivia
	Kuwait	St. Vinc./Grens	Bosnia/Herz..
	Lesotho	UAE	Botswana
	Liechtenstein	Uruguay	Brazil
	Luxembourg		Brunei
	Maldives		Bulgaria
	Malta		Burkina Faso
	Marshall Is.		Burma
	Palau		Cambodia
	Poland		Cameroon
	Portugal		Canada
	Saint Lucia		Cent. Afr. Rep.
	Samoa		Chad
	Sao Tome/Prin.		Chile
	Saudi Arabia		China
	Seychelles		Colombia
	Slovenia		Comoros
	Swaziland		Congo/Brazz.
	Tonga		Congo/Kinsh.
	Tunisia		Costa Rica
	Tuvalu		Cote d'Ivoire
			Croatia
			Denmark

APPENDIX 1
(*continued*)

0: (11/6%)	1: (35/18%)	2: (18/9%)	3+: (127/67%)
			Ecuador
			Egypt
			El Salvador
			Eq. Guinea
			Eritrea
			Ethiopia
			Fiji
			Finland
			France
			Gabon
			Gambia, The
			Georgia
			Ghana
			Greece
			Guatemala
			Guinea
			Guinea-Bissau
			Guyana
			Honduras
			Hungary
			India
			Indonesia
			Iran
			Iraq
			Italy
			Jordan
			Kazakhstan
			Kenya
			Kyrgyzstan
			Laos
			Latvia
			Lebanon
			Liberia
			Libya
			Macedonia
			Madagascar
			Malawi
			Malaysia
			Mali
			Mauritania
			Mexico
			Micronesia

APPENDIX 1
(*continued*)

0: (11/6%)	1: (35/18%)	2: (18/9%)	3+ : (127/67%)
			Moldova
			Mongolia
			Morocco
			Mozambique
			Namibia
			Nepal
			Nicaragua
			Niger
			Nigeria
			Pakistan
			Panama
			Papua N.G.
			Paraguay
			Peru
			Philippines
			Romania
			Russia
			Senegal
			Sierra Leone
			Slovakia
			Solomon Is.
			Somalia
			South Africa
			Spain
			Sri Lanka
			Sudan
			Suriname
			Sweden
			Switzerland
			Syria
			Tajikistan
			Tanzania
			Thailand
			Togo
			Turkey
			Turkmenistan
			Uganda
			Ukraine
			United Kingdom
			United States
			Uzbekistan
			Vanuatu

APPENDIX 1
(*continued*)

0: (11/6%)	1: (35/18%)	2: (18/9%)	3+ : (127/67%)
			Venezuela
			Vietnam
			Yemen
			Yugoslavia
			Zambia
			Zimbabwe

0 = intermingled; 1 = homogeneous or one concentrated group with dispersed minorities; 2 = two concentrated groups with or without dispersed minorities; 3+ = three or more concentrated groups.

APPENDIX 2

Minorities at Risk Cases and Key Variables ($n = 270$)

Country	Group	Rebel8095[1]	Settpat[2]	Homeland[3]	Duration[4]	Resource[5]	Ethnic Profile[6]
Afghanistan	Hazaras	7		1	3	0	3
Afghanistan	Pashtuns	7		1	3	0	3
Afghanistan	Tajiks	0		0	3		3
Afghanistan	Uzbeks	7		0	3		3
Albania	Greeks	0		0	3	1	3
Algeria	Berbers	0		1	3	0	3
Angola	Bakongo	0		1	3	1	3
Angola	Cabinda	4	3	1	3	1	3
Angola	Ovimbundu	7		1	3	1	3
Argentina	Indigenous Peoples	0	2	1	3	1	3
Australia	Aborigines	0	0	1	3	0	2
Azerbaijan	Armenians	7	3	1	3	0	3
Azerbaijan	Lezgins	0		1	3	0	3
Azerbaijan	Russians	0	1	0	2	0	3
Bahrain	Shi'is	0	0	1	3	0	1
Bangladesh	Biharis	0	1	0	1	0	3
Bangladesh	Chittagong Hill	7	3	1	3	0	3
Bangladesh	Hindus	0	0	0	3	0	3
Belarus	Poles	0	3	1	3	1	3
Belarus	Russians	0	0	1	2	0	3
Bhutan	Lhotshampas	3	3	0	2	0	3
Bolivia	Highland PPLS	1		1	3	1	3
Bolivia	Lowland PPLS	1	3	1	3	1	3
Bosnia	Croats	7		1	3	1	3

Country/Group		Rebel8095[1]	Settpat[2]	Homeland[3]	Duration[4]	Resource[5]	Ethnic Profile[6]
Bosnia	Muslims	0	1	1	3	0	3
Bosnia	Serbs	7		1	3	1	3
Botswana	San Bushmen	0	3	1	3	1	3
Brazil	Afro-Brazilians	0		1	3		3
Brazil	Amazonian Indians	3	2	1	3	1	3
Bulgaria	Roma	0	0	0	3	0	3
Bulgaria	Turks	0		0	3	1	3
Burma	Kachins	7	3	1	3	0	3
Burma	Karens	7	2	1	3	0	3
Burma	Mons	5		1	3	1	3
Burma	Rohingya	4	2	1	1		3
Burma	Shans	5	2	1	3	0	3
Burma	Zomis (Chins)	5	3	1	3	0	3
Burundi	Hutus	5	0	1	3	0	0
Burundi	Tutsis	1	0	1	3	0	0
Cambodia	Vietnamese	0	0	0	1	0	3
Cameroon	Bamileke	0	3	1	3	1	3
Cameroon	Kirdis	0	3	1	3	1	3
Cameroon	Westerners	0	2	1	3	1	3
Canada	French Canadians	0	0	1	3	0	3
Canada	Indigenous Peoples	3	0	1	3	0	3
Canada	Québécois	0	3	1	3	1	3
Chad	Southerners	6	3	1	3	1	3
Chile	Indigenous Peoples	1	3	1	3	1	3

Country	Group						
China	Hui Muslims	0	0	1	3	0	3
China	Tibetans	1	3	1	3	0	3
China	Turkmen	0	2	1	3	0	3
Colombia	Blacks	0		1	3	1	3
Colombia	Indigenous Peoples	1		1	3	1	3
Costa Rica	Antillean Blacks	0	2	1	2	1	3
Croatia	Serbs	7		1	3	1	3
Cyprus	Turkish Cypriots	0	3	1	3	0	2
Czech Rep.	Roma	0	0	0	3	0	2
Czech Rep.	Slovaks	0	3	0	3	1	2
Dem. Rep. Congo	Hutus	0	2	0	1	1	3
Dem. Rep. Congo	Luba	0		1	2	0	3
Dem. Rep. Congo	Lunda, Yeke	0		1	3	0	3
Dem. Rep. Congo	Ngbandi	0		1	3	0	3
Dem. Rep. Congo	Tutsis	0	2	0	1	1	3
Djibouti	Afars	7	3	1	3	0	2
Dominican Rep.	Blacks	0		0	1	1	2
Ecuador	Blacks	0	3	1	3	1	3
Ecuador	Highland PPLS	0	3	1	3	1	3
Ecuador	Lowland PPLS	0	2	1	3	1	3
Egypt	Copts	0		1	3		3
El Salvador	Indigenous Peoples	0	2	1	3	1	3
Eritrea	AFARS	6	3	1	3		3
Estonia	Russians	0	3	0	1		2
Ethiopia	Afars	6	3	1	3	0	3
Ethiopia	Amhara	6	3	1	3	1	3
Ethiopia	Oromo	5	3	1	3	1	3
Ethiopia	Somalis	4	3	1	3	0	3

APPENDIX 2
(*continued*)

Country/Group		Rebel8095[1]	Settpat[2]	Homeland[3]	Duration[4]	Resource[5]	Ethnic Profile[6]
Ethiopia	Tigreans	7	3	1	3	1	3
Fiji	East Indians	0	0	0	2	0	3
Fiji	Fijians	0	0	1	3	0	3
France	Basques	2	2	1	3	0	3
France	Corsicans	2	3	1	3	0	3
France	Muslims	0	1	0	1	0	3
France	Roma	0	0	0	3	0	3
Georgia	Abkhazians	7	2	1	3	1	3
Georgia	Adzhars	0	3	1	3	1	3
Georgia	Ossetians (South)	0	3	1	3	0	3
Georgia	Russians	7	1	0	2	0	3
Germany	Turks	0	1	0	1	0	2
Ghana	Ashanti	0	3	1	3	1	3
Ghana	Ewe	1		1	3	0	3
Ghana	Mossi-Dagomba	0		1	3	0	3
Greece	Muslims	0	2	0	3	0	3
Greece	Roma	0	0	0	3	0	3
Guatemala	Indigenous Peoples	6	3	1	3	1	3
Guinea	Fulani	0	3	1	3	0	3
Guinea	Malinka	0		1	3	1	3
Guinea	Susu	0		1	3	1	3
Guyana	Africans	0	1		3	0	3
Guyana	East Indians	0	0		2	0	3
Honduras	Black Karibs	0	2	1	3	1	3

Country	Group						
Honduras	Indigenous Peoples	0	3	1	3	1	3
Hungary	Roma	0	0	0	3	0	3
India	Assamese	4	3	1	3	1	3
India	Bodos	5	3	1	3	0	3
India	Kashmiris	6	3	1	3		3
India	Mizos	4	3	1	3		3
India	Muslims	0	0	1	3	0	3
India	Nagas	4	3	1	3	0	3
India	Sikhs	6	3	1	3	0	3
India	Tripuras	6	2	1	3	1	3
Indonesia	Acehnese	5	3	1	3	1	3
Indonesia	Chinese	0	1	0	2	0	3
Indonesia	East Timorese	5	3	1	3	0	3
Indonesia	Papuans	5	3	1	3	1	3
Iran	Arabs	2	3		3		3
Iran	Azerbaijanis	0	3	1	3	0	3
Iran	Baha'is	0	1	1	2	0	3
Iran	Bakhtiari	0			3	0	3
Iran	Baluchis	4	3	1	3	0	3
Iran	Christians	0	1	1	3	0	3
Iran	Kurds	6	3	1	3	0	3
Iran	Turkmen	4		0	3	0	3
Iraq	Kurds	7	3	1	3	1	3
Iraq	Shi'is	7		1	3	1	3
Iraq	Sunnis	0	1	1	3	0	3
Israel	Arabs	1	3	1	3		2
Israel	Palestinians	2	3	1	3	0	2
Italy	Roma	0	0	0	3	0	3

APPENDIX 2
(continued)

Country	Group	Rebel8095[1]	Settpat[2]	Homeland[3]	Duration[4]	Resource[5]	Ethnic Profile[6]
Italy	Sardinians	1	2	1	3	0	3
Italy	South Tyrolians	2	3	1	3		3
Japan	Koreans	0	1	0	2	0	1
Jordan	Palestinians	0	0	1	3	0	3
Kazakhstan	Germans	0	3	0	1		3
Kazakhstan	Russians	0	3	1	3	1	3
Kenya	Kalenjins	0		1	3	1	3
Kenya	Kikuyu	0	3	1	2	1	3
Kenya	Kisii	0	2	1	3	1	3
Kenya	Luhya	0	3	1	3	1	3
Kenya	Luo	0		1	3	1	3
Kenya	Maasais	0	2	1	3		3
Kyrgyzstan	Russians	0	1	0	2	0	3
Kyrgyzstan	Uzbeks	0	3	0	2	0	3
Laos	Hmong	4		1	2	0	3
Latvia	Russians	0	0	0	1	0	3
Lebanon	Druze	7	3	1	3	0	3
Lebanon	Maronite Christians	7	3	1	3	0	3
Lebanon	Palestinians	7		0	1		3
Lebanon	Shi'is	7	3	1	3	0	3
Lebanon	Sunnis	7	0	1	3	0	3
Lithuania	Poles	0	3	1	3	0	2
Lithuania	Russians	1	0	0	1	0	2
Macedonia	Albanians	3	3	1	3	1	3

Macedonia	Roma	0		0	3	3
Macedonia	Serbs	0		0	3	3
Madagascar	Merina	3		1	3	3
Malaysia	Chinese	0	0	0	2	3
Malaysia	Dayaks	0	2	1	3	3
Malaysia	East Indians	0		0	2	3
Malaysia	Kadazans	0	3	1	3	3
Mali	Tuareg	0		1	3	3
Mauritania	Black Moors	0	0	1	3	3
Mauritania	Kewri	4		1	3	3
Mexico	Mayans	6		1	3	3
Mexico	Other Indigenous	0	0	1	3	3
Mexico	Zapotecs	3	3	1	3	3
Moldova	Gagauz	0	2	1	2	3
Moldova	Slavs	5	3	0	1	3
Morocco	Berbers	0		1	3	3
Morocco	Saharawis	7	3	1	3	3
Namibia	Basters	0	3	1	2	3
Namibia	Europeans	0	1	1	2	0
Namibia	San Bushmen	0		1	3	0
New Zealand	Maori	0		1	3	2
Nicaragua	Indigenous Peoples	6	2	1	3	1
Niger	Tuareg	5		1	3	0
Nigeria	Ibo	0	3	1	3	1
Nigeria	Ogani	0	3	1	3	1
Nigeria	Yoruba	0	3	1	3	1
Pakistan	Ahmadis	0	0	1	2	0
Pakistan	Baluchis	1	3	1	3	0

APPENDIX 2
(continued)

Country/Group		Rebel8095[1]	Settpat[2]	Homeland[3]	Duration[4]	Resource[5]	Ethnic Profile[6]
Pakistan	Hindus	0	2	0	3		3
Pakistan	Mohajirs	2	1	0	1	0	3
Pakistan	Pashtuns (Pushtuns)	6	3	1	3	0	3
Pakistan	Sindhis	4	3	1	3	1	3
Panama	Blacks	0	1	1	2	0	3
Panama	Chinese	0	1	0	1	0	3
Panama	Indigenous Peoples	0		1	3	1	3
Papua N.G.	Bouganvilleans	4	3	1	3	0	3
Peru	Blacks (Afro-Peruvians)	0		1	3		3
Peru	Indigenous Highland PPLS	0	2	1	3	1	3
Peru	Lowland Indigenous PPLS	0		1	3	1	3
Philippines	Igorots	5		1	3	0	3
Philippines	Moros	6	3	1	3	0	3
Romania	Magyars	0	2	1	3	1	3
Romania	Roma	0	0	0	3	0	3
Russia	Avars	1		1	3		3
Russia	Buryat	0	2	1	3	1	3
Russia	Chechens	7	3	1	3	1	3
Russia	Ingush	3	3	1	3	0	3
Russia	Karachay	0	2	1	3	0	3
Russia	Kumyks	0	2	1	3	1	3
Russia	Lezgins		0	1	3	0	3
Russia	Roma	0	0	1	3	0	3
Russia	Tatars	0	3	1	3	1	3

Country	Group						
Russia	Tuvinians	0	3	1	3	1	3
Russia	Yakut	0	3	1	3	1	3
Rwanda	Hutus	2	0	1	3	0	0
Rwanda	Tutsis	7	0	1	3	0	0
Saudi Arabia	Shi'is	1	2	1	3	1	1
Senegal	Diolas in Casamance	4	3	1	3	1	3
Sierra Leone	Creoles	0	1	0	2	0	3
Sierra Leone	Limba	0		1	3	0	3
Sierra Leone	Mende	0		1	3	1	3
Sierra Leone	Temne	6	3	1	3	0	3
Singapore	Malays	0	0		1	0	0
Slovakia	Hungarians	0	2	1	3	1	3
Slovakia	Roma	0	0	0	3	0	3
Somalia	Issaq	7		1	3	0	3
South Africa	Asians	0	1	0	2	0	3
South Africa	Coloreds	0	3	1	3		3
South Africa	Europeans	1	0	1	3	0	3
South Africa	Xhosa	2	3	1	3	0	3
South Africa	Zulus	0	3	1	3	0	3
South Korea	Honamese	1	3	1	3	0	1
Spain	Basques	2	3	1	3	1	3
Spain	Catalans	2	3	1	3	1	3
Spain	Roma	0	0	0	3	0	3
Sri Lanka	Indian Tamils	0	2	0	2	0	3
Sri Lanka	Sri Lankan Tamils	7	3	1	3	1	3
Sudan	Southerners	7	3	1	3	1	3
Switzerland	Jurassians	2	2	1	3	0	3
Syria	Alawi	0	3	1	3	0	3

Country	Group	Rebel8095[1]	Settpat[2]	Homeland[3]	Duration[4]	Resource[5]	Ethnic Profile[6]
Taiwan	Aboriginal Taiwanese	0	2	1	3	0	2
Taiwan	Mainland Chinese	0	1	0	1	0	2
Taiwan	Taiwanese	0	0	1	3	0	2
Tajikistan	Russians	0	3	0	2	0	3
Thailand	Chinese	0	1	1	2	0	3
Thailand	Malay-Muslims	2	3	0	3		3
Thailand	Northern Hill Tribes	0		1	3	0	3
Togo	Ewe	7		1	3	1	3
Togo	Kabre	3		1	3	1	3
Turkey	Kurds	0		1	3	1	3
Turkmenistan	Russians	0	1	0	2	0	3
Uganda	Acholi	5		1	3	0	3
Uganda	Baganda	7	3	1	3	0	3
Ukraine	Crimean Russians	0	3	1	1	0	3
Ukraine	Crimean Tartars	0	2	1	3	0	3
Ukraine	Russians	0	2	1	2	1	3
United Kingdom	Afro-Caribbeans	0	1	0	1	0	3
United Kingdom	Asians	0	1	0	1	0	3
United Kingdom	Catholics in N. Ireland	2	2	1	3	0	3
United Kingdom	Scots	1	3	1	3	0	3
United States	African Americans	0	0	1	3	0	3
United States	Hispanics	2		0	3		3
United States	Native Americans	0	2	1	3		3
United States	Native Hawaiians	0	0	1	3	0	3

Uzbekistan	Russians	0	1	0	2	0	3
Venezuela	Blacks	0	1	1	3	1	3
Venezuela	Indigenous Peoples	1	1	1	3	0	3
Vietnam	Chinese	0	1	1	2	0	3
Vietnam	Montagnards	1	2	1	3	0	3
Yugoslavia	Croats	0	2	1	3	1	3
Yugoslavia	Hungarians	0	3	1	3	1	3
Yugoslavia	Kosovo Albanians	3	3	1	3	1	3
Yugoslavia	Roma	0	0	0	3	0	3
Yugoslavia	Sandzak Muslims	0	3	1	3	0	3
Zambia	Bemebe	3	3	1	3	1	3
Zambia	Lozi	3	3	1	3	0	3
Zimbabwe	Europeans	0	1	1	1	0	3
Zimbabwe	Ndebele	4	3	1	2	1	3

[1] This variable indicates the level of rebellion for 1980–95: 0 indicates no rebellion, and 7 indicates a protracted civil war. Other scores indicate the level of rebellion between these extremes.

[2] SETTPAT describes the settlement pattern of the ethnic group: 0 indicates dispersed, 1 indicates urban, 2 indicates concentrated minority, and 3 indicates concentrated majority.

[3] HOMELAND indicates whether the group regards the region in which they are residing as part or all of their homeland territory: 0 indicates they do not, and 1 indicates they do.

[4] DURATION indicates how long a group has resided in a given place: 0 indicates residence since 1945, 1 indicates residence beginning between 1800 and 1945, and 2 indicates residence since before 1800.

[5] RESOURCE indicates the resource richness of the region in which the group resides: 0 indicates that the region contains no natural or man-made resources, and 1 indicates that it does. I have a fuller form of this variable, which indicates whether the resources are man-made, natural, or both. Readers can contact me directly for these data.

[6] ETHNIC PROFILE indicates the number of ethnic groups that make up the state in which the group resides: 0 indicates the state has only dispersed groups, 1 indicates the state is homogeneous or contains one concentrated group with dispersed minorities, 2 indicates two concentrated groups with or without dispersed minorities, and 3 indicates that the state contains three or more concentrated groups with or without dispersed minorities.

APPENDIX 3

Ethnic Data for Autonomous Units of Russian Federation[a]

	Total Population	Titular Nation	% Titular	# of Titulars	% Russian	# of Russians	% of Total in RF in Region
Republics							
Adygey	432,046	Adygey	22.1	95,439	68.0	293,640	77.7
Altay	190,831	Altay	31.0	59,130	60.4	115,118	85.2
Bashkortostan	3,943,113	Bashkirs	22.9	863,808	39.3	1,548,291	29.2
Buryatia	1,038,252	Buryats	24.0	249,525	70.0	726,165	59.3
Checheno-Ingushetia	1,270,429	Chechens	57.8	734,501	23.1	293,771	81.7
		Ingush	12.9	163,762	—	—	76.1
Chuvashia	1,338,023	Chuvash	67.8	906,922	26.7	357,120	77.4
Dagestan[b]	1,802,188		80.2	1,444,795	9.2	165,940	51.1
Kabardino-Balkaria	752,531	Kabards	48.2	363,494	32.0	240,750	94.2
		Balkars	9.4	70,793	—	—	90.4
Kalmykia	322,579	Kalmyks	45.4	146,316	37.7	121,531	88.2
Karachay-Cherkessia	414,970	Karachay	31.2	129,449	42.4	175,931	86.1
		Cherkess	9.7	40,241	—	—	79.3
Karelia	790,150	Karelians	10.0	78,928	73.6	581,571	63.2
Khakassia	566,861	Khakass	11.1	62,859	79.5	450,430	80.1
Komi	1,250,847	Komi	23.3	291,542	57.7	721,780	86.7
Mari El	749,332	Mari	43.3	324,349	47.5	355,973	50.4
Mordva	963,504	Mordva	32.5	313,420	60.8	586,147	29.2
North Ossetia	632,428	Ossetians	53.0	334,876	29.9	189,159	83.2
Sakha (Yakutia)	1,094,065	Yakuts	33.4	365,236	50.3	550,263	96.1

Region	Nationality						
Tatarstan	Tatars	3,641,742	48.5	1,765,404	43.3	1,575,361	32.0
Tuva	Tuvinians	308,557	64.3	198,448	32.0	98,831	96.3
Udmurtia	Udmurts	1,605,663	30.9	496,522	58.9	945,216	69.5
Oblasts							
Birobidzhan	Jews	214,085	4.2	8,887	83.2	178,087	1.7
Okrugs							
Buryatia	Buryats	77,188	54.9	42,362	40.8	31,473	10.1
Chukchi	Chukchi	163,934	7.3	11,914	66.1	108,297	78.5
Evenki	Evenksi	24,769	14.0	3,480	67.5	16,718	11.6
Khanty-Mansi	Khanty	1,282,396	0.9	11,892	66.3	850,297	60.4
	Mansi		0.5	6,562	—	—	
Komi-Permyak	Komi-Permyak	158,526	60.2	95,415	36.1	57,272	64.8
Koryak	Koryaks	39,940	16.5	6,572	62.0	24,773	34.9
Nentsy	Nentsy	53,912	11.9	6,423	65.8	35,489	18.3
Taymyr	Dolgans	55,803	8.9	4,939	67.1	37,438	7.0
	Nentsy		4.8	2,446	—	—	
Ust'-Orda Buriyat	Buryats	135,870	36.2	49,298	56.5	76,827	11.7
Yamalo-Nenets	Nentsy	494,844	4.2	20,917	59.2	292,808	59.8

a Tabulated using data from the *1989 Soviet Census* 7, part 1, table 4, pp. 104–680.

b For Dagestan, the category of titular nation includes 10 ethnic groups under the category "The Peoples of Dagestan." These people include the following nationalities and their respective percentages and numbers: Avars, 27.5 (496,077); Aguls, 0.8 (13,791); Dargins, 15.6 (280,431); Kumyks, 12.9 (231,805); Laks, 5.1 (91,682); Lezgins, 11.3 (204,370); Nogais, 1.6 (28,294); Rutuls, 0.8 (14,955); Tabassarans, 4.3 (78,196); and Tsakhurs, 0.3 (5,194). They total 80.2 percent of the population, and none of the groups constitutes a majority.

Notes

Notes to Chapter 1
The Forgotten Meaning of Territory

The poem by Uzbek poet Cholpan Ergash is reprinted in Connor, "The Impact of Homelands," p. 17.

1. Fearon, "Rationalist Explanations for War."

2. Whereas Fearon largely rejects the indivisibility (obstacle) as a cause of war, others do not, including Thomas Schelling (*Strategy of Conflict*); Fred C. Iklé (*How Nations Negotiate*); Glenn Snyder and Paul Diesing (*Conflict among Nations*, chaps. 2 and 3); Janice Gross Stein (*Getting to the Table*, chap. 8); Alexander George and Gordon Craig (*Force and Statecraft*, chap. 12); Roger Fisher ("Fractionating Conflict," pp. 91–109; John Vasquez ("The Tangibility of Issues," pp. 179–92); and Paul F. Diehl ("What Are They Fighting For?" pp. 333–44). A more general social science treatment can be found in Elster's, *Solomonic Judgements*.

3. Previous research falls under two disciplinary rubrics. International relations scholars tend to restrict their analysis to material considerations (for example, resources) and to impute state motivations to ethnic groups (if they consider ethnic groups at all). Comparativists and area specialists often ignore material considerations and state motivations (that is, they do not consider the interests of the state acting in the capacity of an international actor) and focus on nonmaterial factors (language rights, status), or they produce analyses that are largely sui generis and are not easily generalized. By restricting the analysis to only one type of actor or by assuming symmetrical interests, this research does not pay sufficient attention to the full range of motivations that different actors might bring when bargaining over territory.

4. International relations scholars have tended to equate ethnic groups and nations with states in their application of tenets of neorealism to internal conflicts. Although their approach is consistent with the applicability of such notions as anarchy and self-help at both levels of analysis, these other approaches have tended to emphasize material factors and the balance of capabilities as causes of conflict. Security of identity, attachment to territory, and legitimacy tend not to be considered. International relations scholarship that conflates ethnic groups with states includes Van Evera's "Hypotheses on Nationalism and War," Posen's "Security Dilemma and Ethnic Conflict," and Wagner's "Causes of Peace." An exception is Waever, Buzan, Kelstrup, and Lemaitre's *Identity, Migration, and the New Security Agenda*. For an excellent review and critique of neorealism and its application to internal wars, see David's "Internal War." For a fine review of international relations studies of ethnicity and nationalism, see Lars-Erik Cederman, "Nationalism and Ethnicity."

5. Fearon and Laitin, "Explaining Interethnic Cooperation." The literature on the politics of ethnic conflict and its management is vast. Some of the best treat-

ments include Byman, *Keeping the Peace*; Esman, *Ethnic Politics*; McGarry and O'Leary, *The Politics of Ethnic Conflict Regulation*; Montville, *Conflict and Peacemaking*; and Horowitz, *Ethnic Groups in Conflict*.

6. Wallensteen and Sollenberg, "Armed Conflicts."

7. Trachtenberg, "Intervention in Historical Perspective," p. 31.

8. See Kaufmann's, "Possible and Impossible Solutions," Schaeffer, *Warpaths*, and Kumar, "The Troubled History of Partition."

9. Cf. Blainey, *Causes of War*, and Walt, *Revolution and War*. On ethnic conflicts in particular, see Lake and Rothschild, *The International Spread of Ethnic Conflict*. This last volume presents both pessimistic and optimistic assessments on the likelihood of the spread of ethnic conflict across interstate boundaries.

10. On refugee flows and other problems associated with ethnic conflicts, see Newland, "Ethnic Conflict and Refugees"; Weiner, "Bad Neighbors, Bad Neighborhoods"; and Ryan, *Ethnic Conflict*.

11. This was less true prior to World War I, when the principle of national self-determination was elevated to the status of an international and legitimate norm. Prior to World War I, defeated peoples often resented defeat but accepted it nonetheless. Once the principle of national self-determination became a norm, then the very idea of rule by "others" was considered an affront. Ethnic and national conflict subsequently emerged as the rule rather than the exception. Fortunately, most contemporary ethnic and national conflicts—and these are hardly restricted to the developing world—remain nonviolent.

12. The number of recently published edited volumes demonstrates the multitude of scholars and practitioners interested in understanding the dynamics of nationalism, ethnicity, and violence since the end of the cold war. See, for example, Brown, *Ethnic Conflict and International Security*; Tiech and Porter, *The National Question in Europe*; Kupchan, *Nationalism and Nationalities*; Brown, *The International Dimensions of Internal Conflict*; Brown and Ganguly, *Government Policies*; Lake and Rothschild, *The International Spread of Ethnic Conflict*; Carment and James, *Peace in the Midst of Wars*; Walter and Snyder, *Civil Wars*; and Szayna, *Identifying Potential Ethnic Conflict*.

13. Within the vast modernization and development literature, logical arguments and evidence have supported contradictory claims. Donald Horowitz, for example, hypothesizes that the level of economic development among an ethnic group and the region in which it resides contributes to separatism; low development on both dimensions equals danger. Jean LaPonce argues that both economically advanced and backward groups and regions might seek independence. Research has supported both sets of hypotheses. See Horowitz, *Ethnic Groups in Ethnic Conflict*, especially chap. 6, and LaPonce, *Languages and Their Territories*, especially pp. 137–49. The seminal work is Deutsch's, *Nationalism and Social Communication*. For critiques, see Hecter's *Internal Colonialism*. Also see his "Dynamics of Secession" and, with Levy, "The Comparative Analysis of Ethnoregional Movements"; Tiryakian and Rogowski, *New Nationalisms*; and Coakley, *Territorial Management*, for more general accounts of national regional movements.

14. Anderson, *Imagined Communities*; Gellner, *Nations and Nationalism*; Hobsbawm, *Nations and Nationalism*. Also see Hroch, *Social Preconditions*.

15. See Wolf, *Peasant Wars.*

16. For an excellent review of this literature, see Saul Newman, "Does Modernization Breed Ethnic Political Conflict?" More recent research within this materialist tradition is being conducted under the auspices of the World Bank, stressing economic variables and development as causes of civil war more generally; see Collier and Hoeffler, "Justice-Seeking."

17. Walker Connor spells out this logic in "Eco- or Ethno-Nationalism?"

18. See Davies, "The J-Curve"; Gurr, *Why Men Rebel*; and Olzak, *The Dynamics of Ethnic Competition.*

19. Within this interethnic-competition approach, some scholars argue that because ethnic groups occupy distinct economic niches, which have discrete territorial locations, conflicts often become geographically based. The argument works best for immigrant groups who try to move beyond their particular niche; different groups then compete for the same resources. The seminal work on this is Barth, *Ethnic Groups.* Thinking along similar lines about "middleman minorities" can be found in Horowitz's *Ethnic Groups in Conflict*, especially pp. 116–24. Again, a crucial element is some sort of identity marker, such as ethnicity.

20. Timor Kuran goes one step further in the critique and argues that not only can we as outsiders not know each individual's "tipping point" of dissatisfaction, but we do not and cannot even know our own. Predicting violence based on relative deprivation is impossible. See Kuran, "Now out of Never."

21. For a discussion of the value of territory, see Diehl and Goertz, "Entering International Society." Diehl and Goertz also consider the "relational" value of the territory in which the actors attach some sort of historical or identity-based value to the territory, and this value varies with the actors. Yet the indicators they use in their model are "materially-based," and the value of the territory is considered only from the perspective of the state or imperial power.

22. Traditional and contemporary international relations theories lead us to expect that strategic or intrinsic worth should cause the strongest reaction from the state. And, indeed, Paul Huth found that a powerful predictor of territorial disputes among states was the desire to control strategically located territory. Further, Huth found that the presence of a bordering minority with linguistic or cultural ties to a challenger state was "*not a primary cause* of territorial disputes between states in the post–World War II period. Huth, *Standing Your Ground*, chap. 4 (p. 81 for quotation, his emphasis).

23. A state's concern with economic autarky is the most obvious manifestation. See, for example, Snyder, *Myths of Empire*, pp. 3–4, 24–25; Gilpin, *War and Change*, chap. 3; Quincy Wright, *A Study of War*, pp. 167–72; and Waltz, *Theory of International Politics*, chap. 7.

24. The "geostrategy school" is epitomized by Mackinder, "Geographical Pivot," and Spykman, *The Geography of Peace*; Sprout and Sprout, *Ecological Paradigm.* Whereas Mackinder and Spykman spent much of their energy on identifying key locations, Sprout and Sprout went further in exploring not only how geography informs actors' interests but also how it conditions their behavior.

For more empirical analyses of objective geographic elements, see Harvey Starr's and Benjamin Most's numerous articles testing whether shared borders and the proximity of states to one another contribute to a state's proclivity for war. Starr, "Opportunity and Willingness" and "Joining Political and Geographic Perspectives": Starr and Most, "Contagion and Border Effects" and "Forms and Processes of War Diffusion." Also see Siverson and Starr, *Diffusion of War.* For a review of this literature, see Diehl, "Geography and War." Diehl points out that none of these authors argued that geography is all determinative. Rather, geography is only "one of many influences that defines [*sic*] the possibilities of war" (p. 14). For a general empirical exploration of the role of territory since 1816 in the interstate system, see Goertz and Diehl, *Territorial Changes.* Also see Liberman, "The Spoils of Conquest."

25. Agnew, *Place and Politics.* Agnew parses the meaning of *place* in three ways: locale, location, and "sense of place." Locale refers to the setting of social interactions; location is a wider setting and involves broader social interactions (for example, at the state and international levels); sense of place describes a more subjective, emotive attachment to land in which territory is tied to ancestors and is viewed as the homeland. For an impressive empirical investigation of the former Soviet Union informed by Agnew's framework, see Kaiser, *The Geography of Nationalism.*

26. Brewer, "Social Identity. Brewer and Gardner, "Who Is This 'we'?"

27. Exemplars of this school are Shils, "Primordial, Personal"; Geertz, "Integrative Revolution"; and Isaacs, *Idols of the Tribe.* Bloom's *Personal Identity* and the more empirical account of the Middle East conflict as analyzed in *Self-Involvement in the Middle East Conflict,* by the Committee on International Relations. For an account that combines biology with sociology, see Van den Berghe, "Race and Ethnicity."

28. For an analysis of how cooperation within ethnic groups may foster cooperation between different ethnic groups, see Fearon and Laitin, "Explaining Interethnic Cooperation."

29. The first scholar to apply the security dilemma to ethnic conflict is Posen, "Security Dilemma and Ethnic Conflict." This approach has produced a vast cottage industry. A comprehensive review can be found in Rose's, "Security Dilemma and Ethnic Conflict."

30. For an interesting and important theoretical treatment of other emotions, as well as fear, in relation to status among ethnic groups, see Petersen, *Understanding Ethnic Violence.*

31. These are conditions that Robert Jervis identified as leading to the most intense security dilemma. Jervis, "Cooperation under the Security Dilemma."

32. For recent work in this area, see Glaser, "Political Consequences of Military Strategy" and "Security Dilemma Revisited."

33. Three of the best works on elite-manipulation approaches are Brass, *Ethnicity and Nationalism*; Gagnon, "Ethnic Nationalism"; and Gourevitch, "The Reemergence of Peripheral Nationalisms."

34. Snyder and Ballentine, "Nationalism and the Marketplace."

35. For an interesting discussion of the role of nationalism among Croats and Serbs, see Ignatieff, *Blood and Belonging*, especially pp. 21–28.

36. According to the Kosovo Commission Report, this is precisely what happened to Milosevic: "By playing the nationalist and ethnic card in Kosovo as his path to power, Milosevic had made himself captive of internal ideological forces

that were unwilling to compromise on Kosovo." Independent Commission on Kosovo, *Kosovo Report*, p. 132.

37. Jane Perlez, "Slovak Leader Fans Region's Old Ethnic Flames," *New York Times*, October 12, 1997.

38. Actually, the explanation in such cases reduces to the claim that such actors are in fact not rational. This is hardly satisfactory, however.

39. Ethnic violence can occur in four situations: first; among members of an ethnic group; second, between different ethnic groups; third, between two states; fourth, between an ethnic group and a state. In the first type, referred to as intraethnic, violence occurs when members of an ethnic group resort to violence against their fellow members. The violence is restricted to the group. Because this theory assumes that both actors are unitary, it has little to say about the first type of conflict, that which occurs within a group. In the second type, violence emerges among two different ethnic groups. This type is often referred to as communal violence. The third type of conflict, between two states, is referred to as interstate war. The fourth type of violence occurs between an ethnic group and individuals, usually soldiers, fighting on behalf of the state. It often takes the form of general civil war and may entail fights to control the government or secessionist bids. The last type constitutes the research domain of this book.

40. One scholar found that since 1945 the largest number of conflicts were about territorial questions, and a majority of these involved the search for greater autonomy or secession from the state. See Gantzel, "War in the Post–World War II World." Also see Gantzel and Schwinghammer, *Die Kriege nach dem zweiten Weltkrieg*.

41. Territory is not unimportant in traditional state-to-state interactions but has a different meaning. Kalevi Holsti and John Vasquez (using Holsti's data set) have shown that contests over territory have figured prominently in interstate wars over the last three hundred years. Using a liberal measure of "territorial issues," Vasquez estimates that 149 of the 177 wars (84 percent) involved issues related to territory. Holsti, *Peace and War*, and Vasquez, *War Puzzle*, chap. 4.

42. For the merits of a research design that includes quantitative and qualitative methods, see King, Keohane, and Verba, *Designing Social Inquiry*.

43. The Correlates of War data set, including the more recent section on civil wars, is not helpful here. First, I would like to have variance on both the independent and dependent variables. Examining instances of civil war would preclude variance on the latter. Moreover, of the 106 civil wars, almost all "were between members of the same ethnic or linguistic family." In the case of the U.S. Civil War, Singer and Small stated, "However, the lack of ethnic differences between the two sides, as well as the military contention for control of areas near the capital, clearly place the war in the civil category." Singer and Small seemed biased against including civil wars they deemed "ethnic." Small and Singer, *Resort to Arms*, appendix A, p. 317.

44. Some works on case-study methodology include George's "Case Studies and Theory Development": George and McKeown's "Case Studies and Theories"; King, Keohane, and Verba, *Designing Social Inquiry*, Van Evera, *Guide to Methods*, pp. 49–88; and Bates et al.'s *Analytic Narratives*, pp. 3–22.

45. This collection of maps has two problems, however. First, the data used to

detail the maps are well over thirty years old. Although, for the most part, the territorial distribution of ethnic groups is similar to what it was then (areas that have undergone upheaval and major population movements are excepted), proportional distributions are not. Second, these maps only represent linguistic groups; religious and racial groups are not considered. Thus for cases in which religion served as the underlying cleavage, the Soviet atlas is of limited use. This reliance on linguistic groupings also implies that I had to be careful of the Soviet categorization of peoples and places. The atlas categorizes the population of Birobidzhan not as Jewish but as Yiddish speakers.

46. The tight connection of the "Georgian" ethnicity with the state of Georgia provides for an additional case study. Chapters 6 and 7 spell this out.

47. Nationalist leaders are free to construct national identities, but not to do as they please.

Notes to Chapter 2
Indivisible Territory and Ethnic War

Anthony Smith, *The Ethnic Origins of Nations*, p. 163.

1. See appendix 1.

2. Fearon, "Rationalist Explanations."

3. Barbara Walter's article on how internal wars end, for example, focuses our attention on how third-party intervention can ease the commitment problem and allow actors to reach a negotiated settlement. James Fearon modeled the effects of private or imperfect information on states seeking to resolve disputes. Walter, "Critical Barrier," and Fearon, "Rationalist Explanations."

4. Although this book is about ethnic violence between ethnic groups and states, when an ethnic group dominates a state and when the group sees the same territory as intrinsic to its respective state and ethnic group, then this theory can be readily applied to states. Jürgen Habermas explains this dynamic as a situation in which "[t]his leads to a double coding of membership, with the result that the legal status defined in terms of civil rights also implies membership in a culturally defined community." Habermas, *The Inclusion of the Other*, p. 113.

5. Jerome Segal and his colleagues found that a key issue regarding the division of Jerusalem among the Palestinians and the Israeli Jews they surveyed is their inability and unwillingness to recognize as legitimate the other group's claims to the same territory. See Segal et al., *Negotiating Jerusalem*.

6. Al Aksa refers to the site of the Al Aksa Mosque and the Dome of the Rock shrine, which is venerated by Muslims (called Al Haram al Sharif, or noble sanctuary). This site is also venerated by the Jews, as it is the location of the First and Second Temple. Greenberg, "Chief Rabbis."

7. As noted in chapter 1, it is useful to recall that a theory, by its very nature, abstracts from reality and advances assumptions that may or may not prove true empirically. As a result, many of the statements advanced in this section are not intended to stand as descriptions of empirical reality (though they may reflect it accurately). They are intended to be hypothetical and tentative, not absolute.

8. When I use the terms *ethnic groups* and *states*, in each case I mean the

individuals who are responsible for acting on their behalf. This analytic simplification, which portrays the ethnic group and state as unitary, rational actors, is useful in modeling this kind of interaction. However, it ought not to be mistaken for reality.

9. One way around the indivisibility issue is to admit to the possibility of issue indivisibility rhetorically, but then add the concept of side payments to effectively eliminate issue indivisibility from consideration. Catalan nationalists, for example, may trade political autonomy for increased economic autonomy. Yet this is a troubling approach. It backs us up only one level of analysis: instead of asking, Under what conditions will actors consider a given issue indivisible? we must now ask, Why do some actors accept side payments on indivisible issues while others do not? The Algerians, North Vietnamese, Bengalis, Palestinians, and Chechens were offered side payments and refused.

10. Smith, *Ethnic Origins*, pp. 22–31. Only a handful of ethnic groups lack an association with a given territory.

11. Morley and Robins, "No Place like Heimat," p. 8.

12. For excellent discussions of the state, see Mann, *States, War*, especially chap. 1; Tilly, "Reflections" and "War Making"; Skocpol, "Bringing the State Back In" pp. 3–37; and *States and Social Revolutions*, especially chap. 1.

13. See Waltz, *Theory of International Politics*.

14. On this point in particular, see Scott, *Seeing like a State*.

15. In this book, to "demand sovereignty" means demanding full independence, namely the creation of a new state within the international system of states.

16. An important consideration is exactly how settlement patterns emerged to begin with. Natural processes, mass migration following natural and man-made catastrophes, deportations, ethnic cleansing, genocide, imperial relocation and forced settlements, and natural birthrates are all possible explanations. This analysis takes patterns as a given, although why a pattern has emerged is discussed if it bears directly on the case at hand.

17. Koltso, "Territorialising Diasporas."

18. The Sinhalese are largely seen as being in control of the "state," making this a case for an actor with both ethnic and state-centric interests. If an ethnic group dominates a state, we can expect such actors to be motivated by both sets of interests. Other examples include the former Yugoslavia, where the Serbs were seen as dominant; the former Soviet Union, the Russians; Israel, the Jews; Rwanda, the Tutsi; Turkey, the Turks; Germany, the Germans; and so on.

19. Eelam consists of the Northern and Eastern Provinces. The Tamil United Liberation Front, the main organization committed to the creation of an independent Eelam, claimed, "Whereas throughout the centuries from the dawn of history, the Sinhalese and Tamil nations have divided between them the possession of Ceylon, the Sinhalese inhabiting the interior parts of the country in its southern and western parts . . . and the Tamils possessing the northern and eastern districts." According to the 1981 census, the Sri Lankan Tamils constituted 86 percent of the Northern Province and 41 percent of the Eastern (in these two provinces combined, they comprise 65 percent of the population), and 71 per-

cent of all Sri Lankan Tamils in Sri Lanka lived in these two provinces. An independent Eelam would deprive Sri Lanka of two-thirds of its coastline, and Muslims in the Eastern Province, comprising about 33 percent, fear that the Sri Lankan Tamils will ethnically cleanse the territory. See Peiris, "An Appraisal." Also see K.H.J. Wijayadasa, "Tamil 'Homeland' Theory of EP-A Hoax," *The Island*, March 29, 1998.

20. Riggins, "Sri Lanka."

21. The Tamils fear government settlements of Sinhalese in areas deemed their traditional homeland. See Manogaran, "Sinhalese-Tamil Relations." Available online at www.tamilnation.org/conflictresolution/cnfus96/cnf02.htm.

22. The best treatment of the requirements of collective action remains Tilly's *From Mobilization to Revolution*, chap. 3.

23. For example, a concentrated minority may constitute 49 percent of a region's population, and two other groups may make up about 25 percent of the population. Or conversely, a concentrated-minority might simply be 25 percent of a population of which another group constitutes the remaining 75 percent.

24. Little theorizing exists on legitimacy and ethnic claims. Donald Horowitz argues that prior occupation is the strongest claim to legitimacy. Ernest Gellner touches on some of these issues in his discussion of what should constitute the proper boundaries of political units in "Nationalism in a Vacuum," pp. 243–54. For a discussion of majority rule as a legitimating principle, see Robert Dahl's essay "Democracy, Majority Rule, and Gorbachev's Referendum," *Dissent* (fall 1991) 491–96. Horowitz's discussion can be found in *Ethnic Groups*.

25. The Jews in Israel are a good example. Jews often highlight their achievements in irrigating once fallow land and building viable settlements as a way of enhancing the legitimacy of claims to Israeli-occupied territory.

26. Grant, *Recent British Battles*, p. 345.

27. Tenure may depend on two factors: (1) the longer a group has lived in a particular place and has had historical ties to the land, the more legitimate its claims; and (2) the group that can claim to have occupied the territory first may have a legitimate case, regardless of the number of ethnic brethren who currently inhabit the territory. In most cases, these arguments reduce to the same thing: the first national on the territory has, ipso facto, entitled subsequent nationals to the claim of duration. However, the event that proves the exception is a large diaspora. So, for example, one group occupies a land for fifty years and then subsequently abandons it (perhaps due to a drought). After some time, members of the group return to the abandoned land to find it occupied by another group. In this case the distinction between the two forms holds, because the original inhabitants did not occupy the land as long as its subsequent inhabitants, but they have a claim to have done so "first."

28. There is some disagreement among scholars as to whether majority rule is, or should be, the foundation principle or one of a handful of principles. Regardless of this principle's standing, it is regarded as foundational both among theorists and among those seeking self-determination by democratic means.

29. This matters because the world's most powerful states—including the United States—are democracies, making external support for groups seeking sovereignty both more likely and more useful. Support is more likely due to shared

values, and it is more useful because of the power and resources these states can bring to bear. NATO's 1999 intervention in Kosovo is a case in point.

30. Schelling, *The Strategy of Conflict*, p. 74.

31. An example is Israel's refusal to allow an official census of Palestinians living on "Israeli" territory. See Greenberg, "Palestinian Census."

32. External support matters a good deal in these cases.

33. For an excellent study of population movements, urbanization, and land issues, see Weiner, *Sons of the Soil*. Weiner points out that most of the migration to India's cities is from other urban areas and that migrants tend to be dispersed throughout the country, not concentrated in a particular region (p. 36). David Laitin provides support as well in his research on attitudes of Russians in non-Russian Soviet successor states toward assimilation. He found that only 14 percent believed that the "the future for Russians in their republic was best fulfilled by mobilizing politically as Russians." See Laitin, *Identity in Formation*, p. 202.

34. On the Russian tendency to emigrate back to Russia from the near abroad, see Chin and Kaiser, *Russians As the New Minority*.

35. Precedent setting could still affect relations with other states, however. One state may pressure a binational state to resist sovereignty demands in order not to set a precedent for its own national minorities. The Kurds of Iraq, Iran, and Turkey are the classic case.

36. See appendix 1.

37. Roger Fisher, "Fractionating Conflict," p. 100.

38. A state's concern about precedent setting also makes a powerful appeal to other multinational states, who may be indirectly damaged by another state's acquiescence to a secession. The status quo has itself become a powerful norm of interstate politics, to the degree that the intrinsic legitimacy or merit of claims is often subordinated to the potential of an outcome that might upset the status quo. After the forceful reannexation of Georgia in 1922, Lenin, for example, deflected criticism by placing the spotlight on the British and suggested the following course of action: "First, to evacuate Ireland and conduct a popular referendum there; second, to take the same steps in India; third, to apply the same measures in Korea; fourth, to take the same action in all countries where armies of any of the great imperialist powers are kept." As quoted in Connor, *National Question*, p. 218.

39. Gorbachev was criticized by many of his contemporaries who believed that by granting independence to the Baltic republics he could have prevented or at least delayed the collapse of the Soviet Union. For example, he could have granted independence on the grounds that because they had been independent prior to their forced annexation by the Soviet Union, that is, they had not *voluntarily* joined the union (one of the conditions detailing the status and rights of union republics under the Soviet constitution), their independence could not set a precedent to which any other union republic could appeal (the Baltics were the only union republics that met these strict criteria).

40. An alternative logic might operate as well. If violence is costly and the material or strategic worth of a territory is low, allowing secession might seem the more rational course in the face of a hostile threat to state survival. Facing a tradeoff between a simultaneous internal and interstate war and a low-cost secession, states might simply allow the nation to secede. Two tensions arise with this

argument, however. First and most important, if precedent-setting logic applies most intensely during a time of high perceived external threat, the true choice may be between (1) risking multiple consecutive secessions (or even worse, the alliance of a seceding national territory with a threatening external adversary) or (2) fighting two costly wars: one against a low-priority territory (in order to prevent a precedent) and the other against another state. Second, because even the most rational actors tend to underestimate the costs and risks of war, especially a government opposed to secessionist-minded nations, the risks of initiating war against a nation will generally be discounted compared with the risks of losing land and population in the face of an external threat.

41. The logic here is similar to the chain-store paradox in which a store precludes competition in the long term by forgoing profits and engaging in a price war in the short term in order to eliminate the competition. Selten, "Chain Store Paradox."

42. For an analysis of when an actor should attack given short-term but especially long-term considerations, see Brown, "Deterrence Failures." Donald Horowitz touches on the importance of the timing of action in *Ethnic Groups in Conflict*, p. 625 n. 38.

43. For excellent discussions of Israel's territorial dilemmas, see Lustick, *Unsettled States*, chap. 1; and David Newman, "Real Spaces, Symbolic Spaces."

44. There are also more traditional state justifications for intractability on the issue of exchanging land for peace: Israel is a small state surrounded by more populous enemies. In a war, Israel could exchange territory for time, which would materially improve its chances of survival. Moreover, some of the territory that has caused conflict is of particular strategic worth: the Golan Heights materially improve the offensive capabilities of the state that controls it. Israel's binational structure, however, precludes the operation of precedent setting.

45. I am assuming at least parity of capabilities between states and ethnic groups. In most cases the state will probably possess an abundance of military capability relative to the individual groups.

46. Presumably, they would not resort to arms if they calculated their chance at victory as zero. Also, nations may be able to perceive and pursue an entire range of goals short of what we more typically think of as "victory" in state-state contexts. Their requirements to win may be lower. The maxim that the weak side (that is, ethnic groups) wins by not losing looms large in these interactions. Finally, on-paper balances of forces can shift rapidly once violence starts. Cuba's Batista, for example, appeared to possess an overwhelming military advantage against Castro's revolutionaries, but Batista's ability to *use* his advantages effectively proved to be virtually nil. Whole units deserted or defected, and the tide quickly turned in favor of the "suicidal" revolutionaries.

• 47. Scott Sagan, for example, argues that in the case of the Pacific War, "Deterrence failed in 1941, despite the anticipated 'unacceptable' costs of war to Japan, because the costs of not going to war were considered even higher." Sagan, "Origins of the Pacific War," p. 350. For an examination of the conditions under which small states might attack large states, see Paul, *Asymmetric Conflicts.* For a concise discussion of when to initiate a war, see Mearsheimer, *Conventional Deterrence*, pp. 62–63.

48. Donald Horowitz provides an overview of some mechanisms and conditions that might be involved in the devolution of power within states in chapter 15 of *Ethnic Groups in Conflict*, pp. 601–52.

Notes to Chapter 3
Territory and Violence: A Statistical Assessment

1. These findings are very robust. I first tested some preliminary hypotheses on settlement patterns using phase 1 of the Minorities at Risk data set and found similar results. Subsequent analyses by other scholars have replicated my findings. For my earlier analysis, see Toft, "The Geography of Ethnic Conflict." For later tests of similar hypotheses, see Fearon and Laitin, "Ethnicity, Insurgency, and Civil War."

2. MAR data are available on-line at http://www.cidcm.umd.edu/inser/mar/home.htm. For explanations of the data set and empirical findings derived from MAR, see Gurr, *Minorities at Risk* and *Peoples against States*; and with Marshall and Khosla, "Peace and Conflict." Data for variables that are not included in the main data set can be obtained from me directly.

3. See, for example, Small and Singer, *Resort to Arms*; Licklider, "The Consequences of Negotiated Settlements," and Sambanis, "Partition As a Solution."

4. MAR consists of 275 politically active communal groups, defined as cultural or religious groups that do not have a recognized state or institutionalized status and whose members share a distinctive collective identity based on cultural or ascriptive traits that are salient to both members and nonmembers. To be included, a group must have a population of at least one hundred thousand, or else constitute more than 1 percent of its state's total population. All groups included in the MAR data set suffered from discriminatory policies and/or mobilized to protect or advance their interests. In other words, if a group is included in the data set, ethnic conflict is presumed. My theory makes the same assumption.

From the 275 cases, I excluded five: (1) the foreign workers of Switzerland, (2) the scheduled tribes of India, (3) the Saami of the Nordic countries, (4) the indigenous peoples of Paraguay, and (5) the Roma of Croatia. The first two were excluded because they are "economic groupings" with no attachment to land, and the third because it was categorized not under a particular state but under a region. The last two cases were missing codings for the concentration measures. The Haitian blacks of Dominica were missing a "REG" coding, but they did have codings for the composite concentration measure of GROUPCON. The Scots of the United Kingdom were also miscoded, but I corrected the coding. With the exclusion of these five cases, the total number of cases used in this analysis was 270. See appendix 2 for a listing of the cases and key variables.

5. I considered collapsing intermediate guerrilla activity into the high-intensity rebellion coding, but the scale of activity was sufficiently smaller to justify coding it under low-intensity rebellion. I checked to determine whether this collapsing skewed or changed the results, and it did not. In fact, having a higher threshold for high-intensity rebellion should generate higher confidence in the results.

6. MAR provides variables for the level of rebellion annually from 1985 as well. The values are obviously the same.

7. Although MAR is set up to measure rebellion at five-year intervals, for idiosyncratic reasons, not all of the periods comprise five years.

8. This figure indicates that of a possible mean value between 0 and 7 (from "no rebellion" to "protracted civil war"), these groups averaged 2.78 in the level of rebellious activity. The p-value indicates that the level of violence in these groups is statistically distinguishable from 0 by any conventional standard.

9. Pearson chi2(6) = 41.61, p = .000.

10. Recall that large-scale rebellion refers to engagement in large-scale guerrilla activity or a protracted civil war (that is, a series of 6 or 7 in MAR).

11. The sole urban group identified as engaging in rebellion consisted of the Russians of Georgia. This, however, might be a coding error: it was the former Soviet/Russian military that was engaged in the fighting in Abkhazia, not civilian resident Russians (who fled, along with ethnic Georgians and others).

12. Aside from rebellion and political protest, MAR includes a measure of communal conflict, or conflict with other ethnic groups. Activity under this type of conflict ranges from acts of harassment at one extreme to communal rioting and to communal warfare (defined as protracted, large-scale intergroup violence) at the other. Considering that urbanites and widely dispersed minorities comingle with other groups, we should not be surprised to find them engaged more readily in violence with other ethnic groups. Yet here their frequency of engagement in this type of conflict was equal to that of other groups, which was generally very low, and again, they had among the lowest mean scores. During the 1980s none of the urban or widely dispersed groups were engaged in communal warfare (three dispersed groups were engaged in deadly communal rioting, the Tutsi and Hutu of Burundi and the Muslims of India, but this finding was not statistically significant). Not surprisingly, these urban and widely dispersed groups shared low mean scores of communal conflict with their concentrated counterparts.

13. The only groups that had lower mean scores for nonviolent political protest were categorized under REG6/2 and REG6/3, or widely dispersed minority, interspersed, or degree of integration unknown. My inclination is not to read too much into these scores: the number of REG3/2 cases did not exceed eight, and for the REG3/3 cases, the fact that the degree of integration is unknown makes these cases suspect.

14. Glenny, *The Fall of Yugoslavia*, p. 123.

15. For an excellent discussion of nationalist discourses over Northern Ireland see, McGarry and O'Leary, *Explaining Northern Ireland*.

16. I tested these hypotheses using OLS regression. I also analyzed the data using an ordered probit model. The findings were the same: the coefficients were in the expected direction and were statistically significant. OLS output is presented here because it is simpler to interpret.

17. The independent variables are GNPPRCAP, GROUPCON, CONCENX8, REG1, SEPX, PROT85X, REGMAJD, ATRISK1, LANG, CUSTOM, BELIEF, RELIG, AUTLOST, CATNESS, POLDIS90, and AUTON90.

18. The ethnic-profit variable is a new variable I created for MAR. Coding this variable involved referencing ethnographic maps, reports, surveys, and books to determine where individual ethnic groups reside and whether the state contained one or more regionally concentrated ethnic group. The most helpful sources were

Atlas narodov mira and the multitude of maps produced by the United States Central Intelligence Agency (CIA). The CIA maps are available online at http://www.lib.utexas.edu/maps/index.html. Other sources include David H. Price, *Atlas of World Cultures: A Geographical Guide to EthnographicLiterature* (Newbury Park, Calif.: Sage Publications, 1989), Roland J.-L. Breton, *Atlas of the Languages and Ethnic Communities of South Asia* (Walnut Creek, Calif.: AltaMira Press, 1997), and James Minahan, *Nations without States: A Historical Dictionary of Contemporary National Movements* (Westport, Conn: Greenwood Press, 1996). See appendix 1 for the breakdown of states.

19. The resource-rich variable was coded using a variety of sources including ethnographic maps, United States Geological Survey maps, data from the World Bank, the Economist Intelligence Unit, newspaper accounts of fights over resources, and individual-country economic data. To test whether strategic worth alone affects violence, I created a variable of interstate borders (both land and maritime) and found that it was not statistically significant. Ethnic groups living in regions with interstate borders were neither more nor less likely to experience violence than those that did not have borders.

20. Ethnic groups in states with three or more concentrated groups displayed a mean score of rebellion of 1.90, and those in binational states ($n = 16$ or 6 percent) had a substantially lower score of 0.69. This descriptive statistic is a good indication that ethnic groups in multinational states experience more violence than those in binational states.

Notes to Chapter 4
Russia and Tatarstan

1. The epigraph to this chapter is a corollary to Napoleon Bonaparte's remark "Scratch a Russian and you will find a Tatar." Tatarstan is an autonomous republic within the internationally recognized state of the Russian Federation. It is referred to as Tatarstan or the Tatar Republic. I use the term *Tatars* to refer to people who identify with the group on linguistic, religious, or cultural grounds, whether or not they live within the borders of Tatarstan. I refer to Russia as "Russia" or the "Russian Federation."

2. In fact, because of the weak legitimacy of the independence movement, capabilities as a factor are hardly broached in this case.

3. Wixman, "The Middle Volga," p. 423.

4. After a ban of two centuries, in the eighteenth century Catherine the Great allowed Islam to be practiced again to curry favor with Tatar elites. This recognition lasted for almost a full century, until Islam and Tatar nationalism were deemed threatening to the Russian Empire and imperial control. Rorlich, *The Volga Tatars*, especially chap. 5.

5. Wixman explains that the Tatars and the Russians faced the same dilemma: to become a Tatar or a Russian meant to adopt the language and religion of the other. Hence they saw each other as threatening, and educational policies, especially those dealing with religion and language, were debated with consternation. Wixman, "The Middle Volga," p. 423.

6. These figures were rounded to the nearest thousand and were taken from

the *1989 Soviet Census* 7, part 1, table 2 (p. 10), table 3 (p. 66), and table 4 (p. 178). *Itogi Vsesoiuznoi perepisi naseleniia 1989 goda.* The number of Tatars in the Former Soviet Union includes all Tatars, not just Volga Tatars, who can more readily trace their roots to the region in and around Tatarstan. For a discussion of Crimean and "Kazan" Tatars, see d'Encausse, *Decline of an Empire,* pp. 191–199.

7. See Toropov, *Spravochnik novykh partii,* p. 5, who put the figure at 20–30 percent. Another estimate put the figure at 38 percent for the 1980s. See Raviot, "Tipy Natsionalizma," p. 46.

8. United States Information Agency, "Islam Commands Devotion."

9. Derlugian, "Historical Sociological Interpretations," p. 89.

10. Sheehy, "Tatarstan Asserts Its Sovereignty," p. 2 n. 6.

11. These data were taken from a Tatar Province Party Committee meeting and reported in *Pravda,* September 1, 1990, p. 3.

12. When asked in a unionwide referendum on March 17, 1991, whether they considered "it necessary to preserve the Union of Soviet Socialist Republics as a renewed federation of equal, sovereign republics, in which the rights and freedoms of the people of all nationalities will be completely guaranteed," 87.5 percent of Tatar voters supported sustaining the Soviet Union. The referendum was held in nine republics: Azerbaijan, Byelorussia, Kazakhstan, Kyrgyzstan, Russia, Tajikistan, Turkmenistan, Ukraine, and Uzbekistan. The three Baltic republics, Armenia, Georgia, and Moldova, refused to participate. Overall, 76.4 percent of voters were in favor of sustaining the union.

13. Lithuania's per capita income in the late 1980s was 1,500 rubles, whereas Tatarstan's was a mere 212 rubles. Tatar Province Party Committee meeting, reported in *Pravda,* September 1, 1990, p. 3.

14. The political structure of the Soviet Union was federal, with four levels of administrative divisions. At the top of this structure were the 15 Soviet Socialist Republics, or union republics. Each union republic bordered a foreign state, and all remaining administrative units were contained within and accountable to these 15, including 20 autonomous Soviet Socialist Republics (ASSRs), 8 autonomous areas (*oblasty*), and 10 autonomous districts (*okruga*). Article 80 of the USSR constitution designated only the 15 union republics as founding members of the Soviet Union with the right to secede.

15. By August 1990, seven union republics had issued declarations of sovereignty or independence: Lithuania (March), Estonia (March), Latvia (May), Russia (June), Uzbekistan (June), Ukraine (July), and Byelorussia (July). One study found that among the union republics, concentration of the titular nationality was a strong indicator of an early disposition to secede. See Emizet and Hesli, "Disposition to Secede." For a statistical account of the independence movements in Russia, see Treisman, "Russia's Ethnic Revival."

16. For an account of Gorbachev's maneuvers, see Dunlop, "Russia." Also see Suny, *The Revenge of the Past,* chap. 4.

17. In addition to this law, a related law—the Law on the Procedures for Resolving Questions Related to the Secession of Union Republics from the USSR (O poryadke reshenie voprosov, svyazannykh c vykhodom soyuznoi respubliki iz SSSR)—was adopted. Article 3 stipulated: "The peoples of autonomous republics

and autonomous formations shall retain the right to decide independently the question of staying in the USSR or in the seceding union republic, as well as to raise the question of their own legal state status" (Za narodami avtomnym respublik i avtomnykh obrazovaniy sokhranyaetsya pravo na samostoyatel'noe reshenie v Soyuze SSR ili vykhodyashchey Soyuznoy respublike, a takzhe o svoyem na postanovku voprosa o svoyem gosudarstvenno-pravovom statuse). *Izvestiya*, April 6, 1990.

18. Similar to the former Soviet Union, Russia was a federation. It contained a total of 88 political-administrative units, some of which were ethnically based. The non–ethnically based entities, what were commonly referred to as the "regions," consisted of 49 oblasts, 6 territories (*kraya*), and 2 federal cities. The remaining 31 "autonomous" jurisdictions were created to provide political recognition to ethnic groups and included 16 autonomous republics, 5 autonomous oblasts, and 10 autonomous okrugs. In 1991 the autonomous oblasts, with the exception of the Jewish Oblast, were given the status of autonomous republics, thereby increasing the number to 20 autonomous republics in the Russian Federation. In 1992, with the split of Checheno-Ingushetia, the number increased to 21. The autonomous republics were the most politically developed ethnic entities, due in large measure to the existence of republican legislatures and executive branches. See appendix 3 for the names of the autonomous entities and for population data. Three regions were involved in violence in post-1989 Russia, and they were all areas with concentrated majorities: Chechnya, North Ossetia, and Tuva. For a discussion of the Soviet political structure and its influence on ethnic mobilization, see Roeder, "Soviet Federalism."

19. *Pravda*, September 1, 1990, p. 3. The text of the declaration of sovereignty can be found in *Belaya kniga Tatarstana*, p. 7. The local Parliament, also known as the Supreme Soviet, will be referred to as the Tatarstan Parliament.

20. *Izvestiya*, August 7, 1990, p. 2.

21. See n. 12.

22. The final report of the USSR referendum was published in *Izvestiya*, March 27, 1991, pp. 1 and 3. The results of the Russian referendum were published in *Izvestiya* on March 26, 1991, p. 2.

23. The comments were made on May 12, at a meeting that included Gorbachev and Yeltsin. The meeting came about due to the formula that was established for signing the Union Treaty, which stated that only republics that had attended an earlier meeting, at which the rules were established, could sign the Union Treaty. The participants were the union republics. These included Russia, Ukraine, Byelorussia, Uzbekistan, Kazakhstan, Azerbaijan, Tajikistan, Kyrgyzstan, and Turkmenistan. Estonia, Latvia, Lithuania, Georgia, and Moldova opted out. According to the autonomous republics, their exclusion from the signing of the Union Treaty was a violation of numerous laws (for example, On the Demarcation of the Powers of the USSR and the Members of the Federation) and of the draft of the Union Treaty, which did not distinguish between union and autonomous republics. The autonomous republics argued that since they had the same legal status as the union republics, they too should be afforded the opportunity to sign the Union Treaty independently of Russia. Yet there was a problem for the non-Russian union republics. Should the autonomous republics be granted the

"one vote, one republic" right, then Russia, which would surely strong-arm them, would have not just one vote but sixteen additional ones. The compromise, which Shamiyev rejected, was that the Russian autonomous republics would sign as constituents of both the USSR and Russia. See *Pravda* and *Izvestiya*, May 13, 1991, p. 1, and *Izvestiya*, May 17, 1991, p. 1. For the text of the Union Treaty draft, see *Pravda*, March 9, 1991, pp. 1 and 3, and *Izvestiya*, March 9, 1991, p. 2.

24. Interview in *Pravda*, May 18, 1991, p. 2.

25. *RFE/RL Daily Report*, May 21, 1991.

26. Toropov, *Spravochnik novykh partii*, p. 5.

27. Published in an article by Ittifak activist Fauzia Bairomova in *Shakhrai Kazan* on October 12, 1991, and reprinted in *Izvestiya*, November 25, 1991, p. 4.

28. Toropov, *Spravochnik novykh partii*, p. 5.

29. Ibid.

30. See McAuley, *Russia's Politics*, p. 104.

31. *RFE/RL Daily Report*, May 24, 1991.

32. *Kommersant*, no. 22, p. 12. *Current Digest of the Soviet Press* 43, no. 21 (1991): 24.

33. The contents of this leaflet were reported in *Rossiya*, no. 22 or 23, 1991. *Current Digest of the Soviet Press* 43, no. 21 (1991): 24.

34. *Washington Post*, April 8, 1990, January 14, 1991, and *Guardian* (London), August 22, 1991. On August 23, 1989, more than one million Baltic citizens (13 percent of the population) took part in a four-hundred-mile-long "Baltic Chain" linking the capitals of the three republics to commemorate the fiftieth anniversary of the Molotov-Ribbentrop Pact, which led to their subjugation by the Soviet Union. *New York Times*, August 27, 1989.

35. See *Political Parties in Europe*, Radio Free Europe Research (Munich: Radio Free Europe, Radio Liberty, February 1990).

36. Shamiyev was the only person who managed to collect the required number of signatures to appear on the ballot. Thus he ran uncontested.

37. *RFE/RL Daily Report*, May 29, 1991.

38. Yeltsin won 60 percent of these votes.

39. *Ekspress-Khronika*, June 18, 1991, p. 4. Also *RFE/RL Daily Report*, June 14, 1991.

40. Nationalists formed no concerted counteropposition. If they had been as strong as those in the Baltic states, a more intense opposition to Shamiyev would have developed.

41. For more on the politics of economic interests in Tatarstan, see Giuliano, "Who Determines the Self."

42. *Belaya kniga Tatarstana*, pp. 21–22.

43. Ibid., p. 23.

44. At the time, Communists held 218 of 250 seats in the Supreme Soviet (local parliament) of Tatarstan, and they too supported Shamiyev's stance. *Financial Times*, September 4, 1991.

45. On November 15, 1991, Yeltsin signed ten decrees that gave Russia authority over all financial agencies on its territory. As one reporter exclaimed, "Thus,

Yeltsin, at a single stroke, has taken full economic power into his own hands."
Komsomolskaya pravda, November 19, 1991, p. 1.

46. For various reports from the Soviet press, reactions from the international press, and official documents on the CIS, see *Moskovskaya pravda*, December 10, 1991, p. 1, December 11, 1991, p. 1, December 13, 1991, p. 1; *Trud*, December 10, 1991, p. 1, December 11, 1991, p. 3, December 12, 1991, p. 1, December 24, 1991, p. 1; *Nezavisimaya gazeta*, December 10, 1991, pp. 1 and 2, December 11, 1991, p. 3, December 24, 1991, p. 1; and *Moskovski komsomolets*, December 10, 1991, p. 1.

47. A crucial question here is why Moscow was so nervous about the referendum. Is it because elites viewed the democratic process as legitimate? Since when is it written that because a majority of people in one territory vote a certain way, it necessarily must stand as legitimate? Russian leaders appear to have internalized this norm, or more cynically, they were thinking about what the International Monetary Fund or the international community writ large would say if it "cracked down" on the legitimate national aspirations. Regardless, Russian elite behavior was influenced by this ideal of democracy and majority rule made manifest through referenda sweeping the land.

48. ITAR-TASS, February 25, 1992.

49. *Rossiiskaya gazeta*, March 7, 1992, p. 1.

50. ITAR-TASS, March 8, 1992. Russian radio reported on March 7 that the Parliament considered convening an extraordinary session to reword the referendum question but decided not to, issuing the appeal instead.

51. Sheehy, "Tatarstan Asserts Its Sovereignty," p. 4.

52. *BBC News Service*, March 25, 1992.

53. *Belaya kniga Tatarstana*, p. 27.

54. *RFE/RL Daily Report*, April 3, 1992.

55. Associated Press, April 6, 1993.

56. For a description of the negotiations, see *Belaya kniga Tatarstana* and Walker, "The Dog That Didn't Bark."

57. *RFE/RL Daily Report*, August 31, 1992.

58. Vladimir Morokin, *Rossiiskaya gazeta*, February 7, 1992, p. 1.

59. *Moskovskiye novosti*, September 27, 1992.

60. These findings should be interpreted cautiously, as they are based on data that did not disaggregate ethnic and rural distinctions. The rural areas were largely populated by Tatars. Nevertheless, the rural factor alone does seem to have had at least some independent effect. For an excellent discussion of the rural-urban factor in Tatarstan's politics, see McAuley, *Russia's Politics*, pp. 106–8.

61. Yeltsin's appeal reported by TASS, March 20, 1992, and March 21, 1992. *Rossiiskaya gazeta*, March 21, 1992, p. 1. Yeltsin's appeals were countered on local television by film clips from a 1990 speech in Kazan in which Yeltsin told the republics to determine the fate of their own independence. As reported by *Nezavisimaya gazeta*, March 24, 1992, p. 1.

62. *Christian Science Monitor*, April 23, 1991.

63. Toropov, *Spravochnik novykh partii*.

64. Also reported by *RFE/RL Daily Report*, March 25, 1992.

65. See *Belaya kniga Tatarstana*, pp. 25–27.

66. *RFE/RL Daily Report*, January 15, 1992.

67. See *Izvestiya* of September 16, 1992, for an excellent analysis of Tatarstan's ambiguous position detailed through its draft of a bilateral treaty. It cites a poll that indicated that 60 percent of the residents of Tatarstan did not want to secede from Russia. No source or time of poll is stated.

68. See the interview in *Delovaya zhizn'*, nos. 11–12 (October–November 1992), reprinted in *FBIS-USR-018*, February 16, 1993.

69. See *Izvestiya* of September 16, 1992, p. 2. Economic and budgetary issues dominated.

70. Most representatives came from nationalist parties such as Ittifak and Azat-lyk. Leaders of the TPC and the Tatar Supreme Soviet spoke out against the meeting. *Izvestiya*, February 3, 1992, p. 2, and *Moscow News*, February 23–March 1, 1992, p. 5.

71. United Press International, February 2, 1992. Also see Reuters, February 3, 1992.

72. ITAR-TASS, February 1, 1992.

73. Ibid., February 7, 1992.

74. Reuters, February 3, 1992, referencing Interfax.

75. *RFE/RL Daily Report*, February 5, 1992.

76. ITAR-TASS, February 7, 1992.

77. The constitution was printed in *Sovetskaya Tataria*, December 12 or 13, 1992. Reprinted in *FBIS-USR-024*, March 4, 1993, pp. 1–16. Excerpts can be found in *Belaya kniga Tatarstana*, pp. 14–15.

78. *Izvestiya*, March 7, 1992. Emphasis added.

79. ITAR-TASS, March 11, 1992.

80. TASS, March 20, 1992, and March 21, 1992.

81. TASS, March 19, 1992. The full text of Yeltsin's appeal was printed in *Rossiiskaya gazeta*, March 20, 1992, p. 1.

82. *Rossiiskaya gazeta*, March 21, 1992, p. 1.

Notes to Chapter 5
Russia and Chechnya

1. For purposes of this analysis, I refer to the self-declared sovereign state of the Chechen Republic of Ichkeria as Chechnya, or the Chechen Republic.

2. The Chechen-Ingush Republic was 19,300 square kilometers. It contained 15 rayons and 7 cities. In 1990, 41 percent of the population was urban and 59 percent rural. *Narodnoe khoziaistvo RSFSR v 1990* g., pp. 6 and 78.

3. Lemercier-Quelquejay. "Co-optation of Elites."

4. Nekrich, *Punished Peoples*, pp. 50–51.

5. For a concise overview of Chechnya's historical struggle with Russia, see Lieven, *Chechnya*, chap. 9.

6. General Anton Deniken, the leader of the opposition White Armies, later admitted that he had to dedicate no less than one-third of his forces to the Cau-casus region in his failed effort to defeat the "seething volcano." As relayed by Avtorkhanov, "Chechens and Ingush," p. 157.

7. In a repeat of history, the Red Army general charged with subduing the

revolt that followed the repression and imposition of military rule modeled his plan of action on that of Prince Aleksandr Ivanovich Bariatinskii, the general responsible for defeating the Caucasus during the nineteenth century. Broxup, "Introduction," p. 14.

8. During previous struggles against external authority, different clans from a multitude of ethnic groups were united, be it Russian, Persian, or Ottoman. Some of these people were the ancestors of those who today consider themselves part of the "Chechen" nation.

9. Omrod, "North Caucasus."

10. Avtorkhanov claims that 14,000 men, or 3 percent of the republic's population, were arrested starting on July 31, 1937. Avtorkhanov, "Chechens and Ingush."

11. Nekrich, *Punished Peoples*, p. 116. The decree ordering the deportation of the Chechens and Ingush and the liquidation of their ASSR was dated March 7, 1944. Census data reveal that in 1926 the Chechens constituted 76 percent of the population of the Chechen-Ingush Republic, whereas in 1959 they were 34 percent. During the same period, the Russian population in the region rose from 3 percent to 49 percent. These data were taken from Harris, "Geographic Analysis," table 4, pp. 554–56. Avtorkhanov provides some evidence that the Chechens "appealed" to the Germans to recognize their independence and to help them achieve it, a far cry from Stalin's charge of "aiding an invader." Avtorkhanov, "Chechens and Ingush," p. 183.

12. These numbers are from a recent report by V. Zemskov, a senior research associate with the USSR Academy of Sciences. *Argumenty i fakty*, September 30–October 6, 1989, p. 8. Seven groups were targeted for being collaborators: Balkars, Chechens, Crimean Tatars, Ingush, Kalmyks, Karachais, and Volga Germans. For a critical analysis of the deportations, see Conquest, *Nation Killers*.

13. Nekrich, *Punished Peoples*, p. 60.

14. Conquest, *Nation Killers*, and Nekrich, *Punished Peoples*.

15. *1989 Soviet Census* 7, part 1, table 3 (p. 66).

16. The only other ethnic group sharing this differential was the Ingush. I calculated this from data provided by Harris, "Geographic Analysis," table 11, pp. 572–73.

17. Only half of Tatars and Bashkirs consider themselves Muslim, and no more than a fifth practice Islam. United States Information Agency, "Islam Commands."

18. Ibid.

19. These figures were rounded to the nearest thousand and were taken from the *1989 Soviet Census* 7, part 1, table 2 (p. 10), table 3 (p. 66), and table 4 (p. 196).

20. Muzayev, *Novaya Checheno-Ingushetia*, p. 21.

21. Muzayev's *Novaya Checheno-Ingushetia* and *Chechenskaya respublika* are the most comprehensive treatments of the social and political movements in the Chechen republic, but they do not provide concrete data about the size of membership or the number of activists.

22. Like the Tatars, the Chechens sought union republic status for an increase in autonomy. The Chechens, however, were more concerned with political autonomy than with economic control.

23. Muzayev, *Novaya Checheno-Ingushetia*, p. 12.

24. Although the CNC was set up to represent the rights of the two dominant ethnic groups of the republic—Chechens and Ingush—it nevertheless pressed Chechen issues over broader ones. As a result, the Ingush held a referendum on November 30, 1991, and voted to establish their own republic within Russia. Chechnya accepted the results and the Ingush Autonomous Republic was officially declared in June 1992. *Izvestiya*, December 4, 1991, and Omrod, "North Caucasus," p. 458.

25. Muzayev, *Novaya Checheno-Ingushetia*, p. 12; and Kline, "Conflict in Chechnya."

26. Kline, "Conflict in Chechnya."

27. According to an article in *Izvestiya*, rallies were held throughout Grozny. Democratic forces, which expressed support for the CNC Executive Committee, came out against its violent tactics. *Izvestiya*, October 11, 1991, pp. 1–2.

28. *RFE/RL Daily Report*, October 7, 1991.

29. *Izvestiya*, October 8, 1991, pp. 1–2.

30. *Pravda*, October 10, 1991, p. 2. *RFE/RL Daily Report*, October 9, 1991.

31. *RFE/RL Daily Report*, October 10, 1991.

32. Kline, "Conflict in Chechnya."

33. *Izvestiya*, October 10, 1991, pp. 1–2.

34. Ibid., October 11, 1991, p. 2.

35. *Nezavisimaya gazeta*, October 15, 1991, p. 3.

36. Parliamentary elections were to be held on November 17, 1991.

37. *RFE/RL Daily Report*, October 15, 1991.

38. Ibid., October 23, 1991.

39. There were four candidates for president: Dudayev, chairman of the CNC's Executive Committee; R. Gaitemirov, leader of the Green Movement; M. Sulayev, chairman of the World Democratic Movement; and B. Umayev, director of a military base. *Izvestiya*, October 21, 1991, p. 1.

40. There was much debate about the exact turnout and support for Dudayev. On October 29, 1991, *Izvestiya* reported that approximately 55 percent of eligible voters participated in the election. The opposition claimed that the turnout was only half that, but because CNC members made up the electoral commissions, it would be next to impossible to verify the true count. *Moscow News* reported that 72 percent of eligible voters participated and that Dudayev received 90 percent of the vote. As reported by Kline, "Conflict in Chechnya." The *New York Times* reported that Dudayev had received 85 percent of the vote. *New York Times*, November 11, 1991, p. 7.

41. Four countries recognized Chechnya: Estonia, Iran, Lithuania, and Turkey. *Izvestiya*, November 5, 1991, p. 2.

42. The decree was issued on November 7, 1991. The Supreme Soviet was given seventy two hours to decide whether to confirm or rescind it.

43. Muzayev, *Chechenskaya respublika*, p. 168.

44. *Izvestiya*, November 13, 1991, pp. 1–2.

45. *Rossiiskaya gazeta*, November 12, 1991, p. 1.

46. Arsanov was Yeltsin's representative in the republic. *Pravda*, November 11, 1991, p. 1.

47. On November 15 Moscow Radio reported that the PSC, still recognized by Russia as the sole legitimate body in power in the republic, had disbanded itself. *RFE/RL Daily Report*, 18 November 1991.

48. *RFE/RL Daily Report*, March 16, 1992, and May 27, 1992.

49. *Nezavisimaya gazeta*, January 15, 1993, p. 3.

50. According to one estimate, Chechnya had met between 80 and 90 percent of its planned deliveries to Russian industries, whereas Russia had met only 25 percent of its contracts with Chechnya. Although Chechen minister of finance Taimax Abubarov denied that Chechnya was suffering under the blockade, the April 1993 demonstrations, provoked in part by unpaid wages and student grants, revealed otherwise. *Nezavisimaya gazeta*, January 13, 1993, p. 3.

51. Goldenberg, *Pride of Small Nations*.

52. Muzayev, *Chechenskaya respublika*, p. 147.

53. Galeotti, "Chechnya."

54. ITAR-TASS, April 17, 1993.

55. The Chechen conflict had striking parallels to the situation in Russia over the division of power between the Parliament and the president. The conflict in Moscow led to the storming of the parliamentary building in September. Yeltsin, a strong president, won out in the Russian case, as did Dudayev in Chechnya. At the time of the crisis, Russia's Parliament was headed by Ruslan Khasbulatov, who later became a contender in the race to replace Dudayev. The similarities between the two confrontations may have led Dudayev to view Yeltsin in a more sympathetic light: during the confrontation, he issued a statement backing Yeltsin and condemned the Russian Parliament's attempt to impeach him. *RFE/RL Daily Report*, September 23, 1993.

56. It is unclear how many people were killed. Numbers varied from as few as four to as many as sixty. United Press International, June 4, 1993.

57. *RFE/RL Daily Report*, June 4 and 7, 1993. United Press International, June 4, 1993.

58. Another opposition force, the Chechen Republic Provisional Council, was in place by December 1993 under the leadership of Umar Avturkhanov. He became the head administrator of the Nadterechny rayon, which ultimately became the only region beyond Dudayev's control. Avturkhanov had strong ties to Moscow, and it seemed that by the winter of 1993, he and his supporters were ready to displace Dudayev from his stronghold. Yet this group was not able or willing to broach the issue of Chechen sovereignty and its political status in Russia because of its strong ties to Moscow. Therefore, its "popular" support remained severely limited, and it relied heavily on Moscow's help in opposing the Dudayev regime. For an overview of this group, see *Segodnya*, May 12, 1994, p. 3.

59. *RFE/RL Daily Report*, November 3, 1993.

60. During a speech on April 20, 1993, Russian legislator Ruslan Khasbulatov (a Chechen) revealed the arrogance of Moscow officials about their ability to steer events in Grozny. Khasbulatov remarked that the Dudayev regime was still in power because it was favored by Russia. If it were otherwise, he argued, the regime would have collapsed long ago. *RFE/RL Daily Report*, April 21, 1993.

61. Ibid., January 25, 1994.

62. Ibid., March 2, 1994.

63. Ibid., March 31, 1994.

64. Ibid., April 18, 1994.

65. Shakrai was seen as the "crafter" of Moscow's conditions for negotiations (its refusal to recognize Chechnya's independence) and of the move to work with Dudayev's opposition rather than recognize Dudayev as the legitimate leader. Regardless of how much Shakrai was individually responsible for the conduct of negotiations, his tactics had Moscow's tacit approval until his dismissal.

66. There was evidence that even if Moscow was not directly behind the attempts, it condoned them. See *Moskovskiye novosti*, no. 22, May 29–June 5, 1994, p. A9. Also see *RFE/RL Daily Report*, May 24, May 30, May 31, 1994.

67. Yeltsin admitted creating the Provisional Council during an interview on Russian television on August 11, 1993. *RFE/RL Daily Report*, August 12, 1994. Also see *RFE/RL Daily Report*, September 8, 1994.

68. Ibid., August 4, 10, and 11, 1994.

69. Ibid., August 9, 1994.

70. Ibid., August 22 and September 7, 1994.

71. In several of the engagements, the helicopters, artillery, and tanks were reported to bear the markings of the Russian military. The Russian Ministry of Defense denied such reports. Russia's Duma, however, seemed more willing to admit the "official" involvement of Russian forces, especially after Chechen forces had captured troops belonging to the Russian army. The chairman of the State Duma's Defense Committee admitted that three prisoners had been identified as Russian army captains but claimed that "[I]t is not clear whether they appeared in Chechnya under orders from the Defense Ministry or did it on their own." Defense Minister Pavel Grachev continued to deny Russian involvement; he finally admitted it on December 5, 1994. *RFE/RL Daily Report*, November 21 and 29 and December 6, 1994.

72. *RFE/RL Daily Report*, November 28, 1994.

73. Ibid., October 19, December 5 and 6, 1994.

74. Ibid., December 15, 1994.

75. *Official Kremlin International Broadcast News*, August 12, 1992.

76. Kline, "Conflict in Chechnya."

77. The Russian military's overestimation of its chances of success in Chechnya should now be ranked among legendary miscalculations.

78. *RFE/RL Daily Report*, December 13, 1994; emphasis added.

79. Yeltsin, *Midnight Diaries*, pp. 58–59; emphasis added.

80. For such a discussion see, *Nezavisimaya gazeta*, November 26, 1991, p. 3.

81. For a discussion of the budget wars and the distribution of resources, see *Izvestiya*, January 5, 1993, pp. 1–2.

82. Tatarstan's industrial output was impressive, ranking it eleventh among Russia's eighty-nine constituencies. Chechnya contributed less than 1 percent of the total Russian industrial output, ranking it at the bottom. As reported in *Novaya Rossiya*, p. 265.

83. She was dismissed from her position on November 4, 1992. *RFE/RL Daily Report*, December 20, 1991. 83

84. See "Political Parties in Europe."

85. Fifty thousand had come out in support following the seizure of power in October 1991. Kline, "Conflict in Chechnya."

86. In most of these post-Soviet regimes, the structural arrangements adopted were based on the principle of majority rule rather than the mechanism of proportional representation.

87. On Russia's unwillingness to negotiate, see Lapidus, "Contested Sovereignty," pp. 24–25.

Notes to Chapter 6
Georgia and Abkhazia

1. Suny, *The Making of the Georgian Nation*, p. 47.

2. Pipes, *The Formation of the Soviet Union*, p. 212.

3. For purposes of this analysis, the self-declared sovereign state of the Republic of Abkhazia is referred to as Abkhazia, or the Abkhaz Republic. Ajaria is an autonomous republic within the internationally recognized state of the Republic of Georgia. It is referred to as Ajaria or the Ajar Republic. Finally, Georgia, formerly the Georgian Soviet Socialist Republic, is now officially the Republic of Georgia and referred to here as Georgia. Tbilisi is the capital of Georgia, Sukhumi of Abkhazia, and Batumi of Ajaria.

4. During one of his weekly interviews, Georgian premier Eduard Shevardnadze put it in the following stark terms: "Of course I think of the ideals of mankind because the implementation of these ideals depends significantly on Russia. But I also think of my motherland, my little country, first of all. Because, if democracy fails to win there, Georgia will be drowned in blood. It will find itself in an even deeper pool of blood." Georgian radio, Tbilisi, October 4, 1993. Transcript provided by the British Broadcast Corporation (BBC), October 6, 1993. Also see Colarusso, "Abkhazia," and Lynch, *Conflict in Abkhazia*, pp. 16–17.

5. These lands had not been united under a single political authority since the fifteenth century. Eastern Georgia (Kartli and Kakheti) was absorbed into the Russian Empire in 1801, Mingrelia in 1803, Imeretia in 1804, and Abkhazia in 1810. John F. R. Wright, "The Geopolitics of Georgia," p. 136.

6. Suny, "Georgia and Soviet Nationality Policy," p. 207.

7. In 1936 the Republic of Transcaucasia was parceled into three entities: Armenia, Azerbaijan and Georgia.

8. See Pipes, *The Formation of the Soviet Union*, pp. 266–93.

9. Suny, for example, argues that the 1956 student demonstrations in commemoration of Stalin (in reaction to Khrushchev's de-Stalinization campaign) were the result of patriotic pride for a fellow Georgian and indicated a growing national awareness. The severe crackdown by Moscow, resulting in dozens killed and hundreds wounded, revealed a nervous and confused state. Suny, *The Making of the Georgian Nation*, pp. 302–4.

10. Ibid., p. 290.

11. Suny points out that although the rate of Georgia's national income grew at the third lowest rate in the USSR from 1960 to 1971, in 1970 Georgians had savings accounts nearly double those of average Soviet citizens. Suny, "Georgia and Soviet Nationality Policy," p. 213.

12. Suny, *The Making of the Georgian Nation*, p. 318.

13. Azerbaijani birthrates were almost double those of Georgians. Ethnic-bal-

ance concerns were a consistent theme among Georgian intellectuals, described as a sort of paranoia. There was speculation that the resettlement of Georgians with "exceptionally high birth-rates" following natural disasters to areas where the Georgian population was "under siege" was in part designed to bolster the Georgian presence in those regions. Fuller, "Disastrous Weather," p. 1, and "Marneuli," p. 4. Also see her "Georgian Writers."

14. These figures were rounded off and taken from the *1989 Soviet Census 7*, part 1, table 1 (p. 8), and part 2, table 13 (p. 444). *Itogi Vsesoiuznoi perepisi naseleniia.*

15. Only one nationality surpassed Georgians: Lithuanians, with 95.3 percent. Latvians shared the Georgian percentage. *Narodnoe khozyaistvo SSSR*, p. 81.

16. Comrie, *The Languages of the Soviet Union*, p. 197.

17. The linguistic differences among these three groups continue to influence the play of politics. Many Georgians living in Abkhazia speak Mingrelian or Svanetian, and not the more dominant Kartvelian. Thus Abkhaz people had relatively little interaction with the official Georgian language, which was actually Kartvelian. Further, the homelands of Svanetia and Mingrelia are contiguous to Abkhazia. Svanetia is located along the southern slopes of the Caucasus range in western Georgia and shares its northern border with Russia, and Mingrelia is to the south. Both share western borders with Abkhazia. I refer to the Kartvelians, Mingrelians, and Svans as Georgians, unless indicated otherwise.

18. Among republican titular nations, Georgians shared similar language patterns with the Tajiks, Turkmen, and Uzbeks. *Narodnoe khozyaistvo SSSR*, p. 77.

19. Bennigsen and Wimbush, *Muslims of the Soviet Empire*, p. 127.

20. *Official Kremlin International News Broadcast*, August 28, 1992.

21. Bennigsen and Wimbush estimate the percentage of Muslim adherents among the Abkhaz to be 50 to 70 percent, and Clogge estimates it at 20 to 40 percent. Bennigsen and Wimbush, *Muslims of the Soviet Empire*, pp. 129, 213–14; Clogge, "Religion."

22. Comrie, *The Languages of the Soviet Union*, pp. 196–98.

23. The *1989 Soviet census*. Data taken from *Narodnoe khozyaistvo SSSR*, p. 79.

24. Hewitt, "Abkhazia."

25. Ibid.

26. See Zurab Papaskiri, "Some Reflections on the Past of Abkhazia and Georgian-Abkhazian Relations," *Demokraticheskaya Abkhazia*, September 30, 1989, as cited in Chervonnaya's, *Conflict in the Caucasus*, p. 2 n. 7. Also see Otyrba, "War in Abkhazia," p. 282.

27. These figures were rounded from those in the *1989 Soviet Census 7*, part 1, table 2 (p. 14) and part 2, table 13 (p. 444).

28. Armenians constituted 15 percent, Russians 14 percent, Greeks 3 percent, and Ukrainians 2 percent.

29. According to Zaal Anjaparidze, there are some 250 Abkhaz villages throughout Turkey and about 100,000–150,000 in Turkish cities and towns. There may be an additional 5,000 Abkhaz living in Syria and a small number in Jordan and Iraq. Those Abkhaz living abroad identify themselves as Circassians, however, and not Abkhaz with distinct ties to Abkhazia. Data from personal correspondence with Zaal Anjaparidze of the Caucasian Institute for Peace, Democ-

racy, and Development, Tbilisi, Georgia, and from Bennigsen and Wimbush, *Muslims of the Soviet Empire*, p. 213.

30. Suny may see a true choice here, or it may be the case that the structure of demography and historical experience made this outcome of division and violence more likely and even probable. Suny, *The Making of the Georgian Nation*, p. 318.

31. Ethnic tensions had surfaced prior to 1978 as well. In 1973, for example, Georgian Communist Party elites complained about the insistence of minorities on having equitable representation: "in Abkhazia a half-baked 'theory' according to which responsible posts should be filled only by representatives of the indige-nous nationality has gained a certain currency. . . . No one has been given the right to ignore the national composition of the population or to disregard the continual exchange of cadres among nations and the interests of all nationalities." Suny, *The Making of the Georgian Nation*, p. 307, referencing *Zaria vostoka*, April 27, 1973.

32. After 1985, Shevardnadze became the Soviet foreign minister under Gor-bachev. He resigned in 1990, warning of a creeping dictatorship, only to return to the post following the August 1991 coup. He remained foreign minister until the dissolution of the USSR in December 1991.

33. Suny, *The Making of the Georgian Nation*, p. 309.

34. The degree of discrimination and equitable access in Abkhazia is unclear. According to Communist Party rolls in Abkhazia, Georgians constituted 51 per-cent of the party membership but only 44 percent of the population. Yet, accord-ing to *Pravda*, the Abkhaz constituted only 17 percent of the population but filled some 40 percent of the cadre positions. *Pravda*, September 21, 1989, p. 4. For the party figures, see Darrell Slider, "Crisis and Response," p. 53. Ethnic Georgians constituted 80 percent of the deputies to the Georgian Supreme Soviet and the contingent from the Republic of Georgia and 66 percent to the USSR Supreme Soviet. The Abkhaz comprised 8 percent of the former and 3 percent of the latter. Thus, the Abkhaz did seem to have less representation in the institu-tions at the republican level than at the all-union level (although in both cases they were overrepresented, given that the level of the total Abkhaz population in Georgia was just under 2 percent). See *Narodnoe khozyaistvo Gruzinskoi SSR*, p. 31.

35. d'Encausse, *The End of the Soviet Empire*, p. 78.

36. Fuller, "New Abkhaz Campaign."

37. D'Encausse, *The End of the Soviet Empire*, pp. 82–91.

38. Black Sunday is considered one of the main events that led to the dissolu-tion of the Soviet Union. The violence used by the federal troops, and the per-mission granted by the Georgian government under Jumbar Patiashvili, chairman of the Georgian Communist Party, were roundly condemned. In addition to the terms "Bloody Sunday" and "Black Sunday," the term "Tbilisi Syndrome" was coined, referring to Moscow's inability to use force to impose its will. See Suny, *The Revenge of the Past*. For a fuller discussion of these events and the implica-tions for the Soviet Union, see d'Encausse, *The End of the Soviet Empire*, pp. 73–95.

39. Fuller and Ouratadze, "Georgian Leadership."

40. Zviad Konstantinovich Gamsakhurdia was born in 1939. The son of a lead-

ing Georgian literary figure, he obtained his doctorate in philology. He became a scholar of Shakespeare, a writer, and an editor of samizdat papers and journals. During the Soviet period, Gamsakhurdia was a leading and respected human rights activist. He cofounded the Tbilisi branch of the Helsinki group and was arrested several times for his views. From 1977 to 1979 he was imprisoned. The fact that his father was a major Georgian novelist and that he himself was involved in the human rights movement for more than two decades impressed many Georgians.

41. Suny, *The Making of the Georgian Nation*, p. 324.

42. Rogers Brubaker explores the connection between national minorities and nationalizing states in his *Nationalism Reframed*. For a slightly different approach to state building and territorial issues, see Lustick, *Unsettled States.*

43. On August 25, 1990, the Parliament of the Abkhaz Autonomous SSR adopted a resolution, "the Conception of the Abkhaz Autonomous SSR under the Conditions of Self-Management, Self-Financing, and the Changeover to a Regulated Market (Kontseptiya Abkhazskoi ASSR v ucloviyakh samoypravleniya, samofinansirovaniya i perekhoda k reguliruemomu rynku). It also approved a document entitled "On Legal Guarantees to Protect Abkhazia's Statehood" (Opravovykh garantiyakh v zashchitu gosudarstvennosti Abkhazii) and a declaration, On Abkhazia's State Sovereignty (O gosudarstvennom suverenitete Abkhazii). The deputies of Georgian nationality refused to participate in the session. Only 72 of 140 deputies were present—not enough for a quorum. *Pravda*, August 26, 1990, p. 2.

44. No united national opposition or Baltic-style popular front formed in Georgia. All of the national parties-blocs that formed, however, were united in opposing the Communist Party and in advancing Georgia's independence. The Round Table was the party best organized to slate candidates, and it was also one of the most nationalistic in terms of advancing a Georgia for the protection of Georgian identity. See Slider, "Democratization in Georgia," pp. 170–71, and Hunter, *Transcaucasus in Transition*, pp. 118–20.

45. Slider, "Democratization in Georgia," pp. 170–71.

46. Ardzinba was a member of the Communist Party of the Soviet Union since 1967, and from 1988 he was a deputy in the Supreme Soviet of the USSR and chairman of the Commission for Autonomous Entities. He was elected on the basis of his position in the Communist Party and because of his reputation as a legislator who sought to protect the rights of minorities more generally. He was a vocal advocate of the Abkhaz nation, but at a time and in a context in which such advocacy had little political impact. Ardzinba was also a doctor of history, specializing in the history and culture of the peoples of the ancient Orient and Asia Minor. He lived in Moscow until 1988, where he was with the Institute of Oriental Studies. In 1989 he became the director of the Abkhazian Gulia Institute of Language, Literature, and History.

47. Fuller, "Abkhazia on the Brink," p. 2.

48. Reuters North American Wire, March 15, 1991. The same article notes that some twenty thousand people demonstrated in Sukhumi in support of the referendum of March 17.

49. For the USSR as a whole, 76.4 percent (with 80 percent of the electorate

participating) voted yes. In Georgia proper central republic referendum commissions were not created. Local soviets, labor collectives, public associations, and commands of military units independently made arrangements for citizens to take part in the referendum. Thus the number of citizens on the voting lists was quite low, recorded at 45,696. Of these, 99.9 percent voted in favor of the union. This is not surprising, given that these voters were largely organized by party organizations (Communist) and the military. The results were reported by the Central Commission for USSR Referendums in *Izvestiya*, March 27, 1991, pp. 1 and 3.

50. *Vestnik gruziya*, April 2, 1991, p. 1, and *Svobodnaya gruziya*, October 29, 1991, p. 1. In Abkhazia 64 percent of the electorate participated, and of these, 85 percent voted in favor of Georgia's independence. *Nezavisimaya gazeta*, April 2, 1991, p. 3.

51. The Central Electoral Commission reported that 83.4 percent of the electorate participated, but only 79.4 percent submitted ballots. Gamsakhurdia received 86.5 percent of the vote. Voting did not take place in either Abkhazia or South Ossetia. *Izvestiya*, May 27, 1991, p. 1.

52. Chervonnaya, *Conflict in the Caucasus*, p. 91. Shevardnadze made the remark before a session of the Georgian Parliament. Chervonnaya references *Demokraticheskaya Abkhazia*, 25 November 1992, p. 2.

53. Fuller, "Abkhazia on the Brink," p. 4. Also TASS, September 30, 1991.

54. Gamsakhurdia's opposition used his actions during the coup in Moscow as a pretext. Not only had Gamsakhurdia not come out against the coup in Moscow, but he had accepted the Soviet military commander's order to disband the National Guard units in Georgia. Tengiz Kitovani, the commander of the National Guard, refused the order and moved his troops from the capital to the Rkoni gorge. He was joined by the chairman of the Council of Ministers, Tengiz Sigua, who resigned. The opposition held demonstrations demanding an explanation for Gamsakhurdia's behavior during the August coup.

55. Divisions and rivalries among Georgian elites failed to produce a united anti-Communist front, resulting in multiple nationalist-oriented parties backed by armed militias. The Mkhedrioni was one of the first militias to appear on the Georgian scene and had three to five thousand troops at any one time. Its leader was Jaba Ioseliani, who was imprisoned by Gamsakhurdia in an effort to control the armed opposition to him. Ioseliani, who had been a close aide to Shevardnadze when he was the KGB boss in Georgia, was to join the coalition to overthrow Gamsakhurdia and bring Shevardnadze to power. Hunter, *Transcaucasus in Transition*, p. 129.

56. *Izvestiya*, October 5, 1991, p. 1.

57. For reports on events, see *Izvestiya*, December 23, 1991, p. 1, December 24, 1991, p. 1, and December 25, 1991, p. 1.

58. There is evidence to support this conjecture. Gamsakhurdia did not endorse any sort of union with Moscow, and as such, he was seen as an obstacle to those who wanted to sustain some sort of union. For a discussion of Moscow's desire to oust Gamsakhurdia, see Hunter, *Transcaucasus in Transition*, pp. 128–29. Also see *BBC World Service* report, March 17, 1993.

59. *Megapolis-Express*, December 19, 1991, p. 12.

60. Daily rallies in support of Gamsakhurdia continued following his departure.

Note, however, that one of the first acts of the Military Council was to ban public rallies and demonstrations, so these occurred in a very hostile environment. *Izvestiya*, January 16, 1992, pp. 1–2, and *Nezavisimaya gazeta*, January 14, 1992, p. 1.

61. This appointment was not a surprise. Shevardnadze had been in touch with and had indicated his support for the opposition months earlier. Shortly after the opposition seized power, during an interview on French television on January 5, Shevardnadze called on Gamsakhurdia to resign to prevent further bloodshed. Western news agencies reported at the time that the Military Council had already offered him the position of head of state. *RFE/RL Daily Report*, January, 7 1992.

62. Fuller, "Abkhazia on the Brink," p. 4.

63. Chervonnaya, *Conflict in the Caucasus*, pp. 108–9. On June 15, 1992, Russian Parliament chairman Ruslan Khasbulatov threatened Georgia with Russian intervention in order to stabilize the situation in South Ossetia, prevent genocide against Ossetians by the Georgian military, and stop the flow of refugees. He stated that the Russian Parliament might consider South Ossetia's request to join Russia. Shevardnadze accused Moscow of interfering and worsening Georgia's already chaotic internal politics. By June 21, 1992, the number of refugees fleeing north was put at one hundred thousand. *Moskovskiye novosti*, June 21, 1992, p. 4. *RFE/RL Daily Report*, June 16, 1992.

64. Otyrba, "War in Abkhazia," p. 287.

65. In an interview, Zurab Achba, deputy chariman of the Standing Committee on Legal Matters of the Abkhaz Republic, explained why the 1925 constitution was so vital to Abkhazia's position. He explained the importance of three documents in particular: the 1921 Federation Treaty (ratified in February 1922), the 1925 Abkhaz constitution, and the 1978 Georgian constitution. The 1921 Federation Treaty merged Abkhazia with Georgia. The 1925 constitution proclaimed Abkhazia a sovereign state, affiliated with Georgia and the USSR through the Transcaucasia Federation. The 1978 constitution subordinated Abkhazia to Georgia as an autonomous republic. When Georgia declared its independence, it revoked the 1978 constitution, thereby invalidating the Abkhaz constitution, since it was based on the Georgian and Soviet ones. Thus the Abkhaz turned to the 1925 Constitution, which, not surprisingly, granted the republic the highest degree of autonomy with respect to Georgia. *Official Kremlin International News Broadcast*, August 28, 1992. Also see Lak'oba, "History."

66. Article 4 of the 1925 Abkhaz constitution declared that relations between Georgia and Abkhazia were based on a union treaty, and article 5 declared the right of Abkhazia to secede from the Trancaucasian Republic as well as from the USSR. Applied to the current situation, Abkhazia now had the right to secede from Georgia. *Nezavisimaya gazeta*, July 25, 1992, p. 1.

67. They also made the case that the 1925 constitution never really existed, except in draft form. So the whole idea of reinstating this constitution was somewhat ludicrous. *Izvestiya*, July 27, 1992, p. 1.

68. Chervonnaya, *Conflict in the Caucasus*, p. 113.

69. *Izvestiya*, July 27, 1992, p. 1.

70. *Nezavisimaya gazeta*, August 15, 1992, p. 1.

71. One problem with this line of argumentation was that even during the

Soviet period, federal troops could not enter an autonomous republic without the permission of the Supreme Soviet of that republic. They did have permission, but for a different mission. Georgia had also notified the United States, Germany, Russia, and Turkey of the intended action. *Izvestiya*, August 17, 1992, pp. 1–2.

72. *RFE/RL Daily Report*, August 17, 1992.

73. *Izvestiya*, August 17, 1992, pp. 1–2. *RFE/RL Daily Report*, August 18, 1992.

74. *RFE/RL Daily Report*, August 24, 1992.

75. Ibid., August 26, 1992.

76. See Otyrba, "War in Abkhazia," p. 289.

77. *Izvestiya*, August 26, 1992, pp. 1–2.

78. Ibid., September 4, 1994, pp. 1–2.

79. Ibid. Also see *Belaya kniga Abkhazii*, pp. 46–49.

80. *Izvestiya*, October 5, 1992, pp. 1–2.

81. Ibid.

82. Ibid., October 15, 1992, p. 2.

83. However important this endorsement was to Shevardnadze as, it never quite overcame the patina of illegitimacy that surrounded his coming to power in the first place, circumstances that his Abkhaz rival, Ardzinba—as a legitimately elected representative of his people—had never allowed him to forget. In Abkhazia and South Ossetia voting did not take place.

84. *Izvestiya*, December 18, 1992, p. 1.

85. Ibid.

86. Ibid., February 25, 1993, p. 2.

87. In an effort to obtain concrete evidence (for example, a letter or telegram) of Russia's involvement in the civil war, I conducted a series of interviews with officials from Georgia who were advising Shevardnadze during this period. None of them could provide solid material evidence. Rather, each more or less asserted that everyone knew Russia was involved; all one had to do was look at the military equipment, which bore Russian markings.

88. *Izvestiya*, March 17, 1993, p. 1.

89. The Russian Ministry of Defense denied that it took part in the offensive against Sukhumi and claimed that all Russian units in Abkhazia were maintaining strict neutrality. *Izvestiya*, March 17, 1993, p. 2.

90. Ibid., p.1.

91. Ibid., September 22, 1993, pp. 1–2.

Notes to Chapter 7
Georgia and Ajaria

1. Bennigsen and Wimbush, *Muslims of the Soviet Empire*, p. 208.

2. The number of ethnonational groups in the Soviet census declined from 192 in 1926 to 97 in 1939. This "decline" in the number of groups has been attributed to two related factors: (1) a change in the terminology used to categorize people, from the more particular *narodnost'* (people) to the larger *natsional'nost'* (nationality), and (2) the desire to show that the peoples of the USSR were coming together. See Silver, "Ethnic and Language Dimensions."

3. Shireen Hunter points out that as soon as the "Georgians" were offered a chance to debate the nature of their political system, the idea of a "theo-democracy," or "a Christian state ruled on democratic but not secular principles," was advanced. See Hunter, *Transcaucasus in Transition*, p. 112. Also see Aves, "Rise and Fall," p. 159.

4. For one view of the damage that Islam has done to Georgian identity, language, and Ajaria, see Khalvashi's article "Belief in the Existing." Khalvashi was the head of the Ajar section of the Georgian Writers' Union. This article first appeared in the Ajar Party and government newspaper *Sabchota Achara* in January and was reprinted in *Komunisti* a month later. *Komunisti* was the newspaper of the Georgian Party and government and had a circulation of seven hundred thousand.

5. See Fuller, "Islam in Ajaria" and "Disastrous Weather in Georgia."

6. By contrast, Azeris, would remain Azeris regardless of their faith.

7. The problem with this argument is that if the two groups are ethnically identical, then the difference in birthrates logically inheres in their religious differences. It follows that conversion could be expected to regularize birthrates (in this case, downward) across both groups. However, the Muslim Georgians were chiefly rural, and so the differences in birthrates may correspond to this or some other salient difference, such as overall income or education.

8. Fuller, "Islam in Ajaria."

9. A census was also taken in 1937, and the Ajars were listed as a distinct group. They totaled 88,230 in the Soviet Union, and of these, 88,217 lived in the Georgian Republic. This census was not officially published or publicly available. The official reason provided was that it was statistically flawed and underestimated the size of the population. Western scholars believe that one reason was that the census revealed the substantial impact of the purges and collectivization. The 1937 census has since been published. See *Vsesoyuznaya perepis' naselniia*, pp. 83 and 95. For a discussion of the 1937 Soviet census, see Lee Schwartz, "A History of the Russian and Soviet Censuses"

10. The total population of Georgia was roughly 5.4 million.

11. Data obtained from Bennigsen and Wimbush, *Muslims of the Soviet Empire*, p. 208. Bennigsen and Wimbush are the leading experts on the peoples of this region, which is why I rely on their estimates. Estimates from more general sources have put the number as high as 200,000. The *1995 World Factbook* estimates that 11 percent of Georgia's population is Muslim. If we subtract the percentages of known non-Ajar Muslims—the 6 percent who are Azeris and the 1 percent who are Abkhaz, and another 1 percent for Kurds and Muslim Ossetians—we are left with a figure of 3 percent Muslim. Three percent of 5.4 million equals 162,000, which is consistent with Bennigsen and Wimbush's high estimate. This figure is also consistent with the 1926 census, which officially recorded the Ajar population as just under 4 percent of the total Georgian population.

12. Personal correspondence with Zaal Anjaparidze, head of information at the Caucasian Institute for Peace, Democracy, and Development in Tbilisi, Georgia. More than 90 percent of all Georgians worldwide and 95 percent of FSU Georgians live in Georgia. When asked about the number of Ajars, Anjaparidze equated Ajars with Georgians: "Ajarians (called in such a way after the region of

their residence) consider themselves an integrated part of the Georgian nation but not a separate ethnic group, despite their Muslim belief." E-mail, April 22, 1998.

13. Fuller, "Zviad Gamsakhurdia."

14. Jones, "Georgia," p. 297.

15. Fuller, "Gamsakhurdia's First One Hundred Days," p. 10.

16. This polling was practically the inverse of the election outcome in Georgia proper, where the Round Table won with 62 percent and the Communists got 26 percent.

17. Although he modified his position somewhat, Gamsakhurdia did not acknowledge publicly that his statement on the abolition of the republic weakened support for his Round Table coalition. Rather, he blamed it on subversive imperialist agents operating in the republic. See Suny, *The Making of the Georgian Nation*, p. 400 n. 26, and Fuller, "Zviad Gamsakhurdia," p. 14.

18. *Svobodnaya gruziya*, 25 September 1991, p. 1. Reprinted in FBIS-SOV-91-195, October 8, 1991, p. 81.

19. Fuller, "Zviad Gamsakhurdia," p. 14.

20. The following discussion draws heavily on Fuller's "Georgia's Adzhar Crisis."

21. Ibid., p. 9.

22. Abashidze's appointment did not occur without some opposition. He was a Muslim and drew much of his support from the Muslim population in Ajaria. Thus, it is not surprising that much of his opposition came from Christian Georgians living in Ajaria. Nonetheless, he was seen as a Communist functionary whose most recent post under the Soviet system was head of the Ministry of Communal Services in Tbilisi. Abashidze was born in 1938 to a princely family that ruled Ajaria until the nineteenth century. He was trained as an economist, and like to Gamsakhurdia, he was a philologist. Fuller, "Aslan Abashidze," p. 23.

23. This was the second delay. The elections had been originally scheduled for March 3, 1991.

24. Fuller, "Georgia's Adzhar Crisis," p. 12.

25. This bloc consisted of the Republican Party and the Georgian Popular Front, two opposition parties with similar platforms to Round Table. The other major contender was the Ajar Oblast Organization of the Georgian Communist Party.

26. *Svobodnaya gruziya*, 25 September 1991, p. 1.

27. Mayak Radio, August 15, 1992. Reported by the British Broadcasting Corporation, August 17, 1992.

28. Fuller, "Aslan Abashidze."

29. They also protested the way Abashidze was elected into office: not by secret ballot, but by a show of hands. This was done at the insistence of Gamsakhurdia so that he could see who was supporting whom. "I want to see who is going to vote for whom, and in general, clear up for myself who is who." *Megapolis-Express*, no. 32 (1991): 19. Provided by Russian Press Digest, August 10, 1991.

30. He also acknowledged the influence and authority that Shevardnadze had to offer Georgia. *Nezavisimaya gazeta*, October 6, 1993, p. 3.

31. Ibid., June 27, 1992, p. 3. Emphasis added.

32. Ibid., June 27, 1992, p. 3.

33. *Trud*, October 20, 1994, p. 5.

34. Moscow Russian Television Network, October 3, 1994. Reprinted in FBIS-SOV-94-193, October 5, 1994, p. 44.

35. *Trud*, October 20, 1994, p. 5.

36. A similar line of argument could be made of Belgrade's reaction to the secessions of Slovenia and Croatia, whereby Belgrade was fighting to preserve as much of Yugoslavia as it could while defending the rights of ethnic Serbs.

37. *Izvestiya*, April 9, 1991, p. 1.

38. There is no controversy on this point. See, for example, the Stockholm International Peace Research Institute's, *SIPRI Yearbook 1994: Armaments, Disarmament, and Security* (Oxford: Oxford University Press, 1994), p. 108, which concludes that "the technical supply and support provided by the Russian armed forces was crucial for the success of the Abkhazian party."

39. *BBC Summary of World Broadcasts*, August 13, 1992. The interview with Shevardnadze first appeared in *Nezavisimaya gazeta*, August 11, 1992.

40. United States Information Agency, "Urban Georgians."

41. *BBC Summary of World Broadcasts*, August 4, 1993.

42. *Official Kremlin International News Broadcast*, September 28, 1992.

43. *Moscow News*, September 13, 1992.

44. Press conference by the Abkhaz government and Parliament members on the situation in the republic. *Official Kremlin International News Broadcast*, August 28, 1992.

45. *Official Kremlin International News Broadcast*, August 28, 1992.

46. Interfax, November 28, 1995.

47. Compared with Russian intervention in Abkhazia, any meaningful Russian military support for Ajaria would have been much more expensive and complicated, because unlike the former conflict, Russia did not share a border with Ajaria.

48. This gives rise to a puzzle: why would a loyal Georgian consider the intervention of the very state that had held Georgians in patronizing and humiliating bondage for centuries? The answer is that like Shevardnadze, Abashidze is much more of a statesman than a nationalist; his first concern throughout the crisis was the safety and security of his people, not that of an Ajar people. If security matters more than identity, then Russian intervention made sense, since it would have prevented bloodshed, though only at the cost of swallowing a healthy dose of nationalist pride.

49. *Izvestiya*, March 28, 1991, p. 3.

50. Since the conclusion of the war, most of the blame for the start of the armed conflict in Abkhazia and the events in August has come to rest on the shoulders of former defense Minister and National Guard commander Tengiz Kitovani. The consensus that has emerged is that he alone ordered the capture of Sukhumi and the storming of the Parliament building. It is doubtful that this is a fair assessment of responsibility, but it served the political interests of those in power. At the time of the initial offensive, Shevardnadze accepted the deployment of troops as the right of the Georgian state and did not dismiss Kitovani until nine months later.

51. As quoted in Lynch, *Conflict in Abkhazia*, p. 28.

Notes to Chapter 8
Conclusion

1. Lijphart, *Democracy in Plural Societies*. Also see Kymlicka, *Multicultural Citizenship*; Horowitz, *Ethnic Groups in Conflict*, pp. 601–28; and Nordlinger, *Conflict Regulation*.

2. In the case of the Soviet Union, see Hodnett, "Debate over Soviet Federalism," and more recently Roeder, "Soviet Federalism and Ethnic Mobilization" and "Peoples and States after 1989." For an empirical treatment of Russia, see Treisman, "Russia's Ethnic Revival." For a concise history, see Brubaker, *Nationalism Reframed*, chap. 2. A recent critique and more theoretical treatment of the perils of institutions and federalism can be found in Snyder's *From Voting to Violence*.

3. Bunce, *Subversive Institutions*.

4. Ibid., pp. 84–85.

5. Ibid., p. 125.

6. This history is not controversial. The main works I consulted include Leff's *National Conflict in Czechoslovakia* and *Czech and Slovak Republics* and Wolchik's *Czechoslovakia in Transition*.

7. For polling data showing the Slovaks' sense of inequity, see Shabad, Shible, and Zurovchak, "When Push Comes to Shove." On the general suspicions between the Czechs and the Slovaks, see Leff, *National Conflict*, chap. 5.

8. Pehe, "Czech-Slovak Conflict."

9. For accounts of the political bargaining between the Czechs and the Slovaks, Olson, "Dissolution of the State"; Ulc, "Bumpy Road"; Saideman, "Dual Dynamics"; Sevic, "Czechoslovakia's Velvet Divorce"; and Leff, "Could This Marriage Have Been Saved?"

10. Deis, "A Study of Nationalism," p. 11, table 5.

11. "Czechoslovakia Breaks in Two, to Wide Regret," *New York Times*, January 1, 1993.

12. See Silber and Little, *Death of a Nation*.

13. By 1991, 44 percent of the population was Muslim, 31 percent was Serb, and 17 percent was Croat. For an excellent overview of the demographics of Bosnia, see Burg and Sharp, *War in Bosnia-Herzegovina*, chap. 2.

14. Ibid., p. 70.

15. Bunce, *Subversive Institutions*, p. 136.

16. Ibid., pp. 136–37; emphasis added.

17. Ibid., p. 138.

18. Please note the important distinction between theoretical assertions and empirical description. The theory of indivisible territory *posits* a number of claims about actor motivations that are not meant to stand as exhaustive descriptions of how actors actually behave in a crisis or negotiation. Actors and motivations are both ideal types in the Weberian social scientific sense.

19. There is some irony in the fact that Thomas Hobbes, the seventeenth-century philosopher, used the concept of self-preservation (survival) as the starting point in a geometry of human relations whose ultimate aim was a defense and

justification of tyranny (absolute monarchy). He named his essay *Leviathan*. By Hobbes's conception, it would be irrational to prefer a life that was "nasty, brutish, and short" to a life under tyranny (even slavery). But Hobbes can succeed in his argument only by shearing the self of self-preservation of all the qualities that make living worthwhile. For most human beings, life in a coma, a dungeon, or a rape camp is a life not worth living. In such cases, it might be rational to prefer to risk death rather than to go on "living."

20. Ian Fisher, "New Fighting," and editorial, "Africa's Futile War," *New York Times*, February 7, 1999, p. 16.

21. Ian Fisher, "Behind Eritrea-Ethiopia War."

22. See the discussion in n. 19.

23. For an account of the perils of the proliferation of states, see Etzioni, "The Evils of Self-Determination."

24. Kenya provides an excellent example of how violence was averted because urban groups "refused to join in an ethnic war." See Kahl, "Population Growth," p. 116.

25. See Toft, "Differential Demographic Growth."

26. This finding is consistent with findings explaining the relationship between territory and interstate war. John Vasquez, for example, found that territorial disputes have a greater probability of leading to war than other types of disputes, and they are more likely to produce interstate rivals. Suzanne Werner found mixed support. She found that territorial conflicts are more likely to result in a recurrence of low-intensity conflict but not necessarily war. See Vasquez, "Mapping the Probability of War," "The Origins of Interstate Rivalry," and "Territorial Issue." Also see Werner, "The Precarious Nature of Peace."

27. Data taken from Wallensteen and Sollenberg's "Armed Conflicts."

28. Pearson chi2(2) $= 12.39$, $p < .01$. There were 59 armed intrastate conflicts: 28 over territory and 31 over the makeup of the regime. Armed conflicts led to at least 25 battle-related deaths during the year. Included in this analysis are interstate conflicts coded as "terminated." Terminated conflicts are those in which the number of deaths in 1996 did not exceed 25 or, if the conflict was active in 1996, fighting ceased by December 31, 1991, by peace agreement or victory. Peace agreements are defined as "an arrangement entered into by warring parties to explicitly regulate or resolve the basic incompatibility." Victory is "a situation in which one party has been defeated and/or eliminated by the other, or otherwise succumbed to the power of the other (e.g., through capitulation)." Ceasefire-stalemate refers to "a ceasefire agreement between the warring parties and cases where, by 31 December 1996, the final date of data collection, no armed activity above the threshold had been recorded between the actors for at least one year." See ibid., pp. 339 and 357.

29. In September 1999 Russia sent troops to Chechnya on the pretext that a series of terrorist bombings within Russia proper were fomented and directed from Chechnya. As in 1994, Russia expected the 1999 war to last only a few days. As of the writing of this book, the war continues and casualties continue to mount on both sides.

30. On the role of third-party guarantees, see Walter, "Critical Barrier" and "Designing Transitions."

31. Holbrooke, *To End a War*.

32. Kaufmann, "Possible and Impossible Solutions."

33. A surprising but little-noticed fact about partition is that few cases have been successful, and few cases exist today, yet it remains one of the most contested ideas in the press and academic literature. Two reasons might explain this. The first is Bosnia, which seemed a likely candidate for partition. The second is the prominence of some potential cases, such as Palestine, Cyprus, and Northern Ireland.

34. For a similar critique, see Downes, "Holy Land Divided."

35. Reports conflicted. Some claimed the fighters demanded money, and others denied this.

36. The Chechen treatment of Russian theatergoers was probably intended to mirror the treatment of Chechen hostages by Russian armed and secret police forces, who routinely restrict the movement of hostages and force them to defecate in their own clothing as a form of humiliation. See Masha Gessen, "Ignorance Perpetuates the Chechen War," *New York Times*, November 1, 2002.

37. In addition, as with Palestinians in the occupied territories, the wars in Chechnya have come to involve an entire generation of Chechens who know no other life but one of violence and death. See, for example, Sabrina Tabernese, "With Few Ties to Russia, Young Chechens Join Militants," *New York Times*, November 19, 2002.

38. See, for example, Gessen, "Ignorance Perpetuates."

39. See Elaine Sciolino, "Putin Unleashes His Fury against Chechen Guerrillas," *New York Times*, November 12, 2002.

40. In this, he is following the clear precedent established by NATO's 1999 assault on Serbia over the Serbian abuse of ethnic Albanians in Kosovo.

41. The phrase "willingness to suffer" harks back to U.S. calculations of the degree of pain necessary to coerce North Vietnam to abandon its support of Vietcong guerrillas in South Vietnam in the 1960s. In that war, U.S. Secretary of Defense Robert McNamara concluded after careful analysis that no amount of pain that the United States could inflict would succeed in coercing the North. For an analysis of the outcomes of different strategic interactions, see Ivan Arreguín-Toft, "How the Weak Win Wars: A Theory of Asymmetric Conflict," *International Security*, vol. 26, no. 1, Summer 2001, pp. 93–128.

References

Books and Articles

Agnew, John. *Place and Politics: The Geographical Mediation of State and Society.* Boston: Allen and Unwin, 1987.

Anderson, Benedict. *Imagined Communities.* London: Verso, 1983.

Arfi, Badredine. "Ethnic Fear: The Social Construction of Insecurity." *Security Studies* 8, no. 1 (fall 1998): 151–203.

Aves, Jonathan. "The Rise and Fall of the Georgian Nationalist Movements, 1987–1991." In *The Road to Post-Communism: Independent Political Movements in the Former Soviet Union, 1985–1991*, edited by Geoffrey A. Hosking, Jonathan Aves, and Peter J. S. Duncan. New York: Pinter Press, 1992.

Avtorkhanov, Abdurahman. "The Chechens and Ingush during the Soviet Period and Its Antecedents." In *The North Caucasus Barrier: The Russian Advance towards the Muslim World*, edited by Marie Benningsen Broxup. London: Hurst and Company, 1992.

Barth, Frederick, ed. *Ethnic Groups and Boundaries.* Boston: Little, Brown, 1969.

Bates, Robert, et al. *Analytic Narratives.* Princeton: Princeton University Press, 1998.

Belaya Kniga Abkhazii. Moscow, 1993.

Belaya Kniga Tatarstana: Put' k suverenitetu (sbornik ofitsial'nykh dokumentor), 1990–1993. Kazan, 1993.

Bennigsen, Alexandre, and S. Enders Wimbush. *Muslims of the Soviet Empire: A Guide.* Bloomington: Indiana University Press, 1986.

Blainey, Geoffrey. *Causes of War.* 3d ed. New York: Free Press, 1988.

Bloom, William. *Personal Identity, National Identity, and International Relations.* Cambridge: Cambridge University Press, 1990.

Brass, Paul. *Ethnicity and Nationalism: Theory and Comparison.* New Delhi: Sage Publications, 1991.

Breuilly, John. *Nationalism and the State.* Chicago: University of Chicago Press, 1985.

Brewer, Marilyn B. "Social Identity, Distinctiveness, and In-Group Homogeneity." *Social Cognition* 11, no. 1 (spring 1993): 150–64.

Brewer, Marilyn B., and Wendi Gardner. "Who Is This 'We'? Levels of Collective Identity and Self Representations." *Journal of Personality and Social Psychology* 71, no. 1 (1996): 83–93.

Brown, Michael E. "Deterrence Failures and Deterrence Strategies." RAND Paper Series, 77-502-602/2, March 1977.

———. *Ethnic Conflict and International Security.* Princeton: Princeton University Press, 1993.

———. "The Causes and Regional Dimensions of Internal Conflict." In *The*

International Dimensions of Internal Conflict, edited by Michael Brown, 571–601. Cambridge, Mass.: MIT Press, 1996.

Brown, Michael, and Sumit Ganguly, eds. *Government Policies and Ethnic Relations in Asia and the Pacific*. Cambridge, Mass.: MIT Press, 1997.

Broxup, Marie Benningsen. "Introduction: Russia and the North Caucasus." In *The North Caucasus Barrier: The Russian Advance towards the Muslim World*, edited by Marie Benningsen Broxup. London: Hurst and Company, 1992.

Brubaker, Rogers. *Nationalism Reframed*. Cambridge: Cambridge University Press, 1996.

Bunce, Valerie. *Subversive Institutions: The Design and the Destruction of Socialism and the State*. Cambridge: Cambridge University Press, 1999.

Burg, Steven L., and Paul S. Sharp. *The War in Bosnia-Herzegovina: Ethnic Conflict and International Intervention*. Armonk, N.Y.: M. E. Sharpe, 1999.

Byman, Daniel, L. "Divided They Stand: Lessons about Partition from Iraq and Lebanon." *Security Studies* 7, no. 1 (Autumn 1997): 1–29.

———. *Keeping the Peace: Lasting Solutions to Ethnic Conflict*. Baltimore: Johns Hopkins University Press, 2002.

Byman, Daniel, and Stephen Van Evera. "Hypotheses on the Causes of Contemporary Deadly Conflict." *Security Studies* 7, no. 3 (spring 1998): 1–50.

Carment, David, and Patrick James, eds. *Peace in the Midst of Wars: Preventing and Managing International Ethnic Conflicts*. Columbia: University of South Carolina Press, 1998.

Chechenskiya Tragedia: Kto Vinovat. Moscow: Novosti, 1995.

Chervonnaya, Svetlana. *Conflict in the Caucasus: Georgia, Armenia, and the Russian Shadow*. Translated by Ariane Chanturia. Glastonbury, England: Gothic Images Publications, 1994.

Chin, Jeff, and Robert Kaiser. *Russians As the New Minority: Ethnicity and Nationalism in the Soviet Successor States*. Boulder, Colo.: Westview Press, 1996.

Coakley, John. *The Territorial Management of Ethnic Conflict*. London: Frank Cass, 1993.

Colarusso, John. "Abkhazia." *Central Asian Survey* 14, no. 1 (March 1995): 75–96.

Collier, Paul, and Anke Hoeffler. "Justice-Seeking and Loot-Seeking in Civil Wars." World Bank, February 1999. Photocopy.

Committee on International Relations. *Self-Involvement in the Middle East Conflict*, Group for the Advancement of Psychiatry 10, no. 103, November 1978.

Comrie, Bernard. *The Languages of the Soviet Union*. Cambridge: Cambridge University Press, 1981.

Connor, Walker. "Eco- or Ethno-Nationalism?" *Ethnic and Racial Studies* 7 (1984), no. 3:342–59.

———. "A Nation Is a Nation, Is a State, Is an Ethnic Group, Is a . . ." *Ethnic and Racial Studies* 1 (October 1978): 377–400.

———. *The National Question in Marxist-Leninist Theory and Strategy*. Princeton: Princeton University Press, 1984.

———. "The Impact of Homelands upon Diasporas." In *Modern Diasporas in International Politics*, edited by Gabriel Sheffer, 16–46. New York: St. Martin's Press, 1986.

————. *Ethnonationalism: The Quest for Understanding.* Princeton: Princeton University Press, 1994.

Conquest, Robert. *The Nation Killers: The Soviet Deportation of Nationalities.* New York: Macmillan, 1970.

Dahl, Robert. "Democracy, Majority Rule, and Gorbachev's Referendum." *Dissent* (fall 1991): 491–96.

Dale, Catherine. "Turmoil in Abkhazia: Russian Responses." *RFE/RL Research Report* 2, no. 34 (August 27, 1993): 48–57.

David, Steven R. "Internal War: Causes and Cures." *World Politics* 49, no. 4 (July 1997): 552–76.

Davies, James. "The J-Curve of Rising and Declining Satisfaction As a Cause of Revolution and Rebellion." In *Violence in America: Historical and Comparative Perspectives,* edited by Ted Robert Gurr and Hugh Davis, 547–76. Beverly Hills, Calif.: Sage Publications, 1979.

Deis, Michael J. "A Study of Nationalism in Czechoslovakia." *RFE/RL Research Report* 1, no. 5 (January 31, 1992): 8–13.

D'Encausse, Hélène Carrère. *Decline of an Empire: The Soviet Socialist Republics in Revolt.* Translated by Martin Sokolinsky and Henry A. LaFarge. New York: Harper and Row, 1978.

————. *The Great Challenge: Nationalities and the Bolshevik State, 1917–1930.* Translated by Nancy Festinger. New York: Holmes and Meier, 1992.

————. *The End of the Soviet Empire.* Translated by Franklin Philip. New York: Basic Books, 1993.

Derlugian, Georgi Matvee. "Historical Sociological Interpretations of National Separatism in the Four Former Soviet Autonomous Republics: Tataria, Chechnya, Abkhazia, and Ajaria." Ph.D. diss., SUNY Binghamton, N.Y., 1995.

Deutsch, Karl. *Nationalism and Social Communication.* 2d ed. Cambridge, Mass.: MIT Press, 1966.

Diehl, Paul F. "Geography and War: A Review and Assessment of the Empirical Literature." *International Interactions* 17, no. 1 (1991): 11–27.

————. "What Are They Fighting For? The Importance of Issues in International Conflict Research." *Journal of Peace Research* 29, no. 3 (1992): 333–44.

————, ed. *A Roadmap to War: Territorial Dimensions of International Conflict.* Nashville, Tenn.: Vanderbilt University Press, 1999.

Diehl, Paul F., and Gary Goertz. "Entering International Society: Military Conflict and National Independence, 1816–1980." *Comparative Political Studies* 23, no. 4 (January 1991): 497–518.

Dienes, Leslie. "Proposals for Additional Oil Refining in Tatarstan." *Post-Soviet Geography* 33, no. 1 (January 1992): 66–67.

————. "Prospects for Russian Oil in the 1990s: Reserves and Costs." *Post-Soviet Geography* 34, no. 2 (February 1993) 79–110.

Downes, Alexander B. "The Holy Land Divided: Defending Partition as a Solution to Ethnic Wars." *Security Studies* 10, no. 4 (summer 2001): 58–116.

Dunlop, John. "Russia: Confronting a Loss of Empire." In *Nations and Politics in Soviet Successor States,* edited by Ian Bremmer and Ray Taras, 48–51. Cambridge: Cambridge University Press, 1993.

Eismont, Maria. *Prism.* Jamestown Foundation, March 8, 1996. Electronic report.

Ellis, John. *From the Barrel of a Gun: A History of Guerrilla, Revolutionary, and Counter-Insurgency Warfare, from the Romans to the Present.* 2d ed. London: Greenhill Books, 1995.

Elster, Jon. *Solomonic Judgements.* Cambridge: Cambridge University Press, 1989.

Emerson, Rupert. *From Empire to Nation.* Boston: Beacon Press, 1960.

Emizet, Kisangani N., and Vicki L. Hesli. "The Disposition to Secede: An Analysis of the Soviet Case." *Comparative Political Studies* 27, no. 4 (1995): 493–536.

Esman, Milton J. *Ethnic Politics.* Ithaca, N.Y.: Cornell University Press, 1994.

Etzioni, Amitai. "The Evils of Self-Determination." *Foreign Policy* 89 (winter 1992): 21–35.

Eudin, Xenia Joukoff, and Robert C. North. *Soviet Russia and the East, 1920–1927: A Documentary Survey.* Stanford, Calif.: Stanford University Press, 1957.

Fearon, James D. "Rationalist Explanations for War." *International Organization* 49, no. 3 (summer 1995): 379–414.

———. "Commitment Problems and the Spread of Ethnic Conflict." In *The International Spread of Ethnic Conflict: Fear, Diffusion, and Escalation,* edited by David A. Lake and Donald Rothschild, 107–126. Princeton: Princeton University Press, 1998.

Fearon, James D., and David D. Laitin. "Explaining Interethnic Cooperation." *American Political Science Review* 90, no. 4 (December 1996): 715–35.

———. "Ethnicity, Insurgency, and Civil War." *American Political Science Review* 97, no. 1 (February 2003): 75–90.

Fisher, Ian. "Behind Eritrea-Ethiopia War, a 'Knack for Stubbornness.'" *New York Times,* February 14, 1999, p. 3.

———. "New Fighting along Border of Ethiopia and Eritrea." *New York Times,* February 7, 1999, p. 4.

Fisher, Roger. "Fractionating Conflict." In *International Conflict and Behavioral Science,* edited by Roger Fisher. New York: Basic Books, 1964.

Fuller, Elizabeth. "Georgian Writers Discuss the Demographic Situation." *Radio Liberty Research Bulletin* (henceforth abbreviated as RL), 404/84, Radio Liberty Research, October 22, 1984.

———. "Islam in Ajaria." In RL 221/86, Radio Liberty Research, June 4, 1986.

———. "Disastrous Weather in Georgia Accelerates Resettlement of Svans." In RL 134/87, Radio Liberty Research, March 27, 1987.

———. "Marneuli: Georgia's Potential Nagorno-Karabakh?" In RL 477/88, Radio Liberty Research, October 18, 1988.

———. "New Abkhaz Campaign for Secession from the Georgian SSR." *RFE/RL Report on the USSR* 1, no. 14 (April 7, 1989): 27–28.

———. "Georgian Alternative Election Results Announced." *RFE/RL Report on the USSR* 2 (October 26, 1990): 23–24.

———. "Georgia on the Eve of the Supreme Soviet Elections." *RFE/RL Report on the USSR* 2 no. 45 (November 9, 1990): 18–21.

———. "Zviad Gamsakhurdia Proposes Abolition of Adzhar Autonomy." *RFE/RL Report on the USSR* 2, no. 48 (November 30, 1990): 13–14.

———. "Gamsakhurdia's First One Hundred Days." *RFE/RL Report on the USSR* 3, no. 10 (March 8, 1991): 10–13.

———. "Georgia's Adzhar Crisis." *RFE/RL Report on the USSR* 3, no. 32 (August 9, 1991): 8–13.

———. "Abkhazia on the Brink of Civil War?" *RFE/RL Research Report* 1, no. 35 (September 4, 1992): 1–5.

———. "Aslan Abashidze: Georgia's Next Leader?" *RFE/RL Research Report* 2, no. 44 (November 5, 1993): 23–36.

———. "Russia's Diplomatic Offensive in the Transcaucasus." *RFE/RL Research Report* 2, no. 39 (October 1, 1993): 31–32.

Fuller, Elizabeth, and Goulnara Ouratadze. "Georgian Leadership Changes in Aftermath of Demonstrators' Death." *RFE/RL Report on the USSR* 1, no. 16 (April 21, 1989): 28–31.

Gagnon, V. P., Jr. "Ethnic Nationalism and International Conflict: The Case of Serbia." *International Security* 19, no. 3 (winter 1994/95): 130–66.

Galeotti, Mark. "Chechnia: Russia's Sicily?" *Jane's Intelligence Review* 6, no. 3 (March 1, 1994): 128.

Gall, Carlotta, and Thomas de Waal. *Chechnya: Calamity in the Caucasus.* New York: New York University Press, 1998.

Gantzel, Klaus Jürgen. "War in the Post–World II World: Some Empirical Trends and a Theoretical Approach." In *War and Ethnicity: Global Connections and Local Violence*, edited by David Turton, 123–44. Rochester, N.Y.: University of Rochester Press, 1997.

Gantzel, Klaus Jürgen, and Torsten Schwinghammer. *Die Kriege nach dem zweiten Weltkrieg 1945 bis 1992.* Münster: Lit Verlag, 1999.

Geertz, Clifford. "The Integrative Revolution: Primordial Sentiments and Civil Politics in the New States." In *The Interpretation of Cultures.* New York: Basic Books, 1973.

Gellner, Ernest. *Nations and Nationalism.* Ithaca, N.Y.: Cornell University Press, 1983.

———. "Nationalism in a Vacuum." In *Thinking Theoretically about Soviet Nationalities.* New York: Columbia University Press, 1992.

George, Alexander L. "Case Studies and Theory Development: The Method of Structured, Focused Comparison." In *Diplomacy: New Approaches in History, Theory, and Policy*, edited by Paul Gordon Lauren. New York: Free Press, 1979.

George, Alexander L., and Gordon Craig. *Force and Statecraft: Diplomatic Problems of Our Times.* 2d ed. New York: Oxford University Press, 1990.

George, Alexander L., and Timothy McKeown. "Case Studies and Theories of Organizational Decisionmaking." In *Advances in Information Processing in Organizations*, edited by Robert F. Coulam and Richard A. Smith, 2:21–58. Greenwich, Conn.: JAI Press, 1985.

Gilpin, Robert. *War and Change in International Politics.* Cambridge: Cambridge University Press, 1981.

Giuliano, Elise. "Who Determines the Self in the Politics of Self-Determination? Identity and Preference Formation in Tatarstan's Nationalist Mobilization." *Comparative Politics* (April 2000): 295–316.

Glaser, Charles L. "Political Consequences of Military Strategy: Expanding and

Refining the Spinal and Deterrence Models." *World Politics* 44, no. 4 (July 1992): 171–201.

———. "Realists As Optimists: Cooperation As Self-Help." *International Security* 19, no. 3 (winter 1994–95): 50–90.

———. "The Security Dilemma Revisited." *World Politics* 50, no. 1 (October 1997): 171–201.

Glenny, Misha. *The Fall of Yugoslavia*. New York: Penguin Books, 1992.

Goertz, Gary, and Paul F. Diehl. *Territorial Changes and International Conflict*. London: Routledge, 1992.

Goldenberg, Suzanne. *Pride of Small Nations: The Caucasus and Post-Soviet Disorder*. London: Zed Books, 1994.

Gourevitch, Peter. "The Reemergence of Peripheral Nationalisms: Some Comparative Speculations on the Spatial Distribution of Political Leadership and Economic Growth." *Comparative Studies in Society and History* 21, no. 3 (July 1979): 303–22.

Grant, James. *Recent British Battles on Land and Sea*. London: Cassell, 1884.

Greenberg, Joel. "Palestinian Census Ignites Dispute over Jerusalem." *New York Times*, December 11, 1997.

———. "Chief Rabbis Say Israel Must Keep Holy Site." *New York Times*, January 5, 2001.

Gurr, Ted Robert. *Why Men Rebel*. Princeton: Princeton University Press, 1970.

———. "Why Minorities Rebel: A Global Analysis of Communal Mobilization and Conflict since 1945." *International Political Science Review* 14, no. 2 (1993): 161–201.

———. *Minorities at Risk: A Global View of Ethnopolitical Conflicts*. Washington, D.C.: United States Institute of Peace Press, 1993.

———. "Peoples against States: Ethnopolitical Conflict and the Changing World System." *International Studies Quarterly* 38 (1994): 347–77.

———. *Peoples against States: Minorities at Risk in the New Century*. Washington, D.C.: United States Institute of Peace Press, 2000.

———. *Peoples versus States*. Washington, D.C.: United States Institute of Peace Press, 2000.

Gurr, Ted Robert, with Monty G. Marshall and Deepa Khosla. "Peace and Conflict, 2001: A Global Survey of Armed Conflicts, Self-Determination Movements, and Democracy." Center for International Development and Management, University of Maryland, 2000.

Habermas, Jürgen. *The Inclusion of the Other*, edited by Ciaran Cronin and Pablo DeGreiff. Cambridge, Mass.: MIT Press, 1998.

Hardin, Russell. *One for All: The Logic of Group Conflict*. Princeton: Princeton University Press, 1995.

Harris, Chauncy D. "A Geographic Analysis of Non-Russian Minorities and Its Ethnic Homelands." *Post-Soviet Geography* 34, no. 9 (November 1993).

Hecter, Michael. *Internal Colonialism*. Berkeley: University of California Press, 1977.

———. "The Dynamics of Secession." *Acta Sociologica* 35, no. 4 (1992): 267–83.

Hecter, Michael, and Margaret Levy. "The Comparative Analysis of Ethnoregional Movements." *Ethnic and Racial Studies* 2 (July 1979): 260–74.

Heller, Mikhail, and Aleksander Nekrich. *Utopia in Power: The History of the Soviet Union from 1917 to the Present.* Translated by Phyllis B. Carlos. New York: Summit Books, 1986.

Heraclides, Alexis. "Secessionist Minorities and External Involvement." *International Organization* 44, no. 3 (Summer 1990): 341–78.

Herz, John. *Political Realism and Political Idealism.* Chicago: University of Chicago Press, 1959.

Hewitt, B. G. "Abkhazia: A Problem of Identity and Ownership." In *Transcaucasian Boundaries*, edited by John F. R. Wright, Suzanne Goldenberg, and Richard Schofield, 190–225. New York: St. Martin's Press, 1996.

Hewitt, George. ed. *The Abkhazians: A Handbook.* Surrey, England: Curzon Press, 1999.

Hobsbawm, E. J. *Nations and Nationalism since 1780: Programme, Myth, Reality.* Cambridge: Cambridge University Press, 1990.

Hodnett, Grey. "The Debate over Soviet Federalism." *Soviet Studies* 18, no. 4 (1967): 459–69

Holbrooke, Richard. *To End a War.* New York: Random House, 1998.

Holsti, Kalevi. *Peace and War: Armed Conflicts and International Order, 1648–1989.* Cambridge: Cambridge University Press, 1991.

Horowitz, Donald. *Ethnic Groups in Ethnic Conflict.* Berkeley: University of California Press, 1985.

Hroch, Miroslav. *Social Preconditions of National Revival in Europe.* Cambridge: Cambridge University Press, 1985.

Hunter, Shireen T. *The Transcaucasus in Transition.* Washington, D.C.: Center for Strategic and International Studies, 1994.

Huth, Paul. *Standing Your Ground: Territorial Disputes and International Conflict.* Ann Arbor: University of Michigan Press, 1996.

Ignatieff, Michael. *Blood and Belonging.* New York: Farrar, Straus, and Giroux, 1993.

Iklé, Fred C. *How Nations Negotiate.* New York: Praeger, 1964.

Industrial Atlas of the Soviet Successor States, An. Houston, Tex.: Industrial Information Resources, 1994.

Independent Commission on Kosovo, The. *The Kosovo Report.* Oxford: Oxford University Press, 2000.

Isaacs, Harold R. *Idols of the Tribe.* Cambridge, Mass.: Harvard University Press, 1975.

Itogi Vsesoiuznoi perepisi naseleniia 1989 goda: Gosudarstvenny: Komitet SSSR po Statiske. Minneapolis, Minn.: East View Publications, 1992. Microfiche.

Jelavich, Barbara. *History of the Balkans: Twentieth Century.* Cambridge: Cambridge University Press, 1983.

Jervis, Robert. *The Logic of Images in International Relations.* New York: Columbia University Press, 1970.

———. *Perception and Misperception in International Politics.* Princeton: Princeton University Press, 1976.

————. "Cooperation under the Security Dilemma." *World Politics* 30, no. 2 (January 1978): 167–218.

Jones, Stephen F. "Georgia: A Failed Democratic Transition." *Nations and Politics in the Soviet Successor States*, edited by Ian Bremmer and Ray Taras. Cambridge: Cambridge University Press, 1993.

Kahl, Colin. "Population Growth, Environmental Degradation, and State-Sponsored Violence: The Case of Kenya, 1991–1993." *International Security* 23, no. 2 (fall 1998): 80–119.

Kaiser, Robert J. *The Geography of Nationalism in Russia and the USSR*. Princeton: Princeton University Press, 1994.

Kaufman, Stuart J. "Spiraling to Ethnic War: Elites, Masses, and Moscow in Moldova's Civil War." *International Security* 21, no. 2 (fall 1996): 108–38.

Kaufmann, Chaim. "Possible and Impossible Solutions to Ethnic Civil Wars." *International Security* 20, no. 4 (Spring 1996): 136–75.

Khalvashi, Pridon. "Belief in the Existing, or Belief in the Non-Existent." *Komunisti*, no. 1 (February 1986). English translation, *BBC Summary of World Broadcasts*, March 8, 1986.

King, Gary, Robert O. Keohane, and Sidney Verba. *Designing Social Inquiry: Scientific Inference in Qualitative Research*. Princeton: Princeton University Press, 1994.

Kline, Edward. "The Conflict in Chechnya." Working paper, Andrei Sakharov Foundation, March 24, 1995.

Kohn, Hans. *Nationalism: Its Meaning and History*. Malabar, Fla.: Robert E. Krieger Publishing, 1965.

Koltso, Pal. "Territorialising Diasporas: The Case of Russians in the Former Soviet Republics." *Millennium* 27, no. 3 (1999): 607–31.

Kumar, Radha. "The Troubled History of Partition." *Foreign Affairs* 76, no. 1 (Jan.–Feb. 1997): 22–34.

Kupchan, Charles A., ed. *Nationalism and Nationalities in the New Europe*. Ithaca, N.Y.: Cornell University Press, 1995.

Kuran, Timur. "Now out of Never: The Element of Surprise in the East European Revolution of 1989." *World Politics* 44, no. 1, (October 1991): 7–48.

Kymlicka, Will. *Multicultural Citizenship: A Liberal Theory of Minority Rights*. Oxford: Clarendon Press, 1995.

Laitin, David D. *Hegemony and Culture: Politics and Religious Change among the Yoruba*. Chicago: University of Chicago Press, 1986.

————. *Identity in Formation: The Russian-Speaking Populations in the Near Abroad*. Ithaca, N.Y.: Cornell University Press, 1998.

Lake, David A., and Donald Rothschild, eds. *The International Spread of Ethnic Conflict: Fear, Diffusion, and Escalation*. Princeton: Princeton University Press, 1998.

Lak'oba, Stanislav. "History, 1917–1989." In *The Abkhazians: A Handbook*, edited by George Hewitt, 89–101. Surrey, England: Curzon Press, 1999.

Lapidus, Gail W. "Contested Sovereignty: The Tragedy of Chechnya." *International Security* 23, no. 3 (summer 1998): 5–49.

LaPonce, Jean. *Languages and Their Territories*. Translated by Anthony Martin-Sperry. Toronto: University of Toronto Press, 1987.

Leff, Carol Skalnik. *National Conflict in Czechoslovakia.* Princeton, N.J.: Princeton University Press, 1988.

―――. "Could This Marriage Have Been Saved? The Czechoslovak Divorce." *Current History* 95, no. 599 (March 1996): 129–34.

―――. *The Czech and Slovak Republics: Nation versus State.* Boulder, Colo.: Westview Press, 1996.

Lemercier-Quelquejay, Chantal. "Co-optation of Elites of Kabarda and Dagestan in the Sixteenth Century." In *The North Caucasus Barrier*, edited by Marie Bennigsen Broxup, 18–44. London: C. Hurst, 1992.

Liberman, Peter. "The Spoils of Conquest." *International Security* 18, no. 2 (fall 1993): 125–53.

―――. *Does Conquest Pay? The Exploitation of Occupied Industrial Societies.* Princeton: Princeton University Press, 1996.

Licklider, Roy. "The Consequences of Negotiated Settlements in Civil Wars, 1945–1993." *American Political Science Review* 89, no. 3 (September 1995).

Lieven, Anatol. *Chechnya: Tombstone of Russian Power.* New Haven, Conn.: Yale University Press, 1998.

Lijphart, Arend. *Democracy in Plural Societies: A Comparative Exploration.* New Haven, Conn.: Yale University Press, 1977.

Lipset, Seymour Martin. *Political Man: The Social Bases of Politics.* Baltimore: Johns Hopkins University Press, 1981.

Lustick, Ian. *Unsettled States, Disputed Lands.* Ithaca, N.Y.: Cornell University Press, 1993.

Lynch, Dov. *The Conflict in Abkhazia: Dilemmas in Russian "Peacekeeping" Policy.* London: Royal Institute for International Affairs, 1998.

Lysenko, Valentin Ivanovich. *Ot Tatarstana do Chechnii.* Moscow: Instituta Sovremennoi Politiki, 1995.

Mackinder, Halford J. "The Geographical Pivot of History." *Geographical Journal* 23, no. 4 (April 1904): 421–44.

Mann, Michael. *States, War, and Capitalism.* Oxford: Oxford University Press, 1988.

Manogaran, Chelvadurai. "Sinhalese-Tamil Relations and the Prospects for Peace with Justice in Sri Lanka." Paper presented at South Asia Conference on Development, Social Justice, and Peace, Catholic University of America, Washington, D.C., July 19–20, 1996.

McAuley, Mary. *Russia's Politics of Uncertainty.* Cambridge: Cambridge University Press, 1977.

McGarry, John, and Brendan O'Leary, eds. *The Politics of Ethnic Conflict Regulation.* London: Routledge, 1993.

―――. *Explaining Northern Ireland.* Malden, Mass.: Blackwell Publishers, 1995.

Mearsheimer, John. *Conventional Deterrence.* Ithaca, N.Y.: Cornell University Press, 1983.

―――. "Back to the Future: Instability in Europe after the Cold War." *International Security* 15, no. 1 (summer 1990): 5–56.

Mercer, Jonathan. *Reputation and International Politics.* Ithaca, N.Y.: Cornell University Press, 1996.

Mershon, Robert F. *Revolution and Genocide.* Chicago: University of Chicago Press, 1992.

Montville, Joseph, ed. *Conflict and Peacemaking in Multiethnic Societies.* New York: Lexington, 1991.

Morley, D., and K. Robins. "No Place Like Heimat: Images of Homeland in European Culture." *Space and Place: Theories of Identity and Location,* edited by E. Carter et al. London: Lawrence and Wishart, 1993.

Mueller, John. "The Banality of 'Ethnic War.'" *International Security* 25, no. 1, (summer 2000): 42–70.

Muzayev, Timur. *Novaya Checheno-Ingushetia.* Moscow: Informatsionno-ekspertnaya gruppa "Panorama," May 1992.

———. *Chechenskaya respublika: Organi vlasti i politicheskie sily.* Moscow: Informatsionno-ekspertnaya gruppa "Panorama," 1995.

Narodnoe khozyaistvo SSSR v 1990 goda: Statisticheskii ezhegodnik. Moscow: Financi i statistiki, 1991.

Narodnoe khozyaistvo RSFSR v 1990 g.: Statisticheskii ezhegodnik. Moscow: Goskomstat RSFSR, 1991.

Narodnoe khozyaistvo Gruzinskoi SSR za 60 let. Tbilisi: Izdatel'stvo Sabchota Sakartvelo, 1980.

Nekrich, Aleksandr. *The Punished Peoples: The Deportation and Fate of Soviet Minorities at the End of the Second World War.* Translated by George Saunders. New York: W. W. Norton, 1978.

Newland, Kathleen. "Ethnic Conflict and Refugees." In *Ethnic Conflict and International Security,* edited by Michael Brown, 143–63. Princeton: Princeton University Press, 1993.

Newman, David. "Real Spaces, Symbolic Spaces: Interrelated Notions of Territory in the Arab-Israeli Conflict." In *A Roadmap to War: Territorial Dimensions of International Conflict,* edited by Paul Diehl, 3–34. Nashville, Tenn.: Vanderbilt University Press, 1999.

Newman, Saul. "Does Modernization Breed Ethnic Political Conflict?" *World Politics* 43, no. 3 (April 1991): 451–78.

Nichols, Johanna. "Who Are the Chechens." University of California, Berkeley, January 1995.

Nordlinger, Eric A. *Conflict Regulation in Divided Societies.* Cambridge, Mass.: Center for International Affairs, Harvard University, 1972.

Novaya Rossiya, informatsionno-statisticheskii al'manakh. Moscow: Mezhdynarodnaya Akademiya Informatizatsii, 1994.

O'Ballance, Edgar. *Wars in the Caucasus, 1990–1995.* New York: New York University Press, 1997.

Olson, David M. "Dissolution of the State: Political Parties and the 1992 Election in Czechoslovakia." *Communist and Post-Communist Studies* 26, no. 3 (September 1993): 301–14.

Olzak, Susan. *The Dynamics of Ethnic Competition and Conflict.* Stanford, Calif.: Stanford University Press, 1992.

Omrod, Jane. "The North Caucasus: Fragmentation or Federation." In *Nations and Politics in the Soviet Successor States,* edited by Ian Bremmer and Ray Taras, 448–452. Cambridge: Cambridge University Press, 1993.

Otyrba, Gueorgui. "War in Abkhazia." In *National Identity and Ethnicity in Russia and the New States of Eurasia*, edited by Roman Szporluk, 281–309. New York: M. E. Sharpe, 1994.

Paul, T. V. *Asymmetric Conflicts: War Initiation by Weaker Powers*. Cambridge: Cambridge University Press, 1994.

Pehe, Jiri. "Czech-Slovak Conflict Threatens State Unity." *RFE/RL Research Report* 1, no. 1 (January 2, 1992): 83–86.

Peiris, G. H. "An Appraisal of the Concept of a Traditional Tamil Homeland in Sri Lanka." Paper presented at the ICES seminar in Sri Lanka, August 1985. Also published in *The Island*, March 24 and 29, 1999.

Petersen, Roger Dale. *Understanding Ethnic Violence: Fear, Hatred, and Resentment in Twentieth Century Eastern Europe*. Cambridge: Cambridge University Press, 2002.

Pipes, Richard. *The Formation of the Soviet Union: Communism and Nationalism, 1917–1923*. 3d ed. Cambridge, Mass.: Harvard University Press, 1997.

Posen, Barry. "The Security Dilemma and Ethnic Conflict." In *Ethnic Conflict and International Security*, edited by Michael Brown, 103–124. Princeton: Princeton University Press, 1993.

Rahr, Alexander. "The Roots of the Power Struggle." *RFE/RL Research Report* 2, no. 20 (May 14, 1993): 9–15.

Raviot, Jean-Robert. "Tipy natsionalizma obshchestvo i politika v Tatarstane." *Politicheskie Issledovania*, nos. 5–6 (1992).

Riggins, Howard. "Sri Lanka: Negotiations in a Secessionist Conflict," In *Elusive Peace: Negotiating an End to Civil Wars*, edited by William Zartman, 35–58. Washington, D.C.: Brookings Institution Press, 1995.

Roeder, Philip G. "Soviet Federalism and Ethnic Mobilization." *World Politics* 43, no. 2 (1991): 196–232.

———. "Peoples and States after 1989: The Political Costs of Incomplete National Revolutions." *Slavic Review* 59, no. 4 (1999): 854–84.

Rorlich, Azade-Ayse. *The Volga Tatars: A Profile in National Resilience*. Stanford, Calif.: Hoover Institution Press, 1986.

Rose, William. "The Security Dilemma and Ethnic Conflict." *Security Studies* 9, no. 4 (summer 2000): 1–51.

Ryan, Stephen. *Ethnic Conflict and International Relations*. Aldershot, England: Gower Publishing Company, 1990.

Sagan, Scott D. "Origins of the Pacific War." In *The Origin and Prevention of Major Wars*, edited by Robert I. Rotberg and Theodore K. Rabb. Cambridge: Cambridge University Press, 1989.

Saideman, Stephen M. "The Dual Dynamics of Disintegration: Ethnic Politics and Security Dilemmas in Eastern Europe." *Nationalism and Ethnic Politics* 2, no. 1 (spring 1996): 18–43.

Sambanis, Nicholas. "Partition As a Solution to Ethnic War." *World Politics* 52, no. 4 (July 2000): 437–83.

Schaeffer, Robert. *Warpaths: The Politics of Partition*. New York: Wang and Hill, 1990.

Schelling, Thomas C. *The Strategy of Conflict*. Cambridge, Mass.: Harvard University Press, 1960.

————. *Arms and Influence*. New Haven, Conn.: Yale University Press, 1966.

————. *Micromotives and Macrobehavior*. New York: W. W. Norton, 1978.

Schmidt, Fabian. "Kosovo: The Time Bomb That Has Not Gone Off." *RFE/RL Research Report* 2, no. 39 (October 1, 1993): 21–29.

Schwartz, Lee. "A History of the Russian and Soviet Censuses." In *Research Guide to the Russian and Soviet Censuses*, edited by Ralph S. Clem, 48–69. Ithaca, N.Y.: Cornell University Press, 1986.

Scott, James C. *Seeing Like a State: How Certain Schemes to Improve the Human Condition Have Failed*. New Haven, Conn.: Yale University Press, 1998.

Segal, Jerome, et al. *Negotiating Jerusalem*. Albany, N.Y.: State University of New York Press, 2000.

Selten, Reinhard. "Chain Store Paradox." *Theory and Decision* 9 (1978): 127–59.

Sevic, Milan. "Czechoslovakia's Velvet Divorce." *Current History* 91, no. 568 (November 1992): 376–80.

Shabad, Goldie, Sharon A. Shible, and John F. Zurovchak. "When Push Comes to Shove: An Explanation of the Dissolution of the Czechoslovak State." *International Journal of Sociology* 28, no. 3 (fall 1998): 43–74.

Sheehy, Ann. "Recent Events in Abkhazia Mirror the Complexities of National Relations in the USSR." RL 141/78, June 26, 1978.

————. "Tatarstan Asserts Its Sovereignty." *RFE/RL Research Report* 1, no. 14 (April 3, 1992): 1–4.

Shils, Edward. "Primordial, Personal, Sacred, and Civil Ties." *British Journal of Sociology* 8, no. 2 (1957): 130–45.

Silber, Laura, and Allan Little. *Death of a Nation*. New York: Penguin Books, 1995.

Silver, Brian. "Ethnic and Language Dimensions in Russian and Soviet Censuses." In *Research Guide to the Russian and Soviet Censuses*, edited by Ralph S. Clem, 70–97. Ithaca, N.Y.: Cornell University Press, 1985.

Siverson, Randolph, and Harvey Starr. *The Diffusion of War*. Ann Arbor: University of Michigan Press, 1991.

Skocpol, Theda. *States and Social Revolutions*. Cambridge: Cambridge University Press, 1979.

————. "Bringing the State Back In: Strategies of Analysis in Current Research." In *Bringing the State Back In*, edited by Peter B. Evans, Dietrich Rueschemeyer, and Theda Skocpol, 3–37. Cambridge: Cambridge University Press, 1985.

Slater, Wendy. "No Victors in the Russian Referendum." *RFE/RL Research Report* 2, no. 21 (May 21, 1993): 10–19.

Slider, Darrell. "Crisis and Response in Soviet Nationality Policy: The Case of Abkhazia." *Central Asian Survey* 4, no. 4 (1985): 51–68.

————. "Democratization in Georgia." In *Conflict, Cleavages, and Change in Central Asia and the Caucasus*, edited by Karen Dawisha and Bruce Parrott, 158–98. Cambridge: Cambridge University Press, 1997.

Small, Melvin, and J. David Singer. *Resort to Arms: International and Civil Wars, 1818–1980*. London: Sage Publications, 1981.

Smith, Anthony. *The Ethnic Origins of Nations*. Oxford: Blackwell Publishers, 1986.

Smith, Graham, et al. *Nation-Building in the Post-Soviet Borderlands: The Politics of National Identities*. Cambridge: Cambridge University Press, 1998.

Snyder, Glen, and Paul Diesing. *Conflict among Nations*. Princeton, N.J.: Princeton University Press, 1977.

Snyder, Jack. *Myths of Empire*. Ithaca, N.Y.: Cornell University Press, 1991.

———. *From Voting to Violence: Democratization and Nationalist Conflict*. New York: W.W. Norton, 2000.

Snyder, Jack, and Karen Ballentine. "Nationalism and the Marketplace of Ideas." *International Security* 21, no. 2 (fall 1996): 5–40.

Solchanyk, Roman, and Ann Sheehy. "Kapitonov on Nationality Relations in Georgia." RL 125/78, June 1, 1978.

Sprout, Harold, and Margaret Sprout. *An Ecological Paradigm for the Study of International Politics*. Princeton, N.J.: Center for International Studies, 1968.

Spykman, Nicholas J. *The Geography of Peace*. New York: Harcourt Brace, 1944.

Spzorluk, Roman. "The Imperial Legacy and the Soviet Nationalities Problem." In *The Nationalities Factor in Soviet Politics and Society*, edited by Lubomyr Hajda and Mark Bessinger, 1–23. Boulder, Colo.: Westview Press, 1990.

Staff of the U.S. Commission on Security and Cooperation in Europe. "Report on the Tatarstan Referendum on Sovereignty." April 14, 1992.

Starr, Harvey. "Opportunity and Willingness As Ordering Concepts in the Study of War." *International Interactions* 4, no. 4 (1978): 363–87.

———. "Joining Political and Geographic Perspectives: Geopolitics and International Relations." *International Interactions* 17, no. 1 (1991): 1–9.

Starr, Harvey, and Benjamin Most. "Contagion and Border Effects on Contemporary African Conflict." *Comparative Political Studies* 16, no. 1 (April 1983): 92–117.

———. "The Forms and Processes of War Diffusion: Research Update on Contagion in African Conflict." *Comparative Political Studies* 18, no. 2 (July 1985): 206–27.

Starr, Richard F. *The New Military in Russia*. Annapolis, Md.: Naval Institute Press, 1996.

Stein, Janice Gross, ed. *Getting to the Table*. Baltimore: Johns Hopkins University Press, 1989.

Stockholm International Peace Research Institute. *SIPR Yearbook 1994*. Stockholm: Almquist and Wiksell, 1994.

Suny, Ronald Grigor. "Georgia and Soviet Nationality Policy." In *The Soviet Union since Stalin*, edited by Stephen F. Cohen, Alexander Rabinowitch, and Robert Sharlet, 200–26. Bloomington: Indiana University Press, 1980.

———. "Transcaucasia: Cultural Cohesion and Ethnic Revival in a Multinational Society." In *The Nationalities Factor in Soviet Politics and Society*, edited by Lubomyr Hajda and Mark Beissinger, 228–252. Boulder, Colo.: Westview Press, 1990.

———. *The Revenge of the Past*. Stanford, Calif.: Stanford University Press, 1993.

———. *The Making of the Georgian Nation*. 2d ed. Bloomington: Indiana University Press, 1994.

Szayna, Thomas S., ed. *Identifying Potential Ethnic Conflict: Application of a Process Model*. Santa Monica, Calif.: RAND Corporation, 2000.

Tiech, Mikulas, and Roy Porter, eds. *The National Question in Europe in Historical Context*. Cambridge: Cambridge University Press, 1993.

Tilly, Charles. "Reflections on the History of European State-Making." In *The
Formation of National States in Western Europe*, edited by Charles Tilly, 3–84.
Princeton: Princeton University Press, 1975.

———. *From Mobilization to Revolution*. New York: Random House, 1978.

———. "War Making and State Making As Organized Crime." In *Bringing the
State Back In*, edited by Peter B. Evans, Dietrich Rueschemeyer, and Theda
Skocpol, 169–91. Cambridge: Cambridge University Press, 1985.

Tiryakian, Edward A., and Ronald Rogowski, eds. *New Nationalisms of the Developed West: Toward Explanation*. Boston: Allen and Unwin, 1985.

Toft, Monica Duffy. "The Geography of Ethnic Conflict: Do Settlement Patterns
Matter?" Paper presented at the annual meeting of the Midwest Political Science Association, Chicago, Illinois, April 1996.

———. "Multinationality, Regions, and State-Building: The Failed Transition in
Georgia." *Regional and Federal Studies* 11, no. 3 (autumn 2001).

———. "Indivisible Territory, Geographic Concentration, and Ethnic War." *Security Studies* 12, no. 2 (winter 2002/2003).

———. "Differential Demographic Growth in Multinational States: Israel's Two-
Front War." *Journal of International Affairs* 56, no. 1 (fall 2002): 71–94.

———. "The Case of Two-Way Mirror Nationalism in Ajaria." In *The Politics of
the Caspian*, edited by Moshe Gammer. London: Frank Cass, forthcoming
2003.

Toropov, Dmitri. *Spravochnik novykh partii i obshchestvenniykh organizatii Tatarstana*. Moscow: Informatsionno-ekspertnaya gruppa "Panorama," 1992.

Trachtenberg, Marc. "Intervention in Historical Perspective." *In Emerging
Norms of Justified Intervention*, edited by Laura W. Reed and Carl Kaysen, 15–
36. Cambridge, Mass.: Committee on International Security Studies, American
Academy of Arts and Sciences, 1993.

Treisman, Daniel S. "Russia's Ethnic Revival The Separatist Activism of Regional
Leaders in a Postcommunist Order." *World Politics* 49, no. 2 (January 1997):
212–49.

Ulc, Otto. "The Bumpy Road of Czechoslovakia's Revolution." *Problems of
Communism* 41, no. 3 (1992): 19–33.

United States Information Agency. "Urban Georgians Express Confidence in
Shevardnadze and Concern over War in Abkhazia and Economy." Opinion
Research Memorandum M-146–93. Washington, D.C., June 21, 1993.

———. "Islam Commands Intense Devotion among the Chechens." Office of
Research and Media Reaction, Washington, D.C., July 27, 1995.

Van den Berghe, Pierre L. "Race and Ethnicity: A Sociobiological Perspective."
Ethnic and Racial Studies 1, no. 4 (1978): 401–11.

Van Evera, Stephen. "Hypotheses on Nationalism and War." *International Security* 18, no. 4 (spring 1994): 5–39.

———. *Guide to Methods for Students of Political Science*. Ithaca, N.Y.: Cornell
University Press, 1997.

Vasquez, John. "The Tangibility of Issues and Global Conflict: A Test of Rosenau's Issue Area Typology." *Journal of Peace Research* 20, no. 2 (1983): 179–92.

———. *The War Puzzle*. Cambridge: Cambridge University Press, 1993.

———. "Mapping the Probability of War and Analyzing the Possibility of Peace: The Role of Territorial Issues." *Conflict Management and Peace Science* (spring 2001).

———, with Marie T. Henehan. "Territorial Issues and the Probability of War, 1816–1992." *Journal of Peace Research* 38 (March 2001): 123–38.

———, with Christopher S. Leskiw. "The Origins of Interstate Rivalry, 1812–1992." *Annual Review of Political Science* 4 (September 2001): 295–316.

Vsesoyuznaya perepis' naselniia 1937g. Moscow: Institut istoroii SSR, 1991.

Waever, Ole, Barry Buzan, Morten Kelstrup, and Pierre Lemaitre, eds. *Identity, Migration, and the New Security Agenda in Europe*. New York: St. Martin's Press, 1993.

Wagner, R. H. "The Causes of Peace." In *Stopping the Killing: How Civil Wars End*, edited by Roy Licklider, 235–68. New York: New York University Press, 1993.

Walker, Edward. "The Dog That Didn't Bark: Tatarstan and Asymmetrical Federalism in Russia." *Harriman Review* 6, no. 1 (winter 1997): 1–35.

Wallensteen, Peter, and Margareta Sollenberg. "Armed Conflicts, Conflict Termination, and Peace Agreements, 1989–1996." *Journal of Peace Research* 34, no. 3 (1997): 339–58.

Walt, Stephen M. *Origins of Alliances*. Ithaca, N.Y.: Cornell University Press, 1987.

———. *Revolution and War*. Ithaca, N.Y.: Cornell University Press, 1996.

Walter, Barbara F. "The Critical Barrier to Civil War Settlement." *International Organization* 51, no. 2 (spring 1997): 335–64.

———. "Designing Transitions from Civil War: Demobilization, Democratization, and Commitments to Peace." *International Security* 24, no. 1 (spring 1999): 127–55.

Walter, Barbara F., and Jack Snyder. *Civil Wars, Insecurity, and Intervention*. New York: Columbia University Press, 1998.

Waltz, Kenneth N. *Theory of International Politics*. New York: McGraw Hill, 1979.

Weiner, Myron. *Sons of the Soil: Migration and Ethnic Conflict in India*. Princeton, N.J.: Princeton University Press, 1978.

———. "Bad Neighbors, Bad Neighborhoods: An Inquiry into the Causes of Refugee Flows." *International Security* 21, no. 1 (summer 1996): 5–42.

Werner, Suzanne. "The Precarious Nature of Peace: Resolving the Issues, Enforcing Settlement, and Renegotiating the Terms." *American Journal of Political Science* 43, no. 3 (July 1999): 912–34.

Wijayadasa, K.H.J. "Tamil 'Homeland' Theory of EP-A Hoax." *The Island*, March 29, 1998.

Wixman, Ronald. "The Middle Volga: Ethnic Archipelago in a Russian Sea." In *Nations and Politics in the Soviet Successor States*, edited by Ian Bremmer and Ray Taras, 421–47. Cambridge: Cambridge University Press, 1993.

Wolchik, Sharon. *Czechoslovakia in Transition: Politics, Economics, and Society.* New York: Pinter Press, 1991.

Wolf, Eric R. *Peasant Wars of the Twentieth Century.* New York: Harper and Row, 1969.

Wright, John F. R. "The Geopolitics of Georgia." In *Transcaucasian Boundaries*, edited by John F. R. Wright, Suzanne Goldenberg, and Richard Schofield, 134–50. New York: St. Martin's Press, 1995.

Wright, Quincy. *A Study of War.* Abridged edition. Chicago: University of Chicago Press, 1967.

Yeltsin, Boris. *Midnight Diaries.* Translated by Catherine A. Fitzpatrick. New York: Public Affairs, 2000.

Zakaria, Fareed. "Realism and Domestic Politics: A Review Essay." *International Security* 17, no. 1 (summer 1992): 177–98.

Newpapers

Christian Science Monitor
Demokraticheskaya Abkhazia
Ekspress-Khronika
Financial Times
Izvestiya
Komsomolskaya pravda
Megapolis-Express
Moscow News
Moskovskaya pravda
Moskovski komsomolets
Moskovskiye novosti
New York Times
Nezavisimaya gazeta
Pravda
Rossiiskaya gazeta
Segodnya
Svobodnaya gruziya
Trud
Vestnik gruziya
Washington Post

Index

Abashidze, Aslan: and Ajarian political situation, 113–15, 123–24; elected Ajar Supreme Soviet chairman, 111, 197nn. 22, 29; profile of, 197n. 22; and Russian intervention in Ajaria, 123, 198n. 48

Abdullin, Talgat, 60

Abkhaz: as concentrated minority, 21, 87, 93, 119–23, 136–39, 138 table 8.1; as minority in Georgia, 90; population data for, 92–93, 93 table 6.1, 190–91n. 29; in Turkey, 190n. 29

Abkhaz Autonomous Soviet Socialist Republic, 93

Abkhaz identity, 91–92

Abkhaz Parliament, 98, 101–2, 192n. 43

Abkhaz Supreme Soviet, 101–3

Abkhazia: Abkhaz as concentrated minority in, 23; and Black Sunday (April 4, 1989), 95, 191n. 38; and cease-fire negotiations, 103–5; civil war in, 100–106, 125–26; in comparative analysis with Ajaria, 87–88, 115–19, 136–39; constitutions of, 101–2, 194nn. 65, 66, 67; and declaration of independence, 97; and declaration of independence as a federal republic, 101–2; and discrimination against Georgians, 94–95, 191n. 34; and draft treaty with Georgia, 101; and electoral law of Abkhaz minority, 98; Georgia relations of, 12, 87–106, 113, 191n. 34; and Georgian unity, 189n. 5; historical background of, 91–92; and People's Forum of Abkhazia (PFA), 95, 101; political situation of, 97–100; and referendum on the Soviet Union, 97–98; Russian troop involvement in, 105, 195n. 87; territorial dispute over, 93–100; use of term for, 189n. 3

Achba, Zurab, 122, 194n. 65

Ajar identity, 107–10

Ajar Oblast Party Committee, 109

Ajar Republic, 109

Ajar Supreme Soviet, 111

Ajaria: analysis of outcomes in, 115–19; as an autonomous republic, 110–11; in comparative analysis with Abkhazia, 87–88, 115–19, 136–39; and Georgia relations, 12, 107–26; historical background of, 108; nationalist separatism and, 110–12; Russian intervention in, 123, 198nn. 47, 48; territorial dispute over, 110–15

Ajarian Autonomous Soviet Socialist Republic, 93

Ajars: as a concentrated minority, 87, 109–10, 119, 123–24, 136–39, 138 table 8.1; birthrates and ethnic balance in, 109; as an ethnic group, 196–97n. 12; as minority in Georgia, 90; population data for, 108–9, 196nn. 9, 11

Akbulatov, Aslanbek, 77

Akhmadov, Husein, 75

Al Aksa (Jerusalem). *See* Jerusalem

Alars (Iranian), 65

Albanians, and legitimacy issue, 24

All-Union Law on the Demarcation of Powers between the USSR and the Members of the Federation, 49–51, 54, 55, 72, 180–81n. 17, 181–82n. 23

ancient-hatreds argument, 7–8

Anjaparidze, Zaal, 190–91n. 29

Aral Sea basin, effect of economic development projects on, 6

Ardzinba, Vladislav: and cease-fire negotiations in Abkhazia, 103–4; elected Abkhaz Supreme Soviet chairman, 96–97; and elite-manipulation theories, 118–19; on status of Abkhaz republic, 114, 123; profile of, 192n. 46; relations with Shevardnadze, 195n. 83; Russian relations with, 97, 125

Asinba, Zurab, on Abkhaz independence, 97

Atlas Narodov Mira (Atlas of the nations of the world), 13, 172n. 45

Avturkhanov, Umar, 187n. 58

Azatlyk (Tatar nationalist group), 51, 52

Balkans, ethnic conflict in, 17

Baltic Republics, independence movement in, 52–53, 175n. 39, 182n. 34

bargaining theory. *See* dispute settlement
Belarus. *See* Byelorussia
Belyaev, Vladimir, and Soglasie movement, 58
Beppayev, Sufiyan, 104
Black Sunday (April 4, 1989), 95, 191n. 38
Blanca, Antoine, 105
Boer war song, 23–24
Bolgary Velikie, 46
Bonaparte, Napoleon, quoted, 179
Bosnia: ethnic groups in, 7; and motivations for conflict, 8, 130–31; population data for, 199n. 13; Serbian nationalist passions and, 9. *See also* Milosevic, Slobodan
Bosnia-Herzegovina, civil war in, 130
Bunce, Valerie, on ethnofederalism and Yugoslavian disintegration, 128–29, 132
Byelorussia, declaration of independence, 180n. 15

capability, 22–23, 32
case study analysis, 11, 12–13, 44, 134–39; and methodology, 171n. 44; theoretical expectations and research findings for, 138 table 8.1
Caucasian Wars, 65–66
cease-fire agreements, definition of, 200n. 28
Central Intelligence Agency (CIA), map and data resources of, 13
Chavchavadze, Ilia, on Georgian motherland, 107
Chechen identity, 65, 67, 68
Chechen National Congress (CNC), 71
Chechen Parliament, 76–77, 187n. 55
Chechen Provisional Council (CPC), 78–79, 187n. 58
Chechen-Ingush Autonomous Soviet Socialist Republic (ASSR), 67, 71
Chechen-Ingushetia Republic, 70, 185n. 11
Chechens: as a concentrated majority, 79–81, 135–36, 138 table 8.1; deportation of, 68, 185n. 11; historical background of, 65–70; population data for, 69 table 5.1, 69; and suicide martyrs in Moscow theater, 145–46, 201n. 36
Chechnya: as a union republic, 27; civil war and, 77–79, 200n. 29; in compara-
tive analysis with Tatarstan, 81–85; declaration of sovereignty of, 74; and demonstrations on environmental issues, 70; geographic description of, 65; historical background of, 65–70, 184–85n. 7, 185n. 8; independence movement in, 67–75; Islamic religious suppression and, 68–69; map of, 66 fig. 5.1; and negotiations stalemate, 75–77; and People's Front, 70; presidential and parliamentary elections in, 74, 186nn. 39, 40; presidential candidates in, 186n. 39; Provisional Supreme Council (PSC) of, 72–74; Russian economic blockade of, 75–76, 187n. 50; Russian relations with, 12, 64–86, 135–36, 145–48; Russian troop involvement in, 78–79, 188n. 71; settlement patterns and precedent setting in, 79–81; Turkish and Persian domination of, 65; use of term for, 184n. 1; and Vaynakh Democratic Party (VDP), 70–71. *See also* Dudayev, Zhokhar
Chernomyrdin, Viktor, 77
Chigogidsze, Guram, on Ajaria's autonomous status, 110–11
commitment problem, as obstacle to a rational settlement, 2, 17
Commonwealth of Independent States (CIS), 55, 106
concentrated majority: capability for independence of, 22, 26 table 2.1; definition of, 21, 174n. 23; and duration variable, 41; and indivisibility issue theory, 18; and legitimacy of the majority, 24–25, 26 table 2.1; and statistical analysis, 37–38
concentrated minority, 21; and capability for independence, 22, 26 table 2.1; and duration variable, 41; mixed legitimacy of, 25, 26 table 2.1; statistical analysis of, 37–38
conflict bargaining model, 12
Correlates of War data set, 171n. 43
costs of war, 30–31, 176nn. 46, 47
Croatia, independence movement in, 130, 131
Czech Republic, Slovak minority in, 41
Czechoslovakia, former: as a binational state, 26–27; collapse of, 129–30
Czechs, 26

data analysis. *See* statistical analysis

Declaration on State Sovereignty of the Chechen-Ingush Republic, 71

"demand sovereignty." *See* sovereignty demands of ethnic groups

democracy, and majority-rule principle, 24

Democratic Party of Russia (DPR), 52

Deniken, Anton, 184n. 6

development and modernization approach, 5, 168n. 13, 169n. 16

dispersed groups, 21; capability for independence in, 22–23, 26 table 2.1; and duration variable, 41; and indivisibility issue theory, 18; low legitimacy of, 25, 26 table 2.1; and nonviolent political activity, 34, 40; statistical analysis, 38–39; Tatars and legitimacy issue regarding, 57, 183n. 59

dispute settlement: commitment problem in, 2; indivisible issue in, 2; and "Land for Peace" negotiations, 29, 176n. 44; obstacles to, 2–3, 17; private information obstacle to, 2, 172n. 3

divisible territory, as a material/physical object, 1, 10

Dudayev, Zhokhar: assassination attempts on, 78; and Chechnya negotiations for independence, 73–79, 86, 135–36; and confrontation with Chechen Parliament, 76–77, 187n. 55; elected chairman of CNC, 71; elected president of Chechnya, 74, 186nn. 39, 40; and elite-manipulation theories, 84–85, 141; opposition to, 77–79, 187nn. 55, 58, 60, 188n. 65; profile of, 71; public support for, 71–72, 74; speech on Chechen independence of, 80

duration of residence. *See* tenure principle

duration variable, 40–41

East Timor, ethnic conflict, 17

Eelam: description of, 173–74n. 19; as homeland of Tamils, 21; and Tamil conflict in Sri Lanka, 22

elite-manipulation approaches, 8–10, 16; in Abkhazia-Ajaria comparative analysis, 117–19; in Chechnya-Tatarstan comparative analysis, 84–85, 136; as representative of ethnic groups views, 140–41

empirical description, 199n. 18

Ergash, Cholpan, on Homeland's worth, 1

Eritrea-Ethiopian war, 140

Estonia: independence for, 71, 180n. 15; Popular Front membership in, 53

ethnic groups: and data for autonomous units of Russian Federation, 164–65 (tables); definition of, 19; and demand for sovereignty, 21–26; as differentiating from states, 2, 167n. 4; and reasons for risking a "hopeless" war, 31; territorial control and survival for, 19–20, 32; use of term with, 173n. 8; and view of territory, 1

ethnic identity: and ancient-hatreds arguments, 7–8; loss of, 5; and risk of death, 140, 199–200n. 19; securing identity for, 31

ethnofederalism, 128–29

fear factor. *See* precedent setting of states; security-dilemma argument

Fearon, James, 172n. 3

federalism, as factor in ethnic violence, 128

Fisher, Roger, on precedents, 27

Former Soviet Union (FSU): and Aral sea basin policies, 6; debt of, 57; dissolution of, 55; ethnonational groups in, 195n. 2; maps of, 13, 172n. 45; political structure of, 180n. 14; population data for, 13, 195n. 2; and referendum on Soviet Union, 97–98, 192–93n. 49; unionwide referendum on, 180n. 12, 183n. 47

Former Yugoslavia. *See* Yugoslavia, former

Gamsakhurdia, Zviad: as Abkhaz nationalist leader, 95; elected as president of Georgia, 98; and elite-manipulation theories, 118, 140; opposition forces and overthrow of, 99–100, 113, 193nn. 54, 58, 194n. 61; profile of, 191–92n. 40; and Russian relations, 97, 124–25; supporters in Abkhazia for, 102; and views on Ajaria, 110

Georgia: Abkhaz cease-fire negotiations, 103–5; and Abkhaz civil war, 100–106; Abkhaz draft treaty for, 101; and Abkhaz Parliament, 98, 101–2; Abkhazia relations with, 12, 87–106, 113; Abkhazia-Ajaria comparative analysis of, 87–88, 115–19, 136–39; Ajaria relations with, 12, 107–26; ethnic minorities in, 90; geographic description of,

Georgia (*cont.*)
89; historical background of, 89–91; independence movement in, 94–100; map
of, 90 fig. 6.1; and Military Council,
100, 194n. 61; and Round Table, 96,
110, 112, 192n. 44, 197n. 17; use of
term for, 189n. 3; and Zviadists (supporters of Gamsakhurdia), 100–101,
103, 115
Georgian Central Committee, 109
Georgian Communist Party, and minority
representation, 191n. 31
Georgian Democratic Republic, 90
Georgian identity, 89–91, 94, 190n. 17,
196n. 4
Georgian National Guard, in Ajaria, 112
Georgian Parliament, 105
Georgian Supreme Soviet, 110–12
Georgians: as a concentrated majority, 88,
89, 91, 138 table 8.1; birthrates and
ethnic balance in, 189–90n. 13, 196n.
7; population data for, 91
"geostrategy school," 6, 169–70n. 24
Glenny, Misha, 39
Gorbachev, Mikhail: and Baltic independence, 175n. 39; and coup attempt, 54,
72; and dissolution of the Soviet Union,
55; political and economic reforms of,
49–50; and precedent setting, 27, 135
Gurr, Ted Robert, 11

Habermas, Jürgen, 172n. 4
Hobbes, Thomas, 199–200n. 19
Holbrooke, Richard, 144
Holsti, Kalevi, 171n. 41
homeland control, and survival, 20. *See also*
sovereignty demands of ethnic groups
homeland legitimacy. *See* legitimacy
homeland principle, 23, 32–33
homeland variable, 40–41, 43 table 3.7
homelands: attachment to, 34; and ethnic
group identity, 20; historical discourses
on, 16; as an indivisible territory, 1, 20;
intrinsic worth of, 1, 5–6; investment
principle for, 23–24; tenure principle
for, 24, 174n. 27
Hunter, Shireen, 196n. 3
Huth, Paul, 169n. 22

Imeretia, 189n. 5
Imnadze, Nodar, death of, 112

independent states, worldwide listing of,
149–52 (tables)
India, as a multinational state, 27
indivisible territory, 17–33; as a nonmaterial value or subject, 10; and acceptance of side payments, 173n. 9; as an
obstacle to a rational settlement, 2, 17,
167n. 2
indivisible territory theory, 2, 17–33, 132–
33; bargaining model for, 30 table 2.2;
and Chechen-Tatar comparison, 85–86;
for Georgia and Abkhazia, 106, 119–23;
for Georgia and Ajaria, 123–26; hypothesis of, 11, 30; hypothetical nature of,
172n. 7; policy implications of, 141–48;
statistical analysis of, 40–44; theoretical
implications of, 139–41
Ingush Republic, 69
intrinsic worth, of homelands, 1, 5–6,
169nn. 21, 22
investment principle, 23–24
Ioseliani, Jaba, 100, 102
Islamic religious, suppression of, 68–69,
179n. 4
Israeli-Palestinian conflict, 10, 29, 127,
172n. 5, 176n. 44
Ittifak (Tatar nationalist group), 51, 52, 60
Izetbegovic, Alija, 131

Jerusalem: Al Aksa in, 172n. 6; indivisibility issue for, 1, 18, 172n. 6; states
vs. Orthodox Jews' view of, 20
Jewish identity, 29
Jews: as dispersed group, 21; and legitimacy claims in Israel, 174n. 25; and
Warsaw Ghetto Uprising, 31

Karkarashvili, Giorg, 103
Kartvelians, 91, 190n. 17
Kaufmann, Chaim, 144–45
Kavadze, Aleksandr, 121
Kazan, khanate of, 46
Khaindrava, Ivlian, 103
Khakhva, Tengiz, resignation from Ajar Su-
preme Soviet, 111
Khalvashi, Pridon, on Ajaria's autonomous
status, 111
Khasbulatov, Ruslan, 187n. 55, 187n. 60,
194n. 63
Kitovani, Tengiz, and Abkhaz conflict,
100, 198n. 50

Klaus, Vaclav, 129

Kosovo: Albanian legitimacy as majority in, 24; ethnic conflict and violence in, 1, 5; and indivisibility issue, 1; Serbian investment and tenure in, 23–24; Serbian view of loss of, 20

Kuran, Timor, on relative deprivation, 169n. 20

Laitin, David, 175n. 34

"Land for peace" negotiations, 29, 176n. 44

Latvia: independence of, 180n. 15; and People's Front of Latvia, 53; as union republic, 27

Lau, Yisrael Meir (rabbi), 18

leader's role in ethnic conflict. See elite-manipulation approaches

Lebed, Aleksandr, 147

legitimacy principle, 23, 32; Abkhazian autonomy and, 122–23; Chechnya independence demand and, 79; of concentrated majority, 24–25, 26 table 2.1; of concentrated minority, 25, 26 table 2.1; of dispersed groups, 25, 26 table 2.1; and homeland principle, 23, 32–33; and majority-rule principle, 24, 32, 174nn. 24, 28; and precedent setting, 27; Tatarstan's bargaining position and, 57–59; of urban groups, 25, 26 table 2.1

Lijphart, Arend, on federalism, 128

likelihood of violence, 18–19, 34, 133–34; and territorial disputes, 200n. 26

Likhachov, Vasily, on Tatarstan relations with Russia, 59

literature review on ethnic violence, 4–10; for development and modernization, 168n. 13, 169n. 16; for elite-manipulation approaches, 8–10, 170n. 33; for material-based approaches, 5–7; for nonmaterial-based approaches, 7–8

Lithuania: economic situation in, 49; independence of, 53, 180n. 15

Lithuanian Restructuring Movement (Sajudis), 53

locale, definitions of, 170n. 25

Lordkipanidze, Vazha, 123

McNamara, Robert, 201n. 41

majority-rule principle, 24, 32, 174nn. 24, 28

Mamodayev, Yaragai, and Chechnya opposition government, 76–77, 78

material-based approaches, 5–7, 167n. 3; and Abkhazia-Ajaria comparative analysis, 115–19; and Chechnya-Tatarstan comparative analysis, 82–83, 136; and intrinsic worth of territory argument, 5–6, 169nn. 21, 22; political-development and economic-modernization argument regarding, 5, 168n. 13, 169n. 16; and relative deprivation argument, 5; and resource richness, 34, 41–43, 179n. 19

Meciar, Vladimir: and confederal state for Czechs and Slovaks, 129–30; and population transfers, 9

Milosevic, Slobodan: as inciting Serbian nationalist passions, 9; and motivations for Bosnian conflict, 8, 170–71n. 36; on Serbs and Kosovo, 23; and troops to Slovenia, 29

Mingrelia, 189n. 5, 190n. 17

Mingrelians, 91

Minorities at Risk (MAR) data set, 11–12, 34–35, 133–34, 177nn. 2, 4; cases and key variables for, 153–63 (tables); communal conflict in, 178n. 178; duration variable (TRADITN2) for, 40–41, 43 table 3.7; homeland variable for, 40–41, 43 table 3.7; rebellion variable (REBEL) for, 35 table 3.1, 35–36, 36 table 3.2, 177nn. 5, 6, 178nn. 7–11; resource richness variable for, 41–43, 43 table 3.7, 179n. 19; settlement-pattern variable for, 37 tables 3.4, 3.5, 37–40; spatial-concentration variable (REG, or region) for, 36 table 3.3, 36–37; state's ethnic profile variable for, 41–42, 43 table 3.7

Mongol Empire, 46

Morokin, Vladimir, on Tatar independence, 57

Mountain Republic (Gorskaia respublika), 67

Mugadev, Mairbek, 77

multinational states: definition of, 27; and precedent setting, 26–29

Myanmar, as a multinational state, 27

national self-determination principle, 168n. 11

nationalism: and elite-manipulation theories, 9; Welsh homeland and, 19–20 negotiated settlement. *See* dispute settlement

Ninidze, Tedo, on Abkhaz independence, 102

nonmaterial-based approaches, 7–8, 167n. 3; Abkhazia-Ajaria comparative analysis of, 116–17; Chechnya-Tatarstan comparative analysis of, 83, 136

Northern Ireland, ethnic violence, 5, 39–40, 127

Ossetians: Chechens ancestors of, 65; as ethnic minority in Georgia, 90; homeland in North Ossetia for, 97; and South Ossetia Autonomous Oblast, 93, 97; and South Ossetia conflict, 113, 115, 120, 125–26

Ottoman Empire, 65–66, 91, 108

Palestinians, homeland claims, 29

partition, 144–48, 201n. 33

peace agreements, definition of, 200n. 28

Pipes, Richard, on Georgian politics, 87

Pithart, Petr, 130

Poland: as uninational state, 26; and Warsaw Ghetto Uprising in World War II, 31

policy implications, 3–4, 141–48; for ethnic conflict termination, 142–44, 143 fig. 8.1; for partition, 144–48, 201n. 33; for stability vs. justice, 141–42

population exchanges/transfers: of ethnic groups, 144; of ethnic Slovak and Hungarian minorities, 9; in former Yugoslavia, 4

precedent, definition of, 27

precedent setting by states: and cumulative losses, 28; and fear of secession, 2–3, 11, 18–19; and logic for multinational/multiethnic states, 26–29, 175n. 38; logic of, 175–76nn. 38, 40, 41; and relations with other states, 175n. 35; in Russia's bargaining position with Chechnya, 80–81; in Russia's bargaining position with Tatarstan, 59–63; statistical analysis of, 12, 34

private information, as obstacle to rational settlement, 2, 17, 172n. 3

problems of commitment. *See* commitment problem

Putin, Vladimir, Chechnya war policy of, 146–48

Putkaradze, Tengiz, 111

Québécois, sovereignty demands of, 23

rebellion variable (REBEL), 35 table 3.1, 35–36, 36 table 3.2, 177nn. 5, 6, 178nn. 7–11

redistribution of wealth, and ethnic conflict, 7

relative deprivation, 5, 169nn. 19, 20

Republic of Transcaucasia, 90

research methods and procedures, 10–13; case study analysis in, 11, 12–13; statistical analysis in, 11–12

resource competition. *See* relative deprivation

Roma, as dispersed group, 21

Rousseau, Jean-Jacques, 34

Russia: as a multinational state, 27; and bilateral treaty with Tatarstan, 45, 57, 64; Chechnya relations of, 12, 64–86, 135–36, 145–48; and declaration of independence, 180n. 15; and migrations of new-minority Russians, 25, 175n. 34; presidential elections in, 51–53; role of in Abkhaz conflict, 104–6, 124; strategic issues and precedent setting in, 28; Tatarstan relations of, 12, 45–63, 135–36

Russian Federation, 181n. 18

Russian Parliament, 187n. 55

Russian Revolution, 67

Rutskoi, Aleksandr: Chechen relations of, 72–75; on Tatar political situation, 62

Rwanda, ethnic conflict, 17

Sabirov, Mihammat, 56

Sabri, Sheik (mufti of Jerusalem), 18

Schelling, Thomas, on majority rule, 24

Scott, Sir Walter, on my native land, 127

security value of territory, 6

security-dilemma argument, 8, 170n. 29

Segal, Jerome, 172n. 5

Serb identity, 131

Serb nationalism, 9, 131

Serbs: and legitimacy and tenure issues, 23–24; their view of loss of Kosovo, 23

settlement patterns of ethnic groups: analysis of, 173n. 16; concentrated majority in, 21; concentrated minority in, 21;

definition of, 2; dispersed groups in, 21; and frequency of rebellion, 39 fig. 3.1; and indivisibility issue, 2, 18; relative impact of, 34; statistical analysis of, 12, 37 tables 3.4, 3.5, 37–40, 38 table 3.6, 133; and urban groups, 21

settlement-pattern variable, 37 tables 3.4, 3.5, 37–40

Shakrai, Sergei, 78, 188n. 65

Shamil (Imam), 66

Shamiyev, Mintimer: and economic relations, 54; and elite-manipulation theories, 84–85, 141; as leader of the Tatars, 58; and negotiations for independence, 86; on Parliament and congress, 60; on relations with Russia, 55–56, 135; presidential victory of, 53; speeches on nationalism and independence by, 13, 55, 59–60; and Tatarstan declaration, 50; and Union Treaty, 51, 54

Shevardnadze, Eduard: and Abkhaz conflict, 102–6, 198n. 50; elected Georgian Parliament chairman, 105, 195n. 83; and elite-manipulation theories, 118; and Georgian independence and unity, 98, 120–21, 189n. 4; as head of Georgian state, 100–101, 194n. 61, 195n. 83; on racial discrimination/apartheid in Abkhazia, 94; on South Ossetia civil war, 120; and Russian relations in Abkhazia conflict, 124–25; as Soviet foreign minister, 191n. 32

Sigua, Tengiz: and Georgian politics, 96, 99; as prime minister of Georgia, 100, 102

Slovenia: conflict in, 29; independence movement in, 130; and secession from Czechoslovakia, 26, 131; Slovenes as concentrated majority in, 21

Smith, Anthony, on nationalism, 17

Soglasie (Agreement) movement, 52, 58

South Ossetia, civil war conflict, 113, 115, 120, 125–26, 194n. 63

South Ossetia Autonomous Oblast, 93, 97

sovereignty demands of ethnic groups, 21–26; and capability, 22–23, 26 table 2.1, 32; and legitimacy, 23, 26 table 2.1; and likelihood of violence, 18; and settlement patterns, 2, 26 table 2.1; use of term for, 173n. 15

Soviet Union. See Former Soviet Union (FSU)

Spain, ethnic violence, 5, 127

spatial-concentration variable (REG, or region), 36 table 3.3, 36–37

Sri Lanka: ethnic conflict in, 127; Sinhalese minority group in, 21, 173–74nn. 18, 19, 20; Tamil minority group in, 21–22, 173–74nn. 19, 20

Stalin, Joseph: and deportation of Chechens, 68; student demonstrations in commemoration of, 189n. 9

Starovoitova, Galina, on Chechen-Russia relations, 83

states: concern for reputation in (see precedent setting by states); and fear of secession in multiethnic states, 2–3, 11, 18–19, 26–29; listing of, independent states, 149–52 (tables); indivisible territory of and likelihood of violence, 18–19; and securing borders for survival, 31; and territorial control and survival, 19–20, 32; and territorial integrity, 26–29; use of term for, 173n. 8; and view of territory as a material resource, 1, 20; and violence against ethnic groups, 10

state's ethnic profile: as binational state, 26; definition of, 26; as multinational state, 26; and sources for ethnic groups, 178–79n. 18; statistical analysis variable for, 41–42, 43 table 3.7; as uninational state, 26

statistical analysis, 11–12, 34–44, 133–34; duration variable (TRADITN2) for, 40–41, 43 table 3.7; homeland variable for, 40–41, 43 table 3.7; rebellion variable (REBEL) for, 35 table 3.1, 35–36, 36 table 3.2, 177nn. 5, 6, 178nn. 7–11; resource richness variable for, 41–43, 43 table 3.7, 179n. 19; settlement-pattern variable for, 37 tables 3.4, 3.5, 37–40; spatial-concentration variable (REG, or region) for, 36 table 3.3, 36–37; and state's ethnic profile, 41–42, 43 table 3.7, 178–79n. 18

strategic worth of territory, 6, 169–70n. 24

Subversive Institutions (Bunce), 128

Sufism, 69

Suny, Ronald Grigor, on Georgian politics, 87, 93–94

Svanetia, 190n. 17

Svans, 91

Tamil nation, 21–22
Tamil United Liberation Front, 173n. 19
Tamils, in Sri Lanka, 21–22, 173–74nn.
    19, 20
Tatar identity, 47–48, 51, 179n. 5
Tatar Public Center (Tatarskii Ob-
    shchestvennyi Tsentr, TPC), 51, 52
Tatars: as a dispersed group, 57–59, 135–
    36, 138 table 8.1; historical background
    of, 45–48; population data for, 48 table
    4.1, 48, 52, 179–80n. 6
Tatarstan: as a union republic, 27, 49; bar-
    gaining position of and fears of prece-
    dent setting, 59–63; bargaining position
    of and legitimacy issues, 57–59; and bi-
    lateral treaty with Russia, 45, 57, 64,
    184n. 67; and comparative analysis with
    Chechnya, 81–85; congress of and alter-
    native government, 60–61; geographic
    description of, 46; independence move-
    ment of, 48–55, 59–63; map of, 47 fig.
    4.1; Milli Medzhlis (national assembly)
    and, 60; new constitution of, 61; Parlia-
    ment of, 60–61; presidential elections
    in, 53; referendum and negotiated settle-
    ment in, 55–57, 180; rural-urban factor
    in politics of, 183n. 59; Russia relations
    of, 12, 45–63, 135–36; and Soglasie
    (Agreement) movement, 52, 58; use of
    term for, 179n. 1
tenure principle, 24, 34, 174n. 27
terminated conflicts: definition of, 200n.
    28; and policy implications, 142–44,
    143 fig. 8.1
territorial control: and interstate wars,
    171n. 41; number of conflicts and,
    171n. 40; and survival, 19–20, 32
theoretical assertions, 199n. 18
theory of indivisible territory. See indivisible
    territory theory
third-party intervention, in ethnic conflict,
    172n. 3
Tishkov, Valery, on Tatar independence,
    57
Trachtenberg, Marc, on population ex-
    changes, 3–4
trust issues. See commitment problem

Turkey-Greece conflict over Cyprus, 11
types of ethnic violence, 171n. 39

Ukraine: and Crimean Tatar migration,
    145; declaration of independence for,
    180n. 15; independence of, 27–28; stra-
    tegic nuclear resources of, 28
union republics, declarations of indepen-
    dence of, 180n. 15
Union Treaty. See All-Union Law on the
    Demarcation of Powers between the
    USSR and the Members of the
    Federation
urban groups, 21; capability for indepen-
    dence for, 22, 26 table 2.1; and duration
    variable for, 41; and indivisibility issue
    theory, 18; and low legitimacy, 25, 26
    table 2.1; and nonviolent political activ-
    ity, 34, 40; statistical analysis of, 39
Uzbekistan, declaration of independence
    of, 180n. 15

values conflicts, and indivisible-issue obsta-
    cle, 2
Vasquez, John, 171n. 41, 200n. 26

Wales, national anthem of, 19
"willingness to suffer," 201n. 41

Yeltsin, Boris: cease-fire negotiations in Ab-
    khazia, 103–4; and Chechen relations,
    72, 74, 75, 78; and confrontation with
    Russian Parliament, 187n. 55; economic
    reforms of, 54, 182n. 45; and elite-
    manipulation theories, 118; on prece-
    dent setting in Chechnya, 81; and Rus-
    sian independence, 27; and Russian
    relations with republics, 55, 135; and
    Russian troops in Chechnya, 79; and
    Tatarstan relations, 51, 56, 58, 62
Yugoslavia, former: ethnic violence in, 5;
    and Kraijina Serbs in Croatia, 39; and
    population exchange proposal, 4; and
    states view on Kosovo, 20; violent col-
    lapse of, 129–31

Zavgayev, Doku, 71–72